Hands-On Machine Learning with Azure

with Azure

Build powerful models with cognitive machine learning and artificial intelligence

Thomas K Abraham

Parashar Shah

Jen Stirrup

Lauri Lehman

Anindita Basak

BIRMINGHAM - MUMBAI

Hands-On Machine Learning with Azure

Commissioning Editor: Sunith Shetty
Acquisition Editor: Joshua Nadar
Content Development Editor: Karan Thakkar
Technical Editor: Dinesh Pawar
Copy Editor: Safis Editor
Project Coordinator: Nidhi Joshi
Proofreader: Safis Editing
Indexer: Pratik Shirodkar
Graphics: Jisha Chirayil
Production Coordinator: Deepika Naik

First published: October 2018

Production reference: 1311018

Published by Packt Publishing Ltd.
Livery Place
35 Livery Street
Birmingham
B3 2PB, UK.

ISBN 978-1-78913-195-6

www.packtpub.com

mapt.io

Mapt is an online digital library that gives you full access to over 5,000 books and videos, as well as industry leading tools to help you plan your personal development and advance your career. For more information, please visit our website.

Why subscribe?

- Spend less time learning and more time coding with practical eBooks and Videos from over 4,000 industry professionals

- Improve your learning with Skill Plans built especially for you

- Get a free eBook or video every month

- Mapt is fully searchable

- Copy and paste, print, and bookmark content

Packt.com

Did you know that Packt offers eBook versions of every book published, with PDF and ePub files available? You can upgrade to the eBook version at www.packt.com and as a print book customer, you are entitled to a discount on the eBook copy. Get in touch with us at customercare@packtpub.com for more details.

At www.packt.com, you can also read a collection of free technical articles, sign up for a range of free newsletters, and receive exclusive discounts and offers on Packt books and eBooks.

Contributors

About the authors

Thomas K Abraham is a cloud solution architect (advanced analytics and AI) at Microsoft in the South Central Region of the USA. Since January 2016, he's been assisting organizations in leveraging technologies such as SQL, Spark, Hadoop, NoSQL, BI, and AI on Azure. Prior to that, Thomas spent 10 years in Ecolab, where he designed algorithms for IoT devices and built solutions for anomaly detection. In the oil and gas division, he designed and built customer-facing analytics solutions for multiple super majors. His work was focused on preventing equipment failure by modeling corrosion, scale, and other stresses. He has a PhD in Chemical Engineering from The Ohio State University in 2005. His thesis focused on the use of nonlinear optimization with reaction models.

I would like to thank my wife, Dr. Anita Joy-Thomas, for being patient and loving while I hid out in the basement to write these chapters, my children, Rebecca and Matthew, for their love, and my parents and family members, who raised and supported me. I would also like to thank my friends and colleagues, especially those who gave me opportunities and trusted in me at Microsoft and Ecolab, and finally my advisor, Dr. Martin Feinberg, who taught me how to write and think with the highest technical rigor.

Parashar Shah is a Senior Program Manager in the Azure Machine Learning platform team. Currently, he works on making Azure Machine Learning services the best place to do e2e machine learning for building custom AI solutions using big data. Previously at Microsoft, he has been a Data Scientist and a Data Solutions Architect in various Cloud and AI teams.

Prior to joining Microsoft, Parashar worked at Nokia Networks as a Solutions Architect & Product Manager building customer experience analytics solutions for global telcos. He also co-founded a carpooling startup, which helped employees carpool safely. He has 10+ years of global work experience. He is an alum of Indian Institute of Management, Bangalore and Gujarat University.

I would like to thank my mom, Nita, my dad, Dr. Mahendra, and my sister, Vidhi, for their unconditional love and support throughout my life. I am thankful to my co-workers at Microsoft for building our awesome cloud and AI offerings. I am thankful to Kevin Walker for the advanced analytics-related opportunities afforded to me when at Alcatel-Lucent. I would like to thank my teachers who, over the years, taught me how to learn. And finally, thanks to my buddies– Ritu, Dhaval, Nikhil, Dhruvit, Arun, Pradip, Subijay, Shamit, Naufal, Dharmesh, and Vicky for their awesome friendship.

Jen Stirrup is a data strategist and technologist, a Microsoft Most Valuable Professional (MVP), and a Microsoft Regional Director, a tech community advocate, a public speaker and blogger, a published author, and a keynote speaker. Jen is the founder of a boutique consultancy based in the UK, Data Relish, which focuses on delivering successful business intelligence and artificial intelligence solutions that add real value to customers worldwide. She has featured on the BBC as a guest expert on topics relating to data.

Lauri Lehman is a data scientist who is focused on machine learning tools in Azure. He helps customers to design and implement machine learning solutions in the cloud. He works for the software consultancy company, Zure, based in Helsinki, Finland. For the past 4 years, Lauri has specialized in data and machine learning in Azure. He has worked on many machine learning projects, developing solutions for demand estimation, text analytics, and image recognition, for example. Lauri has previously worked as an academic researcher in theoretical physics, after obtaining his PhD on topological quantum walks. He still likes to follow the progress of modern physics and is eagerly a waiting the era of quantum machine learning!

> *I would like to thank my colleague, Karl Ots, for the opportunity to contribute to this book. I also want to thank all my colleagues for creating an awesome environment in which to work !*

Anindita Basak works as a cloud solution architect in data analytics and AI platforms and has been working with Microsoft Azure from its inception. With over a decade of experience, she helps enterprises to enable their digital transformation journey empowered with cloud, data, and AI. She has worked with various teams at Microsoft as FTE in the role of Azure Development Support Engineer, Pro-Direct Delivery Manager, and Technical Consultant. She recently co-authored the book *Stream Analytics with Microsoft Azure,* and was a technical reviewer for various technologies, including data-intensive applications, Azure HDInsigt, SQL Server BI, IoT, and Decision Science for Packt. She has also authored two video courses on *Azure Stream Analytics* from Packt.

> *I'd like to thank to my family for their encouragement and my friend, Ramakrishna, for his support while writing this book. I could not have reached my goal without your contributions.*

About the reviewer

Florian Klaffenbach is currently working as a technology solutions professional at Microsoft. He a well-known expert when it comes to hybrid cloud scenarios, cloud connectivity, and cloud environment optimization. Before he started at Microsoft, he worked at several companies in different roles; as a technical community manager and a solution expert at Dell, and as solutions architect at CGI Germany. He is also one of Packt's authors and has worked on books such as *Implementing Azure Solutions*, First and Second Edition, and *Multicloud for Architect*. He spends his free time with his wife, who is currently awaiting their second child, and his little boy.

Packt is searching for authors like you

If you're interested in becoming an author for Packt, please visit `authors.packtpub.com` and apply today. We have worked with thousands of developers and tech professionals, just like you, to help them share their insight with the global tech community. You can make a general application, apply for a specific hot topic that we are recruiting an author for, or submit your own idea.

Table of Contents

Preface

This book will teach you how advanced machine learning can be performed in the cloud in a very cheap way. You will learn more about Azure Machine Learning processes as an enterprise-ready methodology. This book lets you explore prebuilt templates with Azure Machine Learning Studio and build a model using canned algorithms that can be deployed as web services. It will help you to discover the different benefits of leveraging the cloud for machine learning and AI, deploy virtual machines in AI development scenarios, and how to apply R, Python, SQL Server, and Spark in Azure.

By the end of this book, you will be able to implement machine learning and AI concepts in your model to solve real-world problems.

Who this book is for

If you are a data scientist or developer familiar with Azure Machine Learning and Cognitive Services, and want to create smart models and make sense of data in the cloud, this book is for you. You'll also find this book useful if you want to bring powerful machine learning services into your cloud applications. Some experience with data manipulation and processing, and using languages such as SQL, Python, and R, will help you to understand the concepts covered in this book

What this book covers

Chapter 1, *AI Cloud Foundations*, introduces readers to the Microsoft Azure cloud and the reasons for choosing it as a platform for AI projects. We also describe the important services available to users looking to build AI solutions. This chapter also describes a decision flowchart to help pick and choose the right services on Azure that fit the business needs of an AI project.

Chapter 2, *Data Science Process*, focuses on the frameworks available for data science projects in a structured and organized manner. We will look at the principles of Team Data Science Process (TDSP) and the utilities available to support it. This chapter goes into the details of each step and helps define the criteria for success at every stage of the process.

Chapter 3, *Cognitive Services*, covers Cognitive Services in Azure, which makes it quick and simple to build smart applications. We will take a deep dive at some of the API that can be used to build AI applications without being a machine learning expert.

Chapter 4, *Bot Framework*, explains how to build bots using bot-related services in Azure. We will go through these options in a step-by-step manner to help you get started quickly.

Chapter 5, *Azure Machine Learning Studio*, explores Azure Machine Learning Studio and its advantages, and shows how we can build experiments in Azure Machine Learning Studio.

Chapter 6, *Scalable Computing for Data Science*, covers the vertical and horizontal scaling options in Azure to leverage cloud computing.

Chapter 7, *Machine Learning Server*, explains what the Microsoft Machine Learning Server is and also looks at key parts of the R and Python architecture.

Chapter 8, *HDInsight*, covers various functions of HDInsight in R and how to use them.

Chapter 9, *Machine Learning with Spark*, explains how to use Azure HDInsight in Spark, and explains what machine learning with Azure Databricks is like.

Chapter 10, *Building Deep Learning Solutions*, executes the steps of the popular open source deep learning tool, TensorFlow, on an Azure deep learning VM, and also covers the features of Azure Notebooks. The chapter also highlights the utilization of other deep learning frameworks, such as Keras, Pytorch, Caffe, Theano, and Chainer, using AI tools for Visual Studio/VS code and specifies deeper insights.

Chapter 11, *Integration with Other Azure Services*, covers typical integration patterns with other non-AI services in Azure. The reader will gain a deeper understanding of the options and best practices for integrating with functions, ADLA, and logic apps in AI solutions.

Chapter 12, *End-to-End Machine Learning*, explains how to get started with Azure Machine Learning services for end-to-end custom machine learning.

To get the most out of this book

For this book, you will require a prior knowledge of Azure and have an Azure subscription.

Download the example code files

You can download the example code files for this book from your account at
`www.packt.com`. If you purchased this book elsewhere, you can visit
`www.packt.com/support` and register to have the files emailed directly to you.

You can download the code files by following these steps:

1. Log in or register at `www.packt.com`.
2. Select the **SUPPORT** tab.
3. Click on **Code Downloads & Errata**.
4. Enter the name of the book in the **Search** box and follow the onscreen
   instructions.

Once the file is downloaded, please make sure that you unzip or extract the folder using the
latest version of:

- WinRAR/7-Zip for Windows
- Zipeg/iZip/UnRarX for Mac
- 7-Zip/PeaZip for Linux

The code bundle for the book is also hosted on GitHub at `https://github.com/`
`PacktPublishing/Hands-On-Machine-Learning-with-Azure`. In case there's an update to
the code, it will be updated on the existing GitHub repository.

We also have other code bundles from our rich catalog of books and videos available
at `https://github.com/PacktPublishing/`. Check them out!

Download the color images

We also provide a PDF file that has color images of the screenshots/diagrams used in this
book. You can download it here: `https://www.packtpub.com/sites/default/files/`
`downloads/9781789131956_ColorImages.pdf`.

Conventions used

There are a number of text conventions used throughout this book.

`CodeInText`: Indicates code words in text, database table names, folder names, filenames, file extensions, pathnames, dummy URLs, user input, and Twitter handles. Here is an example: "Alternatively, you can search for `Computer Vision` in the Azure portal".

A block of code is set as follows:

```
vision_base_url =
"https://westus.api.cognitive.microsoft.com/vision/v1.0/"

vision_analyze_url = vision_base_url + "analyze"
```

Bold: Indicates a new term, an important word, or words that you see on screen. For example, words in menus or dialog boxes appear in the text like this. Here is an example: "Click on **Create a resource**, then on **AI + Machine Learning**, and then on **Computer Vision**".

 Warnings or important notes appear like this.

 Tips and tricks appear like this.

Get in touch

Feedback from our readers is always welcome.

General feedback: If you have questions about any aspect of this book, mention the book title in the subject of your message and email us at `customercare@packtpub.com`.

Errata: Although we have taken every care to ensure the accuracy of our content, mistakes do happen. If you have found a mistake in this book, we would be grateful if you would report this to us. Please visit `www.packt.com/submit-errata`, selecting your book, clicking on the Errata Submission Form link, and entering the details.

Piracy: If you come across any illegal copies of our works in any form on the internet, we would be grateful if you would provide us with the location address or website name. Please contact us at copyright@packt.com with a link to the material.

If you are interested in becoming an author: If there is a topic that you have expertise in, and you are interested in either writing or contributing to a book, please visit authors.packtpub.com.

Reviews

Please leave a review. Once you have read and used this book, why not leave a review on the site that you purchased it from? Potential readers can then see and use your unbiased opinion to make purchase decisions, we at Packt can understand what you think about our products, and our authors can see your feedback on their book. Thank you!

For more information about Packt, please visit packt.com.

1
AI Cloud Foundations

Today, every organization aspires to be a leader in adopting the latest technological advancements. The success of such adoption in recent years has been achieved by leveraging the data landscape surrounding businesses. In this chapter, we will talk about how AI can be leveraged using Microsoft's Azure platform to derive business value from that data landscape. Azure offers several hundred services, and choosing the right service is challenging. In this chapter, we will give a high-level overview of the choices a data scientist, developer, or data engineer has for building and deploying AI solutions for their organization. We will start with a decision tree that can guide technology choices so that you understand which services you should consider.

In this chapter, we will cover the following topics:

- Cognitive Services/bots
- Azure Machine Learning Studio
- Azure Machine Learning services
- Machine Learning Server
- Azure Databricks

The importance of artificial intelligence

Artificial intelligence (**AI**) is ever-increasingly being interwoven into the complex fabric of our technology-driven lives. Whether we realize it or not, AI is becoming an enabler for us to accomplish our day-to-day tasks more efficiently than we've ever done before. Personal assistants such as Siri, Cortana, and Alexa are some of the most visible AI tools that we come across frequently. Less obvious AI tools are ones such as those used by rideshare firms that suggest drivers move to a high-density area, and adjust prices dynamically based on demand.

Across the world, there are organizations at different stages of the AI journey. To some organizations, AI is the core of their business model. In other organizations, they see the potential of leveraging AI to compete and innovate their business. Successful organizations recognize that digital transformation through AI is key to their survival over the long term. Sometimes, this involves changing an organization's business model to incorporate AI through new technologies such as the **Internet of Things (IoT)**. Across this spectrum of AI maturity, organizations face challenges implementing AI solutions. Challenges are typically related to scalability, algorithms, libraries, accuracy, retraining, pipelines, integration with other systems, and so on.

The field of AI has been around for several decades now, but it's growth and adoption over the last decade has been tremendous. This can be attributed to three main drivers: large data, large compute, and enhanced algorithms. The growth in data stems mostly from entities that generate data, or from human interactions with those entities. The growth in compute can be attributed to improved chip design, as well as innovative compute technologies. Algorithms have improved partly due to the open source community and partly due to the availability of larger data and compute.

The emergence of the cloud

Developing AI solutions in the cloud helps organizations leapfrog their innovation, in addition to alleviating the challenges described here. One of the first steps is to bring all the data close together or in the same tool for easy retrieval. The cloud is the most optimal landing zone that meets this requirement. The cloud provides near-infinite storage, easy access to other data sources, and on-demand compute. Solutions that are built on the cloud are easier to maintain and update, due to there being a single pane of control. The availability of improved or customized hardware at the click of a button was unthinkable a few years back.

Innovation in the cloud is so rapid that developers can build a large variety of applications very efficiently. The ability to scale solutions on-demand and tear them down after use is very economical in multiple use cases. This permits projects to start small and scale up as demand goes up. Lastly, the cloud provides the ability to deploy applications globally in a manner that's consistent for both the end user and developers.

Essential cloud components for AI

Any cloud AI solution will have different components, all modular, individually elastic, and integrated with each other. A broad framework for cloud AI is depicted in the following diagram. At the very base is **Storage**, which is separate from **Compute**. This separation of **Storage** and **Compute** is one of the key benefits of the cloud, which permits the user to scale one separate from the other. **Storage** itself may be tiered based on throughput, availability, and other features. Until a few years back, the **Compute** options were limited to the speed and generation of the underlying CPU chips. Now, we have options for GPU and **FPGA** (short- for **field-programmable gate array**) chips as well. Leveraging **Storage** and **Compute**, various services are built on the cloud fabric, which makes it easier to use ingest data, transform it, and build models. Services based on **Relational Databases**, **NoSQL**, **Hadoop**, **Spark**, and **Microservices** are some of the most frequent ones used to build AI solutions:

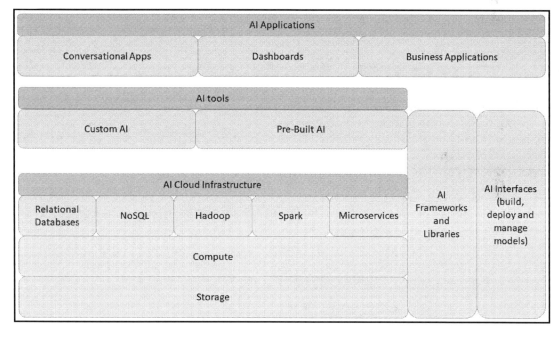

Essential building blocks of cloud AI

At the highest level of complexity are the various AI-focused services that are available on the cloud. These services fall on a spectrum with fully customizable solutions at one end, and easy-to-build solutions at the other. **Custom AI** is typically a solution that allows the user to bring in their own libraries or use proprietary ones to build an end-to-end solution. This typically involves a lot of hands-on coding and gives the builder complete control over different parts of the solution. **Pre-Built AI** is typically in the form of APIs that expose some type of service that can be easily incorporated into your solution. Examples of these include custom vision, text, and language-based AI solutions.

However complex the underlying AI may be, the goal of most applications is to make the end user experience as seamless as possible. This means that AI solutions need to integrate with general applications that reside in the organization solution stack. A lot of solutions use **Dashboards** or reports in the traditional BI space. These interfaces allow the user to explore the data generated by the AI solution. **Conversational Apps** are usually in the form of an intelligent interface (such as a bot) that interacts with the user in a conversational mode.

The Microsoft cloud – Azure

Microsoft's mission is been to empower every person and organization on Earth to achieve more. Microsoft Azure is a cloud platform designed to help customers achieve the intelligent cloud and the intelligent edge. Their vision is to help customers infuse AI into every application, both in the cloud and on compute devices of all form factors. With this in mind, Microsoft has developed a wide set of tools that can help its customer build AI into their applications with ease.

The following table shows the different tools that can be used to develop end-to-end AI solutions with Azure. The Azure Service column indicates those services that are owned and managed by Microsoft (first-party services). The Azure Marketplace column indicates third-party services or implementations of Microsoft products on Azure virtual machines, **Infrastructure as a service (IaaS)**:

	Azure Service	Azure Marketplace
Storage	File, Disk, Blob (Hot/Cool), Queue, Table, Archive	
Compute	VMs (CPU, GPU, FPGA), Functions, Batch, Cloud Services	Data Science VM (DSVM)
Relational Databases	SQL, SQL DW, PostgresSQL, MySQL	Oracle, MySQL, PostgresSQL
NoSQL Databases	CosmosDB, Table Storage	MongoDB, Cassandra
Hadoop	HDInsight (HBase, Hive LLAP, Kafka, Storm)	
Spark	Databricks, HDInsight Spark	
Microservices	Service Fabric, Kubernetes Service, Container Instances	
Custom AI	ML Services, ML Studio, Batch AI, Bot Service	ML Server
Pre-Built AI	Search, Custom Speech, Custom Vision, Language Understanding, Linguistic Analysis, Text Analytics	
Conversational Apps	Bot Service	
Dashboards	Power BI, Timer Series Insights	Tableau, Qlikview
Business Applications	Logic Apps, Web Apps	

Azure services that assist in AI solution building

The preceding table shows the different tools that can be used to develop end-to-end AI solutions on Azure. Due to the pace of the innovation of Azure, it is not easy to keep up with all the services and their updates.

One of the challenges that architects, developers, and data scientists face is picking the right Azure components for their solution.

 Picking the right components for a full, end-to-end solution is outside the scope of this book. Instead, we will focus on just the AI-specific tools that a developer, data engineer, or data scientist will need to use for their solution.

Choosing AI tools on Azure

In this book, we will assume that the you have knowledge and experience of AI in general. The goal here is not to touch on the basics of the various kinds of AI or to choose the correct algorithm; we assume you have a good understanding of what algorithms to choose in order to solve a given business need.

The following diagram shows a decision tree that can help you choose the right Azure AI tools. It is not meant to be comprehensive; just a guide to the correct technology choices. There are a lot of options that cross over, and this was difficult to depict on this diagram. Also keep in mind that an efficient AI solution would leverage multiple tools in combination:

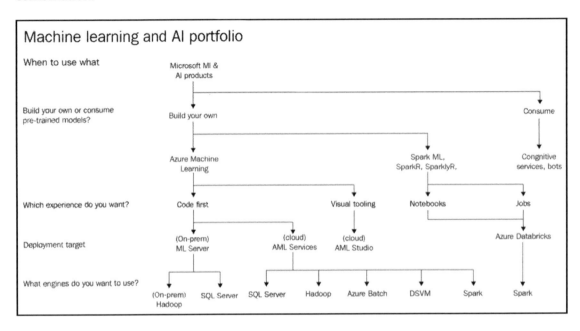

Decision tree guide to choosing AI tools on Azure

The preceding diagram shows a decision tree that helps users of **Microsoft's AI platform**. Starting from the top, the first question is whether you would like to **Build your own models or consume pre-trained models**. If you are building your own models, then it involves data scientists, data engineers, and developers at various stages of the process. In some use cases, developers prefer to just **consume pre-trained models**.

Cognitive Services/bots

Developers who would like to consume pre-trained AI models, typically use one of Microsoft's Cognitive Services. For those who are building conversational applications, a combination of Bot Framework and Cognitive Services is the recommended path. We will go into the details of Cognitive Services in Chapter 3, *Cognitive Services*, and Chapter 4, *Bot Framework*, but it is important to understand when to choose Cognitive Services.

Cognitive Services were built with the goal of giving developers the tools to rapidly build and deploy AI applications. Cognitive Services are pre-trained, customizable AI models that are exposed via APIs with accompanying SDKs and web services. They perform certain tasks, and are designed to scale based on the load against it. In addition, they are also designed to be compliant with security standards and other data isolation requirements. At the time of writing, there are broadly five types of Cognitive Services offered by Azure:

- Knowledge
- Language
- Search
- Speech
- Vision

Knowledge services are focused on building data-based intelligence into your application. QnA Maker is one such service that helps drive a question-and-answer service with all kinds of structured and semi-structured content. Underneath, the service leverages multiple services in Azure. It abstracts all that complexity from the user and makes it easy to create and manage.

Language services are focused on building text-based intelligence into your application. The **Language Understanding Intelligent Service**, **(LUIS)** is one type of service that allows users to build applications that can understand natural conversation and pass on the context of the conversation, also known as **NLP** (short for **Natural-language processing**), to the requesting application.

Search services are focused on providing services that integrate very specialized search tools for your application. These services are based on Microsoft's Bing search engine, but can be customized in multiple ways to integrate search into enterprise applications. The Bing Entity Search service is one such API that returns information about entities that Bing determines are relevant to a user's query.

Speech services are focused on providing services that allow developers to integrate powerful speech-enabled features into their applications, such as dictation, transcription, and voice command control. The custom speech service enables developers to build customized language modules and acoustic models tailored to specific types of applications and user profiles.

Vision services provide a variety of vision-based intelligent APIs that work on images or videos. The Custom Vision Service can be trained to detect a certain class of images after it has been trained on all the possible classes that the application is looking for.

Each of these Cognitive Services has limitations in terms of their applicability to different situations. They also have limits on scalability, but they are well-designed to handle most enterprise-wide AI solutions. Covering the limits and applicability of the services is outside the scope of this book and is well documented.

 Since updates occur on a monthly basis, it is best to refer to the Azure documentation to find the limits of these services.

As a developer, once you, knowingly or unknowingly, hit the limitations of Cognitive Services, the best option is to build your own models to meet your business requirements. Building your own AI models involves ingesting data, transforming it, performing feature engineering on it, training a model, and eventually, deploying the model. This can end up being an elaborate and time-consuming process, depending on the maturity of the organization's capabilities for the different tasks. Picking the right set of tools involves assessing that maturity during the different steps of the process and using a service that fits the organizational capabilities. Referring to the preceding diagram, the second question that gets asked of organizations that want to build their own AI models is related to the kind of experience they would like.

Azure Machine Learning Studio

Azure Machine Learning (Azure ML) Studio is the primary tool, purely a web-based GUI, to help build **machine learning (ML)** models. Azure ML Studio is an almost code-free environment that allows the user to build end-to-end ML solutions. It has Microsoft Research's proprietary algorithms built in, which can do most machine learning tasks with real simplicity. It can also embed Python or R code to enhance its functionality. One of the greatest features of Azure ML Studio is the ability to create a web service in a single click. The web service is exposed in the form of a REST endpoint that applications can send data to. In addition to the web service, an Excel spreadsheet is also created, which accesses the same web service and can be used to test the model's functionality and share it easily with end users.

At time of writing, the primary limitation with Azure ML Studio is the 10 GB limit on an experiment container. This limit will be explained in detail in Chapter 6, *Scalable Computing for Data Science*, but for now, it is sufficient to understand that Azure ML Studio is well-suited to training datasets that are in the 2 GB to 5 GB range. In addition, there are also limits to the amount of R and Python code that you can include in ML Studio, and its performance, which will be discussed in detail later.

ML Server

For a code-first experience, there are multiple tools available in the Microsoft portfolio. If organizations are looking to deploy on-premises (in addition to the cloud), the only option available is **Machine Learning Server** (**ML Server**). ML Server is an enterprise platform that supports both R and Python applications. It supports all the activities involved in the ML process end-to-end. ML Server was previously known as **R Server** and came about through Microsoft's acquisition of revolution analytics. Later, Python support was added to handle the variety of user preferences.

In ML Server, users can use any of the open source libraries as part of their solution. The challenge with a lot of the open source tooling is that it takes a lot of additional effort to get it to scale. Here, ML Server's RevoScaleR and revocalepy libraries provide that scalability for large datasets by efficiently managing data on disk and in memory. In terms of scalability, it is proven that ML Server can scale either itself or the compute engine. To scale ML Server, it is important to note that the only way is to scale up. In other words, this means that you create a single server with more/faster CPU, memory, and storage. It does not scale out by creating additional nodes of ML Server. To achieve scalability, ML Server also leverages the compute on the data engines with which it interacts. This is done by shifting the compute context to distributed compute, such as Spark or Hadoop. There is also the ability to shift the compute context to SQL Server with both R and Python so that the algorithms run natively on SQL Server without having to move the data to the compute platform.

The challenges with ML Server are mostly associated with the limitations surrounding R itself, since Python functionality is relatively new. ML Server needs to be fully managed by the user, so it adds an additional layer of management. The lack of scale-out features also poses a challenge in some situations.

Azure ML Services

Azure ML Services is a relatively new service on Azure that enhances productivity in the process of building AI solutions. Azure ML Services has different components. On the user's end, Azure ML Workbench is a tool that allows users to pull in data, transform it, build models, and run them against various kinds of compute. Workbench is a tool that users run on their local machines and connect to Azure ML services. Azure ML Services itself runs on Azure and consists of experimentation and model management for ML. The experimentation service keeps track of model testing, performance, and any other metrics you would like to track while building a model. The model management service helps manage the deployment of models and manages the overall life cycle of multiple models built by individual users or large teams.

When leveraging Azure ML Services, there are multiple endpoints that can act as engines for the services. At the time of writing, only Python-based endpoints are supported. SQL Server, with the introduction of built-in Python services, can act as an endpoint. This is beneficial, especially if the user has most of the data in SQL tables and wants to minimize data movement.

If you have leveraged Spark libraries for ML at scale on ML Services, then you can deploy to Spark-based solutions on Azure. Currently, these can be either Spark on HDInsight, or any other native implementation of Apache Spark (Cloudera, Hortonworks, and so on).

If the user has leveraged other Hadoop-based libraries to build ML Services, then those can be deployed to HDInsight or any of the Apache Hadoop implementations available on Azure.

Azure Batch is a service that provides large-scale, on-demand compute for applications that require such resources on an ad hoc or scheduled basis. The typical workflow for this use case involves the creation of a VM cluster, followed by the submission of jobs to the cluster. After the job is completed, the cluster is destroyed, and users do not pay for any compute afterward.

The **Data Science Virtual Machine (DSVM)** is a highly customized VM template built on either Linux or Windows. It comes pre-installed with a huge variety of curated data science tools and libraries. All the tools and libraries are configured to work straight out of the box with minimal effort. The DSVM has multiple applications, which we will cover in Chapter 7, *Machine Learning Server*, including utilization as a base image VM for Azure Batch.

One of the most highly scalable targets for running models built by Azure ML Services is to leverage containers through Docker and orchestration via Kubernetes. This is made easier by leveraging **Azure Kubernetes Services (AKS)**. Azure ML Services creates a Docker image that helps operationalize an ML model. The model itself is deployed as containerized Docker-based web services, while leveraging frameworks such as TensorFlow, and Spark. Applications can access this web service as a REST API. The web services can be scaled up and down by leveraging the scaling features of Kubernetes. More details on this topic will be covered in Chapter 10, *Building Deep Learning Solutions*.

The challenge with Azure ML Services is that it currently only supports Python. The platform itself has gone through some changes, and the heavy reliance on the command-line interface makes the interface not as user-friendly as some other tools.

Azure Databricks

Azure Databricks is one of the newest additions to the tools that can be used to build custom AI solutions on Azure. It is based on Apache Spark, but is optimized for use on the Azure platform. The Spark engine can be accessed by various APIs that can be based on Scala, Python, R, SQL, or Java. To leverage the scalability of Spark, users need to leverage Spark libraries when dealing with data objects and their transformations. Azure Databricks leverages these scalable libraries on top of highly elastic and scalable Spark clusters that are managed by the runtime. Databricks comes with enterprise-grade security, compliance, and collaboration features that distinguish it from Apache Spark. The ability to schedule and orchestrate jobs is also a great feature to have, especially when automating and streamlining AI workflows. Spark is also a great, unified platform for performing different analytics: interactive querying, ML, stream processing, and graph computation.

The challenge with Azure Databricks is that it is relatively new in Azure and does not integrate directly with some services. Another challenge is that users who are new to Spark would have to refactor their code to incorporate Spark libraries, without which they cannot leverage the benefits of the highly distributed environment available.

Summary

In summary, this chapter has given a brief overview of all the different services that are available on Azure to build AI solutions. In the innovative cloud world, it is hard to find a single solution that encompasses all the desired outcomes for an AI project. The goal of this book is to guide users on picking the right tool for the right task. Mature organizations realize that being agile and flexible is key to innovating in the cloud. In the next chapter, we will see TDSP stages and its tools.

2
Data Science Process

Over the past decade, organizations have seen a rapid growth in data. Harnessing insight from that data is crucial to the growth and sustenance of these organizations. Yet, groups chartered with extracting value from data fail for various reasons. In this chapter, we will cover how organizations can avoid the potential pitfalls of data science.

There is a larger discussion about the quality and governance of data, which we will not be covering here. Experienced data scientists recognize the challenges with data and account for them in their processes. In general, some of these challenges include the following:

- Poor data quality and consistency
- Silos of data driven by individual business teams
- Technologies that are hard to integrate with other data sources
- The inability to deal with the Vs of big data: volume, velocity, variety, and veracity

In some cases, there are purely organizational challenges that result from a lack of vision and leadership.

On the flip side, data scientists typically come from strong math backgrounds. They end up spending a lot of time refining their models.

TDSP stages

The **Team Data Science Process** (**TDSP**) is a methodology created by Microsoft to guide the full life cycle of data science projects in organizations. It is not meant to be a complete solution, but simply a framework by which teams can add structure to their processes and achieve the full business value of their analytics.

Besides TDSP, the other prevalent methodology that organizations have been adopting is called **CRISP-DM** (short for **Cross-Industry Standard Process for Data Mining**). This methodology has been around since the mid-1990s. There were several attempts to update it in the 2000s, but they were abandoned. The primary focus of CRISP-DM was data mining, but its principles can be extended to data science as well. The major steps listed in CRISP-DM are as follows: business understanding, data understanding, data preparation, modeling, evaluation, and deployment. For practitioners, these steps may seem redundant, but for organizations that are new to deriving value from data, this is a great framework to build a process around. In fact, a lot of the data science tools released on the market by various vendors inherently have functionality that drives users through these steps.

There are several gaps in the CRISP-DM methodology when applied to data science. The most glaring one is the need to connect business outcomes with every step of the process. Challenges in data quality, data sources, biases, algorithm quality, and scalability need to be addressed beyond what is listed here.

TDSP is not an alternative to CRISP-DM, but can be viewed as an additional framework that can be augmented to include existing workflows around data. TDSP is more task-focused, but shares some of the same concepts at a high level with CRISP-DM.

One of the core tenets of TDSP is that the outcome of the data science life cycle as shown in the following diagram is intelligent applications that deliver value to the business. New data science projects can leverage portions of TDSP with the expectation that they will graduate as they become more mature and leverage the other steps of the process. In that sense, TDSP is meant to be iterative and agile. Depending on the nature and maturity of the project, some processes can be eliminated.

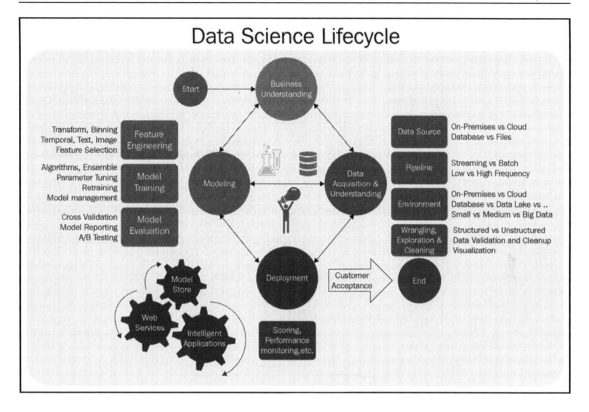

There are five broad stages defined in TDSP, as follows:

- Business understanding
- Data acquisition and understanding
- Modeling
- Deployment
- Customer acceptance

Business understanding

In this stage of TDSP, there are two tasks that drive its goals:

- Defining objectives
- Identifying data sources

Let's break down and analyze each of these tasks and look at how they help derive business understanding.

The defining objectives task includes the following factors:

- **Model targets**: The success of the project is driven by the business goal, which is, in turn, driven by some variable(s) tracked during the analysis. These variables are called **model targets**, and there may be multiple metrics associated with the model targets that predicate their success. An example of frequently used model targets are revenue forecasts, or the probability of a transaction being fraudulent.
- **Relevant questions**: You can define the goals of the project by posing questions to the stakeholders that are relevant, specific, and clear-cut. Typically, questions are answered with numbers or categories/states. Examples of questions include the following:
  - What product(s) are they likely to buy? (Recommendation)
  - How can we group these together? (Clustering)
  - Is this abnormal? (Anomaly detection)
  - How many or how much? (Regression)
  - Which category/state does this belong to? (Classification)

  Some business problems might involve answering more than one of these questions at a time. Understanding which questions are relevant and ascertaining their answers will help clarify the desired business outcomes.

- **Roles and milestones**: The roles and responsibilities of every member of the team will need to be assigned based on the overall project plan. The high-level project plan has milestones that get iterated upon as the project moves along and more details are understood.
- **Success metrics**: There need to be clear criteria for determining the success of the project and these are tied to the business impact. For example, in a predictive maintenance solution, the goal may be to reduce the average period of equipment downtime by x percentage over a span of 6 months. Borrowing from a management concept, we can design the metrics using SMART:
  - Specific
  - Measurable
  - Achievable
  - Relevant
  - Time-bound

For the identifying data sources task, in most cases, there are people within the organization who are trying to answer the same question as the data science problem. Using that as a starting point, it is possible to identify the various data sources that will answer some of the questions laid out in the previous steps.

These data sources may be the following:

- Data that has an impact on the question, directly or indirectly
- Data that directly measures the model target and the important features

Deliverable

The deliverable as follows:

- **Charter document**: This document is used to keep track of the various aspects of the project. These include business background, scope, personnel, plan, architecture, metrics, and communication. A template for this document is provided here: `https://github.com/Azure/Azure-TDSP-ProjectTemplate/blob/master/Docs/Project/Charter.md`.
- **Data sources**: This document describes all the data sources and any required transformations to incorporate them into the project. Any processed data or engineered features are also kept track of. A template of this deliverable is shown here: `https://github.com/Azure/Azure-TDSP-ProjectTemplate/blob/master/Docs/Data_Report/Data%20Defintion.md`.
- **Data dictionaries**: This document provides detailed descriptions for each of the data sources. This may include table schemas and data types with examples. A template for this deliverable is provided here: `https://github.com/Azure/Azure-TDSP-ProjectTemplate/tree/master/Docs/Data_Dictionaries`.

Data acquisition and understanding

In this stage of TDSP, there are three tasks that drive its goals:

- **Ingest data**: To make the exploration and modeling of the data easier, it is ideal to have the source data moved into a single analytics system as much as possible. Within Azure, the ability to move data across the different services is made easy through various tools, keeping these kinds of use cases in mind.

- **Explore data**: Understanding the nature of the data is key to successful analytics projects. In most organizations, data comes with a lot of flaws: outliers, missing values, bad values, and so on. Visualizing the data and analyzing the characteristics of the data is a prerequisite for successful data science projects. This is also typically an iterative process, since some data cleansing is required before other flaws get revealed in the data.

  One of the tools released by Microsoft to assist in this process is an automated utility called **IDEAR** (short for **Interactive Data Exploration, Analysis and Reporting**).The tool has versions for both R and Python, and is available at `https://github.com/Azure/Azure-TDSP-Utilities`. IDEAR can be used to visualize data and prepare reports summarizing data.

  Upon exploring your data, you can start cleaning it up to prepare it for modeling. Some of the typical tasks involved in preparing data for modeling are as follows:

    - Detecting and removing noisy data and outliers
    - Removing or filling in missing values
    - Normalizing data to deal with noise and scale
    - Reducing data records or attributes for easier data handling
    - Discretizing data by converting continuous values into categorical values
    - Removing unwanted characters within data that may create issues when building a model (text analytics)

- **Data pipeline**: In many data science projects, there is the need to refresh the data after the initial dataset is used to build a model. The data may be to score new test data or for the continuous retraining of models. A more robust pipeline is typically built in the deployment phase, but it makes sense to build this pipeline during the current phase in parallel. The constraints and business requirements of the data science project will define the kind of pipeline being set up as either batch, streaming/real-time, or hybrid.

Deliverable

The deliverable as follows:

- **Data quality report**: The IDEAR tool can help create reports that summarize the source data and target variable.
- **Solution architecture**: At this stage of the project, a diagram or description of the data flow can be drawn to show the scoring and retraining (if needed) of pipelines.
- **Checkpoint decision**: Based on the initial evaluation of the data, you can make a decision regarding whether to pursue the project beyond this phase. If the expected business value is not clear at this stage, a decision can be made on getting additional data or discontinuing the project. In some cases, the stakeholders might consider reframing.

Modeling

In this stage, there are three main tasks that deliver its goals:

- **Feature engineering**: In many use cases, the raw data by itself may not be a good indicator of the target variable. Depending on the algorithms being used, it may be necessary to transform some data features into new features that allow its effective use.

  This task is considered part of the art of effective data science projects. It requires an effective combination of the insights obtained from the data exploration task and domain expertise. There is also the predicament of picking the correct number of features to build the model. Using too many variables may add unnecessary noise to the model, while choosing too few may not accurately predict the target variable(s). Any transformational steps carried out on the source data will also need to be carried out on the new data introduced while building a scoring pipeline.

- **Model training**: Choosing the correct algorithm is dependent on the type of problem that the project is trying to solve. The best algorithm will answer the business question in the most impactful manner. Typically, the model training process involves the following tasks:
    - Splitting the input data into a training and test dataset.
    - Building multiple models using the training dataset.

- Evaluating the performance of the model for the given dataset split and comparing multiple algorithms across multiple tuning parameters to establish the best fitting model.
- Establishing which model delivers the best success metric. Sometimes, an ensemble of multiple models may be required to obtain the best metrics.

An automated modeling and reporting utility in R is available here as part of the TDSP utilities from Microsoft: `https://github.com/Azure/Azure-TDSP-Utilities/blob/master/DataScienceUtilities/Modeling/Automated-Modeling-Reporting-Instructions.md`.

Deliverable

The deliverable as follows:

- **Feature sets**: The features chosen to build the model are recorded as part of the Data Definition report. If any of the features are generated from the raw data, the code to generate the features is recorded in this report.
- **Model report**: A standard report will show how each model performed against the various metrics. These metrics may include accuracy metrics, as well as the speed and efficiency of the model.
- **Checkpoint**: Evaluate the performance of the model and determine whether it is good enough to deploy to production systems.

Deployment

The main tasks involved in this stage are to deploy the model and the data pipeline into a production-like environment for consumption by an application.

Once you have a model or collection of models that deliver the required business metrics, you can operationalize them for different applications. Models are typically exposed by some API interface that allows the application to interact with them and generate predictions for various inputs. These APIs can typically handle batch or real-time, or a hybrid of these two, for its input data. The web service itself will be typically resilient, robust, and scalable. This is achieved by keeping track of various metrics of the web service to keep track of the load on the service and help troubleshoot any errors.

Deliverable

The deliverable as follows:

- A dashboard that shows the health and key metrics of the prediction system
- A modeling report that shows the deployment details
- A solution architecture document capturing the various components of the solution

Customer acceptance

The main tasks involved in this stage are as follows:

- **System validation**: Confirming that the deployed model and data pipeline meet the stakeholders needs
- **Project hand-off**: Hand the system off to the group that is going to run the system in production

The customer should verify that the end-to-end solution meets the business needs as defined in the initial business understanding phase. Does the system make timely predictions that satisfy the metrics chosen for the application?

All the documentation is reviewed and finalized and handed off to the group in charge of running operations. This group will be responsible for taking the work done thus far and maintaining it over its life cycle.

Deliverable

An exit report for the project is delivered at the end of this stage. It contains all the details of the project that are required to operate and maintain the system to its full design potential. A template of the exit report is provided here: `https://github.com/Azure/Azure-TDSP-ProjectTemplate/blob/master/Docs/Project/Exit%20Report.md`.

Tools for TDSP

Microsoft has released a set of tools that make it easier for organizations to follow the TDSP process. One of those tools is the IDEAR utility released for CRAN-R, Microsoft R, and Python. Another tool is the **Automated Modeling and Reporting (AMAR)** utility. In this section, we will look into how we can leverage these tools in the TDSP process.

IDEAR tool for R

To install this tool, navigate to `https://github.com/Azure/Azure-TDSP-Utilities/blob/master/DataScienceUtilities/DataReport-Utils/R/Run-IDEAR.R` in order to retrieve the code required for this tool. Download the GitHub repository to make it easier to navigate the different files required for this exercise.

Open R Studio on your computer, navigate to the preceding file, and open it. In the top-right corner of the code tab, click on **Source** to execute the package, as follows:

```
RStudio
File  Edit  Code  View  Plots  Session  Build  Debug  Profile  Tools  Help
                                    Go to file/function        Addins

Run-IDEAR.R

                Source on Save                                    Run        Source

1   repos.date <- "2017-08-01"
2   options(repos = c(CRAN = paste("https://mran.revolutionanalytics.com/snapshot/",
3                                  repos.date,sep="")))
4
5   installed_packages <- rownames(installed.packages())
6   # intall knitr
7   if (!'knitr' %in% installed_packages){
8     install.packages('knitr')
9   } else if ('1.16' != installed.packages()['knitr','version']){
10    remove.packages('knitr')
11    install.packages('knitr')
12  }
13
14  if (!"rmarkdown" %in% installed_packages){
15    install.packages("rmarkdown")
16  }
17
18  if (!"shiny" %in% installed_packages){
```

Then, the following prompt will be shown:

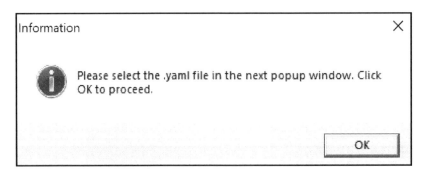

Information   ✕

Please select the .yaml file in the next popup window. Click OK to proceed.

OK

An example `.yaml` file can be loaded from the following location. Select `para-adult.yaml` as follows:

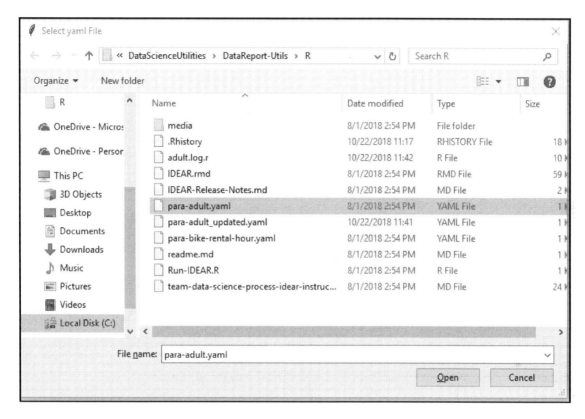

This will open a data quality report for the data example described in the YAML file, as shown in the following screenshot:

You can use the menu on the left-hand side to navigate through the different sections of the output. The first section is the **Task Summary**, which gives a summary of the file read by listing the file location, the names of the different types of variables, and the data science task type (for example, classification):

1 Task Summary

- The metadata (categorical columns, numerical columns, target, etc.) is specified in - *C:/Users/thabraha/Documents/Azure-TDSP-Utilities-master/DataScienceUtilities/DataReport-Utils/R/para-adult.yaml*
- The data location is - *../../../Data/Common/UCI_Income/train.*
- The target is - *label_IsOver50K.*
- The task type is - *classification.*
- The numerical variables are - *age, fnlwgt, educationnum, capitalgain, capitalloss, hoursperweek.*
- The categorical variables are - *workclass, education, maritalstatus, occupation, relationship, race, sex, nativecountry, label_IsOver50K.*

Click on **Data Summary** to get to the next section. Under 2.1 in the following screenshot, you can see a sample of the data by picking the top n number of rows desired:

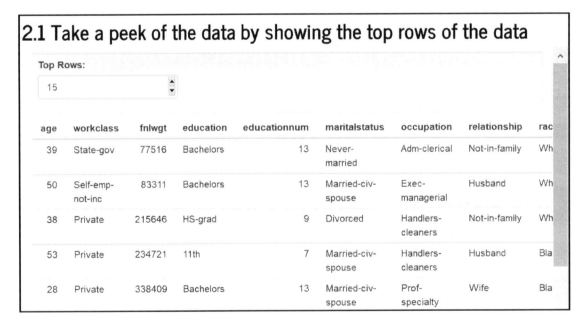

2.1 Take a peek of the data by showing the top rows of the data

Top Rows:

15

age	workclass	fnlwgt	education	educationnum	maritalstatus	occupation	relationship	rac
39	State-gov	77516	Bachelors	13	Never-married	Adm-clerical	Not-in-family	Wh
50	Self-emp-not-inc	83311	Bachelors	13	Married-civ-spouse	Exec-managerial	Husband	Wh
38	Private	215646	HS-grad	9	Divorced	Handlers-cleaners	Not-in-family	Wh
53	Private	234721	11th	7	Married-civ-spouse	Handlers-cleaners	Husband	Bla
28	Private	338409	Bachelors	13	Married-civ-spouse	Prof-specialty	Wife	Bla

This is a great way to visually examine the data that is loaded for discrepancies. Section 2.2 of the following screenshot shows a summary of the data by counting the number of rows and columns:

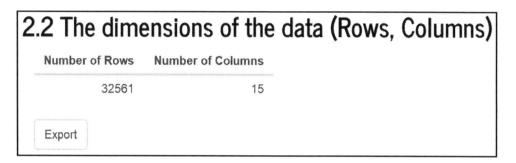

In Section 2.3, the report displays the names and types of the columns, indicating whether they are numeric or categorical:

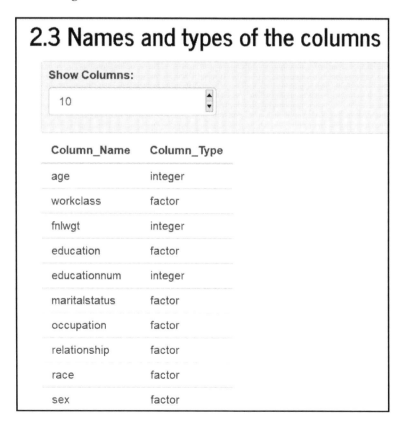

Section 2.4 of the report examines the quality of the data. This report maps the percentage of missing data for each of the variables. The heat map formatting helps to detect any missing data pattern:

2.4 Check the data quality

You can select the number of top variables with the highest rates of missing data, and the number of segments you want to split the data in order to know roughly where missing values exist.

Show Top Variables:	Data Split Segments	Missing Value Symbol
10	10	?

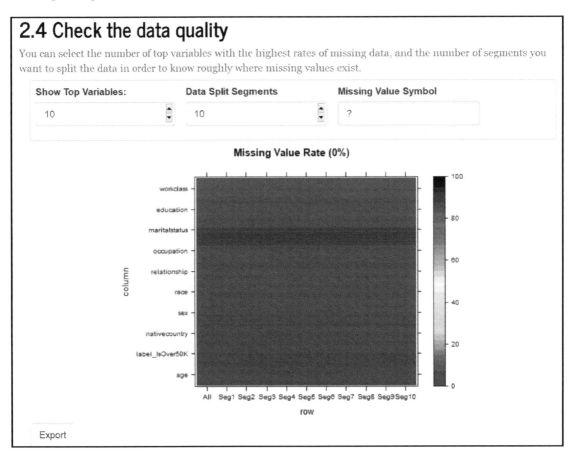

Section 2.5 summarizes the basic statistics of the data by showing the percentiles for the numeric data and the frequency count for the categorical data:

2.5 Summarize basic statisics of the data

Var1	Var2	Freq
	age	Min. :17.00
	age	1st Qu.:28.00
	age	Median :37.00
	age	Mean :38.58
	age	3rd Qu.:48.00
	age	Max. :90.00
	age	NA
	workclass	Private :22696
	workclass	Self-emp-not-inc: 2541
	workclass	Local-gov : 2093
	workclass	? : 1836
	workclass	State-gov : 1298
	workclass	Self-emp-inc : 1116
	workclass	(Other) : 981

Now we move on to Section 3, where we dive deeper into each of the individual variables to investigate them further. In Section 3.1, you can see more detailed statistics of each variable:

3.1 More detailed statistics of each variable

```
age
          n  missing distinct     Info     Mean      Gmd      .05      .10      .25      .50
       .75      .90
     32561        0       73        1    38.58     15.4       19       22       28       37
        48       58
       .95
        63

lowest : 17 18 19 20 21, highest: 85 86 87 88 90
```

```
workclass
          n  missing distinct
     32561        0        9
```

Value	?	Federal-gov	Local-gov	Never-worked	Pri
vate					
Frequency	1836	960	2093	7	2
2696					
Proportion	0.056	0.029	0.064	0.000	0
.697					

Value	Self-emp-inc	Self-emp-not-inc	State-gov	Without-pay
Frequency	1116	2541	1298	14
Proportion	0.034	0.078	0.040	0.000

In Section 3.2, you can visualize the target variable:

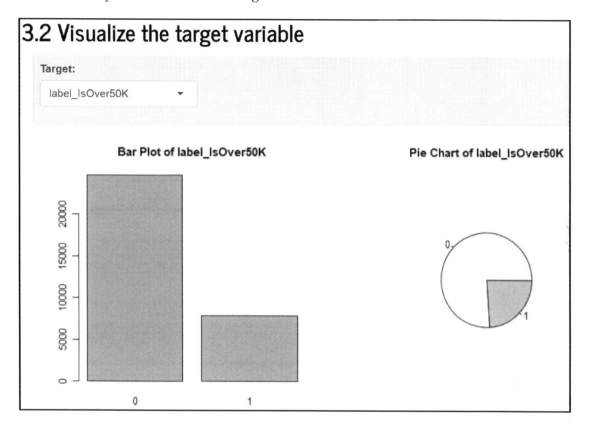

In Section 3.3, you can visualize any of the numerical variables and look at quantiles and the distribution of the data:

3.3 Visualize the numerical variables

You can select the variable from the drop list.

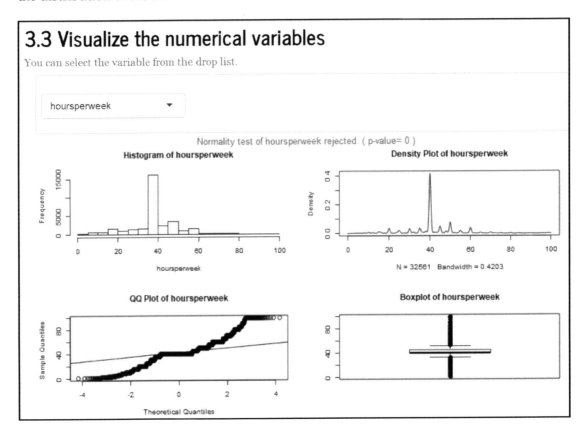

In Section 3.4, you can visualize the categorical variables, showing the frequency of the distinct categories within them:

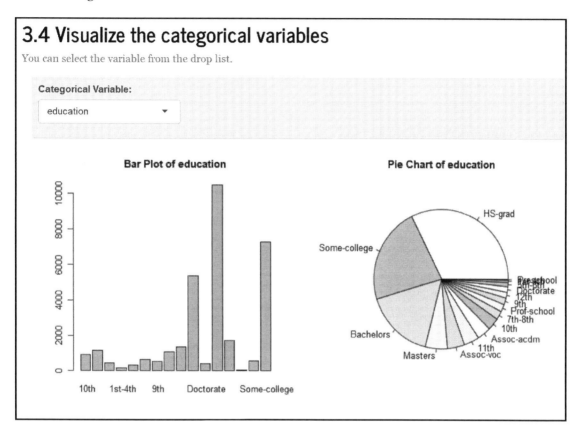

In Section 4, the report helps you to analyze the relationship between the different variables. This is important for understanding which variables are important for building the model, and which can be dropped. In Section 4.1, you can rank the impact of the variables relative to a reference variable:

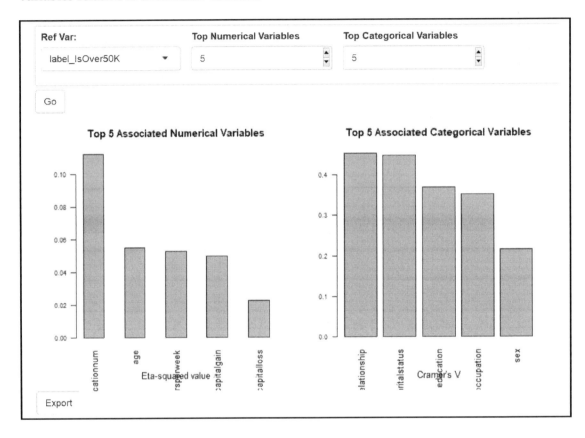

In Section 4.2, you can examine the correlation between two categorical variables. For example, in the following plot, we see that males have more income than females:

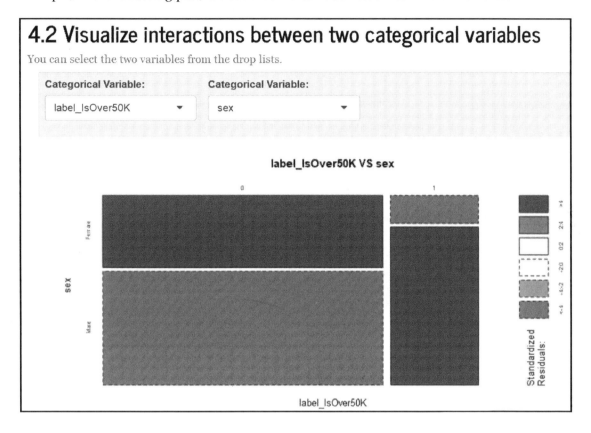

Similarly, in Section 4.3, you can see the interaction between two numerical variables:

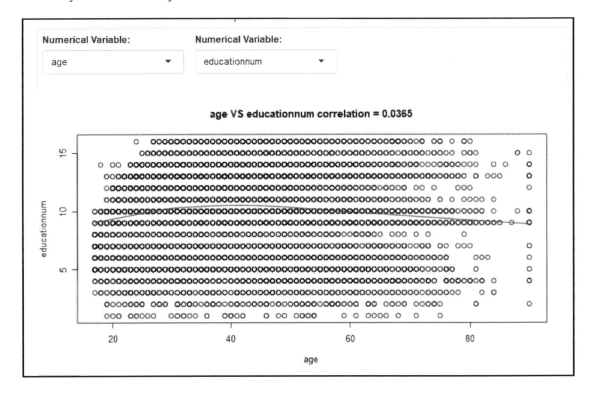

In Section 4.4, you can use different correlation methods to calculate the correlation between numerical variables:

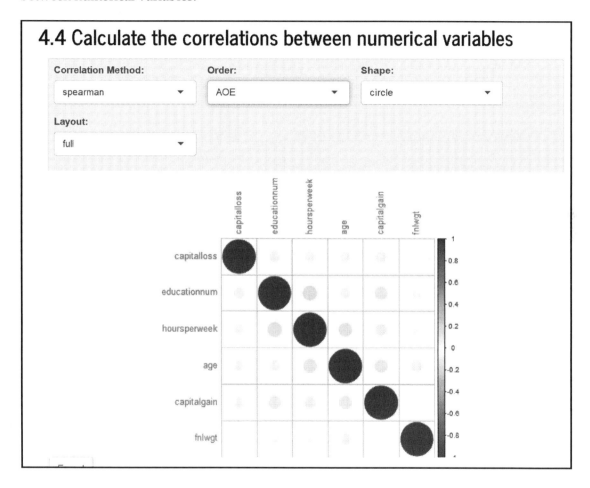

In Section 4.5, you can visualize the interactions between numerical and categorical variables using box plots:

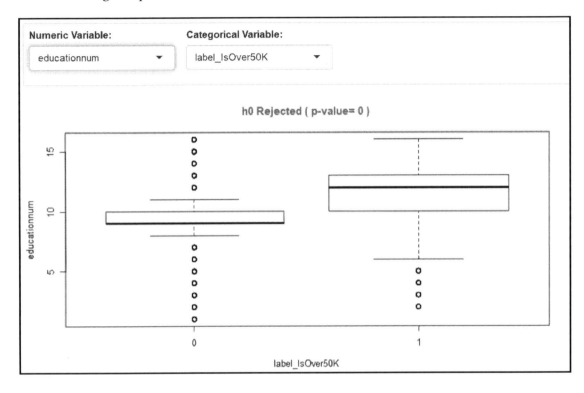

The next three sections focus on multivariate statistics. Section 4.6 leverages **Principal Component Analysis (PCA)** to look at the distribution of data in a reduced variable space:

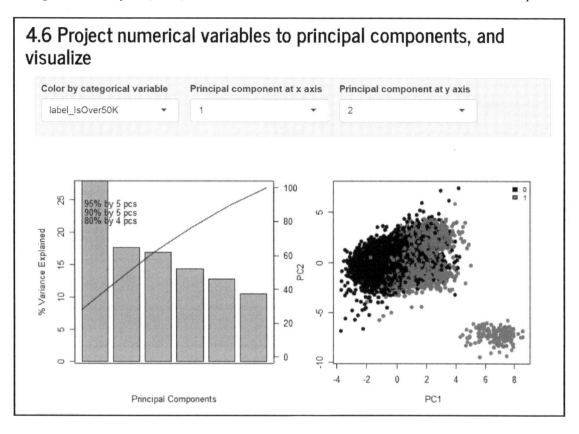

4.6 Project numerical variables to principal components, and visualize

In Section 4.7, you can project numerical variables to 2D space using the t-SNE method. In Section 4.8, you can project both numerical and categorical variables to PCA and visualize them simultaneously:

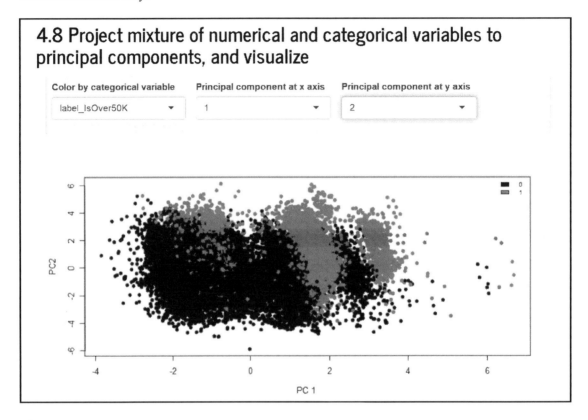

In Section 5, if you click on the **Generate Report** button, it will create a summary report with all the summaries from the preceding sections.

Automated modeling and reporting (AMAR) in R

The AMR tool is a customizable, semi-automated utility built into R to train and evaluate single or multiple machine learning models. It has features such as parameter sweeping to find the model that fits the desired metrics.

Once the report is generated, it contains the following information:

- A model description
- A model evaluation and comparison
- A ranking of the features

In general, the information described in the report can help increase the following:

- The quality of the feature variables
- The level of difficulty for the machine learning task
- Guidance for subsequent feature engineering and modeling

The AMAR tool is available at the following GitHub location: `https://github.com/Azure/Azure-TDSP-Utilities/tree/master/DataScienceUtilities/Modeling`. There are two ways to run the R markdown file that builds the report:

- **Using the R Studio console**: Navigate to the directory where the modeling `.rmd` file exists, and then use the following commands for regression or classification:
    - **Regression**:
      ```
      rmarkdown::render("RegressionModelSelection.rmd")
      ```
    - **Binary classification**:
      ```
      rmarkdown::render("BinaryModelSelection.rmd")
      ```
- **Using the knit function in RStudio**: Open the `.rmd` file in R Studio and click on `knit` at the top:

```
RegressionModelSelection.rmd ×

                    ABC  Q        Knit    ▼   ⚙  ▼
                                 Knit the current
  1 ▾  ---                       document (Ctrl
  2    title: "Automated M  +Shift+K)  ining: Regression"
  3    date: "`r format(Sys.time(), '%B %d, %Y')`"
  4    author: "Team Data Science Process by Microsoft"
  5    output:
  6      html_document:
  7        fig_caption: yes
  8        number_sections: yes
  9        toc: yes
```

The report that is generated is in HTML format and has six sections. We will review the sections in the next few paragraphs. Section 0.1 is an introduction to the machine learning problem and gives details about the specific problem that is being solved. Section 0.2 gives more information about the YAML file used for the report. The YAML file contains all the variable definitions and details about how to run the different machine learning models:

Automated Model training: Binary classification

Team Data Science Process by Microsoft

September 23, 2016

0.1 Introduction

This R Markdown performs **exploratory** model training and evaluation for **binary classification** tasks using the Caret package, which has convenient functions for resampling, hyper-parameter sweeping, and model accuracy comparison. The user can use Caret with R machine learning packages (such as, glmnet, RandomForest, xgboost, etc.). We use these three algorithms with limited paraUsers can customize this template to create their own model training and evaluation process for binary classification tasks.

```
## package 'pROC' successfully unpacked and MD5 sums checked
## package 'ROCR' successfully unpacked and MD5 sums checked
##
## The downloaded binary packages are in
##   C:\Users\remoteuser\AppData\Local\Temp\2\RtmpeExHP1\downloaded_packages
```

0.2 Specify YAML parameter file for input data and modeling

Specify the file which contins the parameter set to train the ML models with. If there are multiple values for each parameter file, then modes ML algorithms will be run with a specified number of random combination of these parameters (currently set to 59).

```
## [1] "Yaml file loc: C:\\Users\\remoteuser\\Source\\Repos\\DGADSCommonUtilities\\DataScienceUtilitie
s\\Modeling\\BinaryClassification\\YamlFiles\\BinaryClassification_UCI_Income.yaml"
```

Section 0.3 gives a summary of the data being input, as well as of how the training and testing data are built:

0.3 Input data, and splitting data into train/test

Once the data is read in, it is split into training and testing. Modeling is run on training data (using CV/bootstrapping and parameter sweeping), and evaluated on the test data.

```
## [1] "Input data description: UCI Adult Census & Income Binary Classification Dataset"
```

```
## [1] "Train/test split percent: 0.75"
```

```
##    income age    type_employer fnlwgt education education_num
## 1     X0  39         State.gov  77516 Bachelors            13
## 2     X0  50 Self.emp.not.inc  83311 Bachelors            13
## 3     X0  38           Private 215646   HS.grad             9
##          marital          occupation relationship  race  sex
## 1    Never.married       Adm.clerical Not.in.family White Male
## 2 Married.civ.spouse   Exec.managerial      Husband White Male
## 3         Divorced Handlers.cleaners Not.in.family White Male
##   capital_gain capital_loss hr_per_week country
## 1         2174            0          40 Vietnam
## 2            0            0          13 Vietnam
## 3            0            0          40 Vietnam
```

In Section 0.4, the report describes the various machine learning algorithms that were used to build this report. It also describes how the features are trained to build the model. As you can see in the following example, this binary classification problem is being trained using the GlmNet, RandomForest, and xgBoost algorithms:

0.4 Model training

0.4.1 Define hyper-parameter sets for glmnet, randomForest and xgBoost

Create the control object for cross validation and parameter sweeping. Here we can use OneSE (one standard error) as selection function. By default, Caret's train uses 'best' model, i.e. the tuning parameters associated with the largest (or lowest for "RMSE") performance. oneSE is a rule in the spirit of the "one standard error" rule of Breiman et al. (1984), who suggest that the tuning parameter associated with the best performance may over fit. They suggest that the simplest model within one standard error of the empirically optimal model is the better choice.

Also, for hyper-parameter sweeping, within a fixed computational time, selecting a random set of parameters (or 'random' search option) is typically a better choise than entire grid search for identifying parameter-set that will provide an optimal model, Bergstra and Bengio, 2012. Therefore, we use a 59 point random grid sample of hyper-parameters. Choosing 59 random points from a hyper-parameter grid will guarantee with 95% confidence that one of the hyper-parameter set will provide a model with accuracy that is within top 5% of the accuracy of all the grid hyper-parameters.

0.4.2 Define train formula based on target and features in parameters file

```
## income ~ age + type_employer + fnlwgt + education + education_num +
##     marital + occupation + relationship + race + sex + capital_gain +
##     capital_loss + hr_per_week + country
```

0.4.3 Train glmnet, randomForest, and xgBoost with parameter sweeping

```
## [1] "Train GlmNet Model: TRUE"
```

```
## [1] "Train RandomForest Model: TRUE"
```

```
## [1] "Train xgBoost Model: TRUE"
```

In Section 0.5, we use different methods to evaluate the model's accuracy and look at which variables impact the target variable the most.

In Section 0.5.1, we look at the accuracy of the three algorithms by looking at their ROC, sensitivity, and specificity:

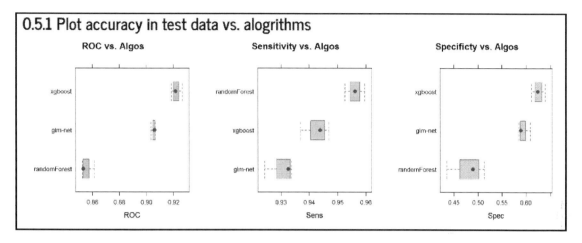

In Section 0.5.2, we can visualize the actual data against the predicted values for each of the different models:

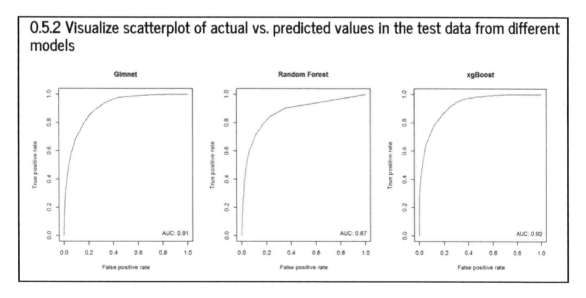

Section 0.5.3 is probably one of the most important sections in exploratory modeling, since it focuses on finding the most important features as described by each of the models. This becomes more relevant in use cases that have too many features, where you need to reduce the number of variables being used in modeling. Section 6 is a summary that can be customized to include any findings from the analysis:

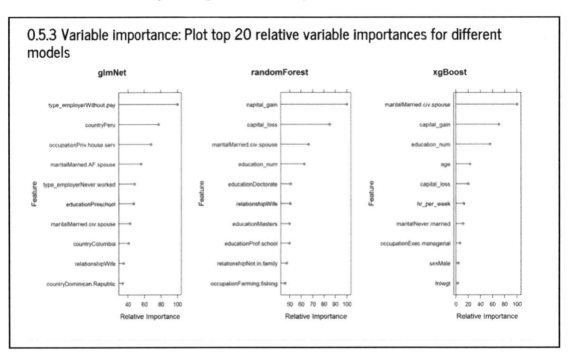

Summary

In conclusion, we have introduced you to the TDSP in this chapter and covered each of the different steps that are involved in detail. This process is meant to augment other existing processes rather than replace them. We also looked at various TDSP utilities that Microsoft has provided that make it easier to build some structure into the data science life cycle. In the next few chapters, we will look at each of the options available within Azure to build AI solutions for your business needs.

3
Cognitive Services

Cognitive Services are a set of pre-trained APIs from Microsoft that allow developers to develop applications that use AI without having to build ML models. With their support for edge deployment, developers can build applications that use powerful AI algorithms to interpret, listen, speak, and see on devices such as a drone.

There are five main categories of APIs:

- Vision
- Language
- Speech
- Knowledge
- Search

Many of these APIs are now customizable to meet the specific needs of companies and their customers. In this chapter, we will look at an overview of each service category and go through a number of examples.

Cognitive Services for Vision APIs

The Vision APIs help you to add image analysis capabilities to your AI application. At the time of writing, there are five Vision APIs included with Cognitive Services:

- Computer Vision
- Face
- Content Moderator
- Video Indexer
- Custom Vision

We will be learning about the first two APIs in this chapter. We will leave the rest for you to explore on your own.

The Computer Vision API

This API provides tags for images based on various recognizable objects, living beings, actions, and scenery. After uploading an image or specifying an image's URL, the algorithm of the Computer Vision API comes up with tags that it identified in the image. This might include the main subject, the setting (indoor or outdoor), furniture, tools, plants, animals, accessories, and gadgets.

Let's take a look at an example image:

We send this to the API and get the output in JSON format. This will show us the tags and the confidence that is associated with each tag:

Tags	```[{ "name": "bench", "confidence": 0.999963641 }, { "name": "outdoor", "confidence": 0.9997799 }, { "name": "grass", "confidence": 0.99955374 }, { "name": "tree", "confidence": 0.994908869 }, { "name": "park", "confidence": 0.9774111 }, { "name": "sitting", "confidence": 0.974007249 }, { "name": "overlooking", "confidence": 0.59242034 }]```

To try out the Computer Vision API quickly, you can go to the following URL: `https://azure.microsoft.com/en-us/services/cognitive-services/computer-vision/`.

As an AI developer, you can use any language to call the API. In this example, we will look at how to call the API using Python, but a similar approach can be used for other programming languages. The steps involved are as follows:

1. Create a Computer Vision API Cognitive Services resource from the Azure portal: `https://portal.azure.com`.

2. Navigate to the API, as shown in the following screenshot. Click on **Create a resource**, then on **AI + Machine Learning**, and then on **Computer Vision**:

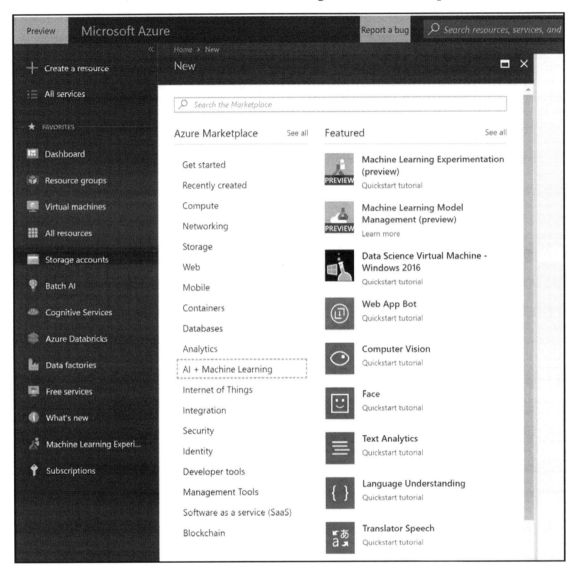

3. Alternatively, you can search for `Computer Vision` in the Azure portal:

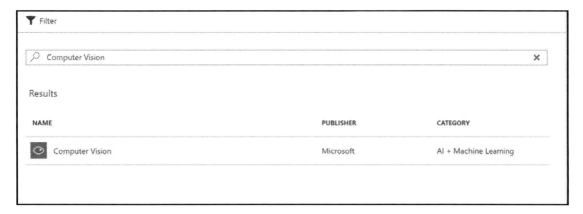

4. Provide a name for your service and then select an appropriate Azure
   subscription, a location, and a pricing tier (either free or paid). You will also need
   to create a new resource group or select an existing one:

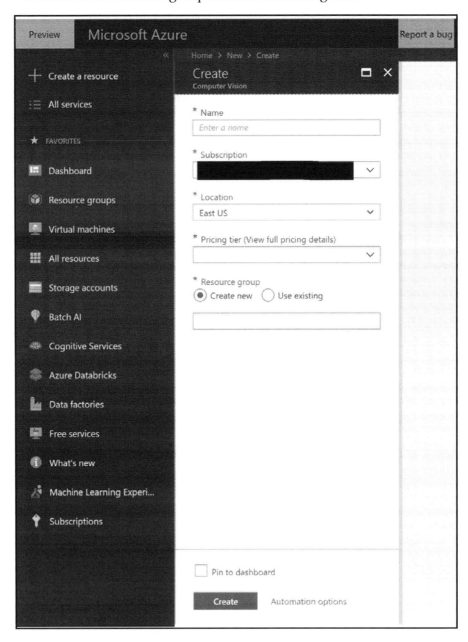

5. It will take less than a minute to create the API. Once it is created, you will see the **Quick start** page, which has links to the API keys and its documentation. You will need the API keys to access the API from your Python (or any other language) code, or the code for whichever language you are using. Once you create the API, you will see the following screen:

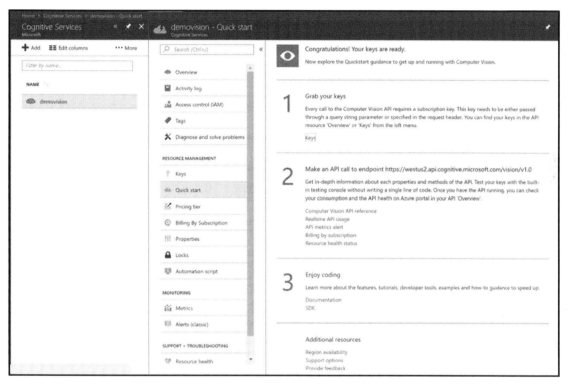

6. Use your favorite Python editor and call the API using the following sample code:

```python
# Replace <Subscription Key> with your valid subscription's api
access key.
subscription_key = "<Access Key>"
assert subscription_key

# Replace the base url with what you see as Endpoint in the portal's
Overview section under your computer vision api
vision_base_url =
"https://westus.api.cognitive.microsoft.com/vision/v1.0/"

vision_analyze_url = vision_base_url + "analyze"
```

```
# Set image_url to the URL of an image that you want to analyze.
image_url =
"https://upload.wikimedia.org/wikipedia/commons/thumb/1/12/" + \
    "Flickr_-_Duncan~_-_London_from_Parliament_Hill.jpg/640px-
Flickr_-_Duncan~_-
London_from_Parliament_Hill.jpg"

import requests
headers  = {'Ocp-Apim-Subscription-Key': subscription_key }
params   = {'visualFeatures': 'Categories,Description,Color'}
data     = {'url': image_url}
response = requests.post(vision_analyze_url, headers=headers,
params=params, json=data)
response.raise_for_status()

# The 'analysis' object contains various fields that describe the
image. The most
# relevant caption for the image is obtained from the
'descriptions' property.
analysis = response.json()
print(analysis)

image_caption =
analysis["description"]["captions"][0]["text"].capitalize()

# Display the image and overlay it with the caption.
# If you are using a Jupyter notebook, uncomment the following
line.

#%matplotlib inline
from PIL import Image
from io import BytesIO
import matplotlib.pyplot as plt
image = Image.open(BytesIO(requests.get(image_url).content))
plt.imshow(image)
plt.axis("off")
_ = plt.title(image_caption, size="x-large", y=-0.1)
```

7. When you run the preceding code, you will see the following output:

```
{'categories': [{'name': 'outdoor_', 'score': 0.02734375, 'detail':
{'landmarks': []}}],
'description': {'captions': [{'text': 'a person sitting on a bench
overlooking the city', 'confidence':
0.9162166873980091}],
'tags': ['bench', 'outdoor', 'grass', 'park', 'sitting', 'picnic',
'overlooking', 'wooden', 'building', 'man',
'field', 'water', 'view', 'green', 'city', 'woman', 'hill', 'lake',
```

```
'table', 'grassy', 'river', 'people']},
'requestId': 'b755820b-f44c-4008-9451-efe6a0db08ae',
'metadata': {'format': 'Jpeg', 'width': 640, 'height': 440},
'color': {'dominantColorForeground': 'Green',
'dominantColorBackground': 'White', 'dominantColors': ['Green',
'White', 'Grey'], 'isBwImg': False, 'accentColor': '866045'}}
```

8. Each transaction equates to one API call. The portal will show you the details that you can monitor, including total calls, errors, latency, and data in/out:

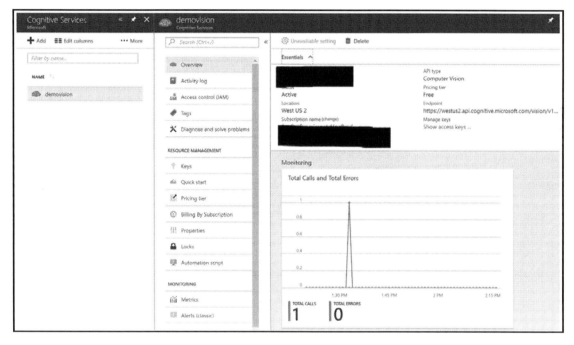

The Computer Vision API has the following requirements:

- The input must be a raw image binary in the form of an application/octet stream or image URL

- The supported image formats are JPEG, PNG, GIF, and BMP

- The image file size must be less than 4 MB

- The image dimension must be greater than 50 x 50 pixels

More information can be found at https://docs.microsoft.com/en-us/azure/cognitive-services/computer-vision/home.

Face API

Let's now look at the next API in the Vision category, the Face API.

This can be used to detect human faces and compare similar ones. It will also indicate facial attributes, including age, emotion, gender, and hair color.

Let's take a look at an example image:

If we send this input image to the API, we get the following output in JSON format:

```
//output omitted
"faceAttributes": {
    "hair": {
      "bald": 0.01,
      "invisible": false,
      "hairColor": [
        {
          "color": "blond",
          "confidence": 1.0
        },
        {
          "color": "brown",
          "confidence": 0.87
        },
      //omitted
      ]
    },
    "smile": 0.018,
    "headPose": {
      "pitch": 0.0,
      "roll": 3.2,
      "yaw": -23.3
    },
```

```
    "gender": "female",
    "age": 24.4,
    "facialHair": {
        "moustache": 0.0,
        "beard": 0.0,
        "sideburns": 0.0
    },
    "glasses": "NoGlasses",        "makeup": {
        "eyeMakeup": true,
        "lipMakeup": true
    },
    "emotion": {
        "anger": 0.001,
        "contempt": 0.002,
        "disgust": 0.002,
        "fear": 0.0,
        "happiness": 0.018,
        "neutral": 0.969,
        "sadness": 0.006,
        "surprise": 0.002
    },
//output omitted
```

To try out the Face API quickly, you can go to the following URL: `https://azure.microsoft.com/en-us/services/cognitive-services/face/`.

Just like the Computer Vision API, you can call the Face API using Python or any other language. The steps for creating the Face API resource are similar to the Computer Vision API, except that you must search for Face API in the portal, as shown in the following screenshot:

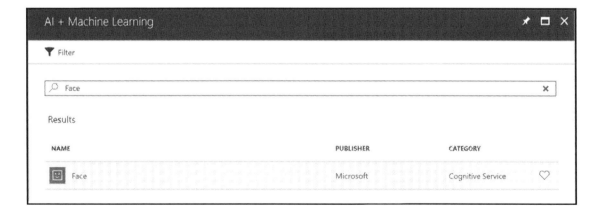

For more information about the remaining Vision APIs, you can go to the following URL: `https://azure.microsoft.com/en-us/services/cognitive-services/directory/vision/`.

Cognitive Services for Language APIs

Language APIs allow us to add text analysis, translation, and other capabilities to our AI applications. At the time of writing, Cognitive Services provide five language APIs:

- Text Analytics

- Translator Text

- Bing Spell Check

- Content Moderator

- Language Understanding

In this chapter, we will just look at the first API. We'll leave the others for you to explore on your own.

Text Analytics

The Text Analytics API can be used to detect sentiment, key phrases, entities, and language from your text. The following is an example that sends an input text to the API and gets the following output in JSON format. The text was as follows: `I am excited about using AI offerings by Microsoft`:

```
{ "languageDetection": {    "documents": [        {          "id":
"fe2529ff-073e-4355-86fa-b927d1b62a23",        "detectedLanguages": [
{          "name": "English",          "iso6391Name": "en",
"score": 1.0          }          ]        }    ],    "errors": []   },
"keyPhrases": {    "documents": [        {        "id":
"fe2529ff-073e-4355-86fa-b927d1b62a23",        "keyPhrases": [
"Microsoft's offerings",        "AI space"        ]        }    ],
"errors": []   },   "sentiment": {    "documents": [      {        "id":
"fe2529ff-073e-4355-86fa-b927d1b62a23",        "score": 0.93527746200561523
}    ],    "errors": []   },   "entities": {    "documents": [      {
"id": "fe2529ff-073e-4355-86fa-b927d1b62a23",        "entities": [
{        "name": "Microsoft",        "matches": [            {
"text": "Microsoft's",        "offset": 25,
"length": 11        }        ],        "wikipediaLanguage":
"en",        "wikipediaId": "Microsoft",        "wikipediaUrl":
"https://en.wikipedia.org/wiki/Microsoft",        "bingId":
"a093e9b9-90f5-a3d5-c4b8-5855e1b01f85"        },        {
"name": "Ai Space",        "matches": [        {
"text": "AI space",        "offset": 50,        "length": 8
}        ],        "wikipediaLanguage": "en",
"wikipediaId": "Ai Space",        "wikipediaUrl":
"https://en.wikipedia.org/wiki/Ai_Space",        "bingId": "2d055fa3-
b3cc-e9f6-776a-77b6ed7f341f"        }        ]        }    ],    "errors":
[]   }}
```

To try out the Text Analytics API quickly, go to the following URL: `https://azure.microsoft.com/en-us/services/cognitive-services/text-analytics/`.

As an AI developer, you can use any language to call the API. In this example, we will look at how to call the API using Python. A similar approach can be used for other programming languages:

1. Create a Text Analytics API Cognitive Services resource from the Azure portal: `https://portal.azure.com`.

2. Navigate to the API, as shown in the following screenshot. Click on **Create a resource**, then **AI + Machine Learning**, and then **Text Analytics**:

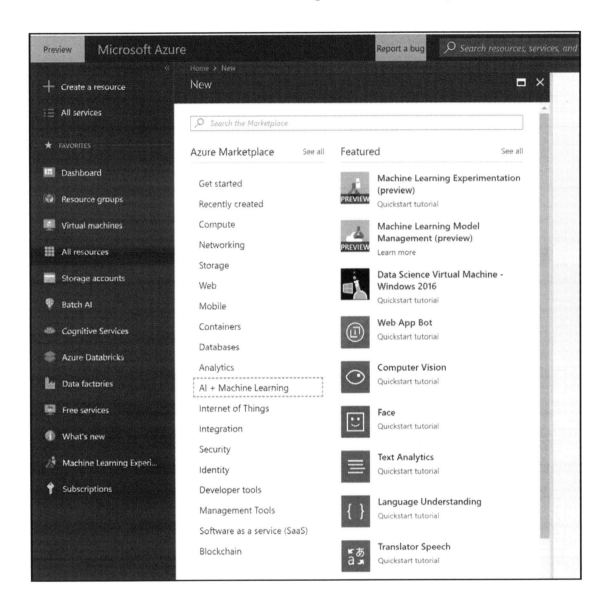

3. Alternatively, you can search for `Text Analytics` in the Azure portal:

4. Provide a name for your service and then select an appropriate Azure subscription, a location, and a pricing tier (either free or paid). You will also need to create a new resource group or select an existing one:

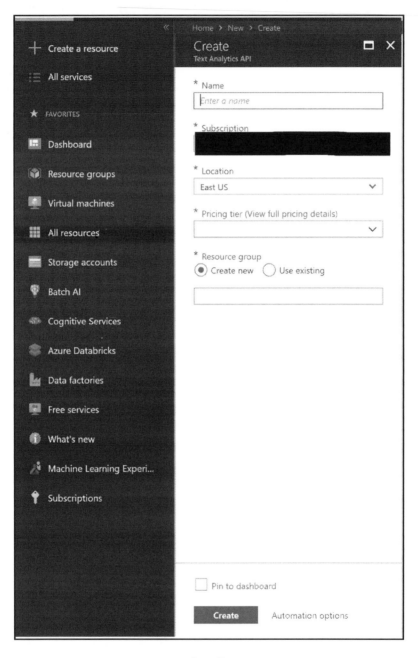

5. It will take less than a minute to create the API. Once it is created, you will see the **Quick Start** page, which has links to the API keys and its documentation. You will need the API keys to access the API from your Python (or any other language) code, or the code for whichever language you are using. Once you create the API, you will see the following screen:

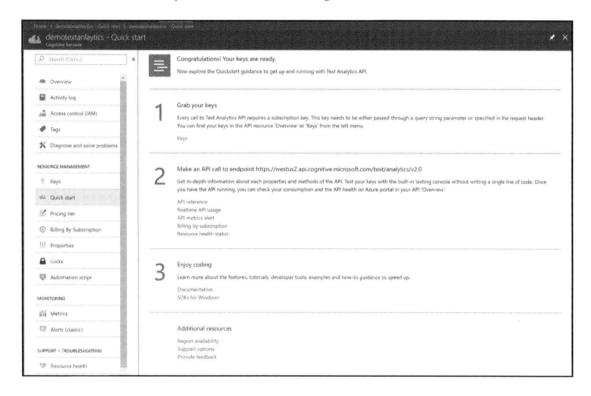

6. Use your favorite Python editor and call the API using the following sample code:

```
# Replace <Subscription Key> with your valid subscription's api
access key.
subscription_key = "<Access Key>"
assert subscription_key

# Replace the base url with what you see as Endpoint in the portal's
Overview section under your api
text_analytics_base_url =
"https://westus2.api.cognitive.microsoft.com/text/analytics/v2.0/"
sentiment_api_url = text_analytics_base_url + "sentiment"

# Send the text you want the api to analyze
```

```
# You can send multiple texts
documents = {'documents' : [
  {'id': '1', 'text': 'I am excited about using AI offerings by
Microsoft.'},
]}

import requests
# Get sentiment of text
headers    = {"Ocp-Apim-Subscription-Key": subscription_key}
response   = requests.post(sentiment_api_url, headers=headers,
json=documents)
sentiments = response.json()
print(sentiments)

# Get the language of text
language_api_url = text_analytics_base_url + "languages"
response   = requests.post(language_api_url, headers=headers,
json=documents)
languages = response.json()
print(languages)

# Get key phrases from text
key_phrase_api_url = text_analytics_base_url + "keyPhrases"
response   = requests.post(key_phrase_api_url, headers=headers,
json=documents)
key_phrases = response.json()
print(key_phrases)

# Get well-known entities
entity_linking_api_url = text_analytics_base_url + "entities"
response   = requests.post(entity_linking_api_url, headers=headers,
json=documents)
entities = response.json()
print(entities)
```

7. When you run the preceding code, you will see an output that looks as follows:

```
{'documents': [{'id': '1', 'score': 0.9388835430145264}], 'errors':
[]}{'documents': [{'detectedLanguages': [{'iso6391Name': 'en',
'name': 'English', 'score': 1.0}], 'id': '1'}], 'errors': []}
{'documents': [{'keyPhrases': ['AI offerings', 'Microsoft'], 'id':
'1'}], 'errors': []}
{'documents': [{'id': '1', 'entities': [{'name': 'Microsoft',
'wikipediaId': 'Microsoft', 'matches': [{'offset': 41, 'length': 9,
'text': 'Microsoft'}], 'bingId': 'a093e9b9-90f5-a3d5-
c4b8-5855e1b01f85', 'wikipediaUrl':
'https://en.wikipedia.org/wiki/Microsoft', 'wikipediaLanguage':
'en'}, {'name': 'Artificial intelligence', 'wikipediaId':
```

'Artificial intelligence', 'matches': [{'offset': 25, 'length': 2, 'text': 'AI'}], 'bingId': '9d99fb44-edac-0e03-1579-19d8d8591a49', 'wikipediaUrl': 'https://en.wikipedia.org/wiki/Artificial_intelligence', 'wikipediaLanguage': 'en'}]}], 'errors': []}

A sentiment score of 0.93 indicates a positive sentiment. The API detected English as the language, and two key phrases and entities.

8. Each transaction equates to one API call. The portal will show details that you can monitor, such as total calls, errors, latency, and data in/out. In the preceding example, we called four different APIs: `sentiment`, `languages`, `keyPhrases`, and `entities`:

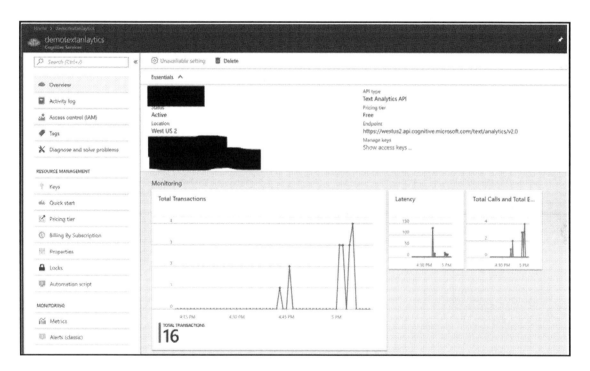

 To find more information about the remaining Language APIs, you can go to the following URL: `https://azure.microsoft.com/en-us/services/cognitive-services/directory/lang/`.

Cognitive Services for Speech APIs

The Speech APIs help you to add various capabilities related to speech-to-text and text-to-speech operations to your AI application.

At the time of writing, Cognitive Services provide four Speech APIs:

- Speech to Text

- Text to Speech

- Speaker Recognition

- Speech Translation

Speech to Text

The Speech to Text API can help convert spoken audio to text. The audio can either be real-time audio or audio that is being streamed from a recording. You can find more information at `https://azure.microsoft.com/en-us/services/cognitive-services/speech-to-text/`.

Cognitive Services for Knowledge APIs

The Knowledge APIs help parse through complex information and map it in a way that makes it easy to consume, based on natural language processing.

At the time of writing, there is one Knowledge API-based service: QnA Maker.

QnA Maker

This API allows you to extract questions and answers quickly from text that is in the form of FAQs by parsing it intelligently. Once this information is available, it can be used to create a question-and-answer bot. You can find more information at `https://azure.microsoft.com/en-us/services/cognitive-services/qna-maker/`.

Cognitive Services for Search APIs

The Search APIs help you search different types of content without having to develop complex search algorithms.

At the time of writing, Cognitive Services provides eight APIs:

- Bing Web Search

- Bing Custom Search

- Bing Video Search

- Bing Image Search

- Bing Visual Search

- Bing Entity Search

- Bing News Search

- Bing Autosuggest

In this chapter, we will discuss one API, Bing Visual Search, and leave you to explore the remaining APIs on your own.

Bing Visual Search

The Bing Visual Search API allows users to identify entities and text within images. This means that they can carry out a range of actions, including deriving information from an image and finding similar images, products, and objects in a range of categories, including fashion, landmarks, flowers, celebrities, and others. Bing Visual Search can extract information from business cards and can be customized for specific domains.

The following screenshot shows an example of an input image that was sent to the API. We then received an output in JSON form, which could be parsed and displayed on the web page, as shown on the right-hand side of the screenshot:

To try out this API or to call the API, programmatically, you can go to the following URL: `https://azure.microsoft.com/en-us/services/cognitive-services/bing-visual-search/`. It also contains the API reference documentation.

> For the remaining Search APIs, you can go to the following URL: `https://azure.microsoft.com/en-us/services/cognitive-services/directory/search/`.

Summary

In this chapter, we have learned how to use Cognitive Services to develop AI applications quickly. In the next chapter, we will learn about the Bot Framework, which is used to build bots.

Reference

- All Cognitive Services can be accessed from the following URL: `https://azure.`
  `microsoft.com/en-us/services/cognitive-services/`

4
Bot Framework

In the previous chapter, we learned about cognitive services, which can help us create an AI application. In this chapter, we will learn about building bots using various Azure services. Microsoft offers a powerful platform that includes the following components to help build and deploy bots:

- Bot builder SDK
- Bot Framework
- QnA Maker
- Bot Service

What is a bot?

A chatbot, or bot, is an application that allows you to have a human-like dialogue via text, image, or speech. A bot can be integrated into either a web app or a mobile app. Different applications, such as Facebook Messenger, Kik, WeChat, or Skype, support various types of bots that might help you to find answers to a specific question, book an appointment at a salon, or book a table at a restaurant. Chatting with a bot should be like chatting with a customer care agent or a friend. Here is an example bot that is helping to answer questions about the weather inside Facebook Messenger. This bot was built by Microsoft, and is known as the Zo bot:

A bot can be deployed in the cloud to help scale the capacity of how much traffic it can handle based on user demand. To give you an idea of how easy it is to create intelligent and powerful bots, we will create a bot using Bot Service, which will cover all of the aforementioned components.

In the following sections, we're going to provide a quick description of each of the components that are available in Azure to help us build bots.

Bot Builder SDK

The Bot Builder SDK enables you to create bots. It supports both .NET and Node.js languages to cover a wide spectrum of developers.

Bot Framework

The Bot Framework enables you to connect bots to various social media channels. You can connect to any number of channels, including Facebook Messenger, Skype, Teams, Kik, or a custom channel.

Alongside the SDK and the Framework, we also have Bot Framework Emulator and Bot Framework Channel Emulator. The Bot Framework Emulator is a desktop application to test your bot, while the Bot Framework Channel Emulator helps you test how your bot will look and work on different channels.

QnA Maker

The QnA Maker service helps us to create basic conversational bots quickly. It can integrate with the **Language Understanding Intelligent Service (LUIS)** to create more intelligent bots. Both QnA Maker and LUIS are cognitive services that we touched upon briefly in `Chapter 3`, *Cognitive Services*.

Bot Service

The Bot Service makes it easy to create bots by combining the Bot Builder SDK and the Bot Framework that we discussed earlier. It supports both .NET and Node.js developers. There are five templates that can be used to create a bot quickly:

- Basic bot
- Form bot
- Language understanding bot
- Question and answer bot
- Proactive bot

Here are the high-level steps that indicate how to create and run a bot using Bot Service:

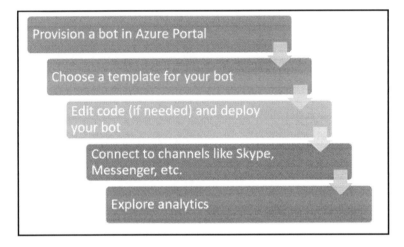

Creating a bot with Bot Service

When we create a bot with Azure Bot Service, Azure does a lot of our work for us. It provisions the bot, creates a bot project based on the bot builder SDK, and publishes the bot. All you need to create a bot in this way is an Azure subscription.

1. To begin with, go to the Bot Framework website at `https://dev.botframework.com`, which will take you to the Azure portal:

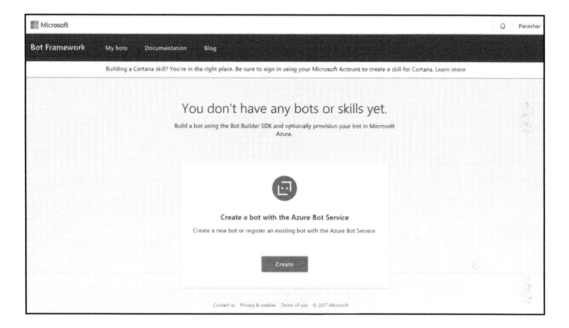

2. Alternatively, we can go directly to the Azure portal at `https://portal.azure.com` and search for `Bot Service`:

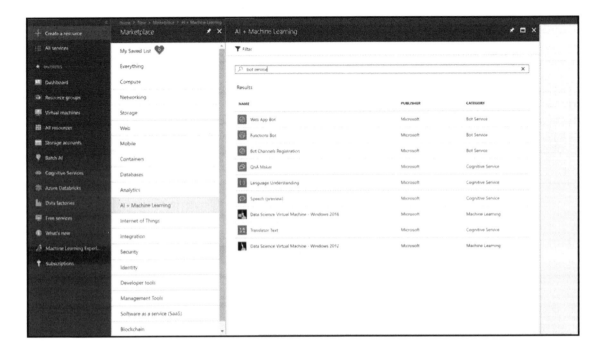

3. For this example, select the **Web App Bot** option:

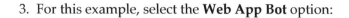
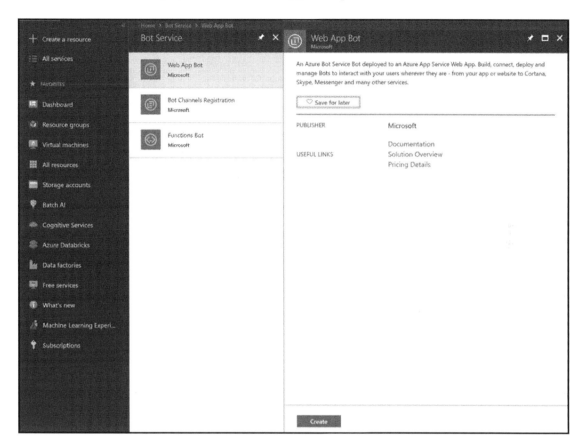

4. After that, provide a bot name, resource group, location, pricing tier, app name, and a programming language for the bot. Currently, C# and Node.js are supported. C# is useful for .Net developers, while Node.js is useful for JavaScript or Node developers.

5. Select a template to set up a bot project. The template will include a library and code samples:

  - A basic bot template creates a simple dialog bot that echoes the user's input
  - A form bot template uses either a form flow with C# or waterfall with Node.js to collect the input from the user during conversation
  - A language understanding bot template uses LUIS for natural language cognitive services

- A question and answer bot uses the QnA Maker cognitive service to create an interactive FAQ-based bot
- A proactive bot uses Azure Functions to trigger actions based on external events

6. For this example, let's select the **Basic** bot template:

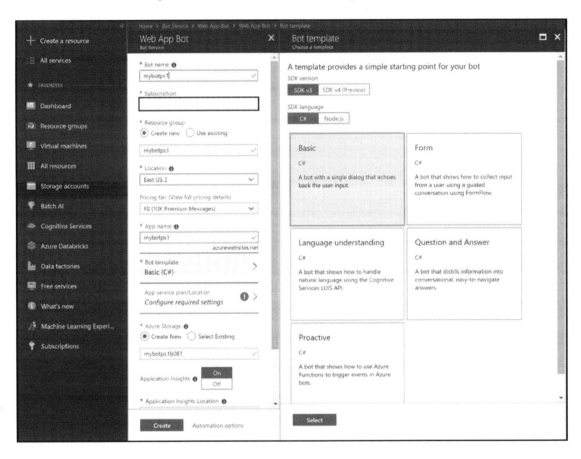

7. Select an app service plan to host your bot:

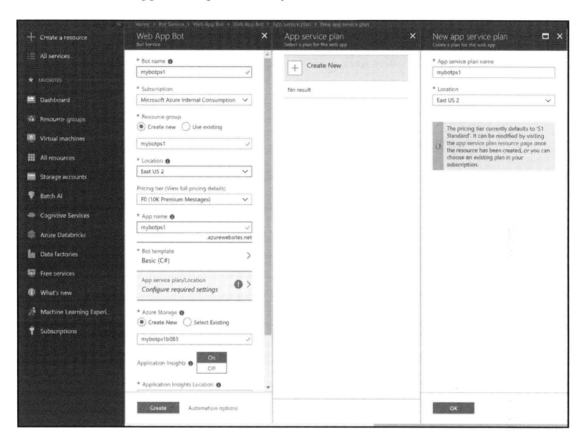

8. Next, select **Auto create App Id and password**:

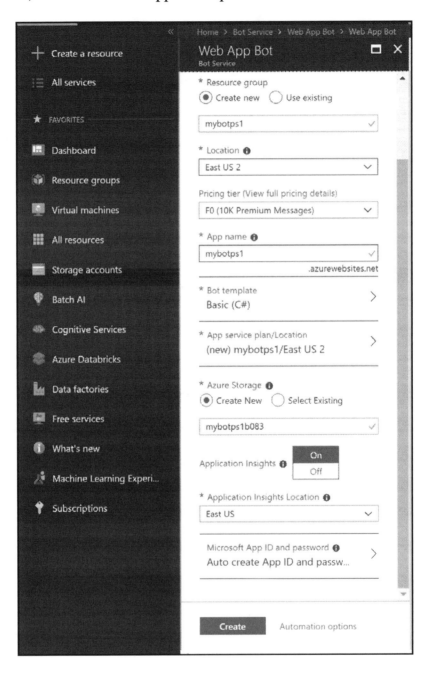

9. After accepting the terms and clicking on **Create**, Azure will provision and set up the bot for you. This may take a little while. Once the bot is created, we will see its overview page, which will look as follows:

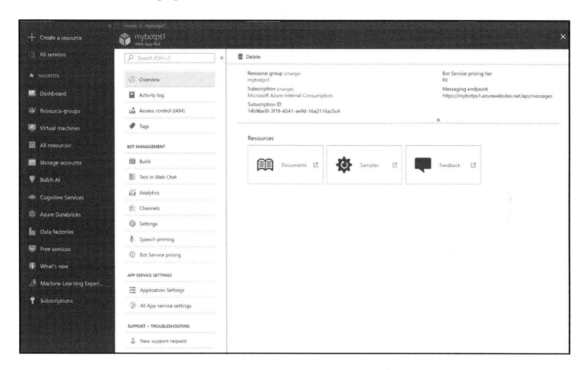

10. We can now click on **Test in Web Chat** and try out the bot from within the portal. Ask a question or say something to the bot and see its reply:

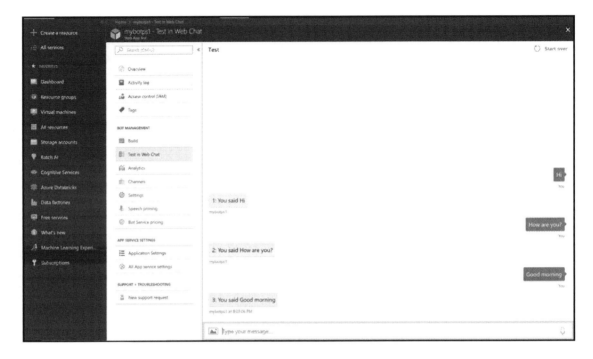

11. We can customize the bot in multiple ways. The source code is available for us to see and edit and we can also use one of the options provided:

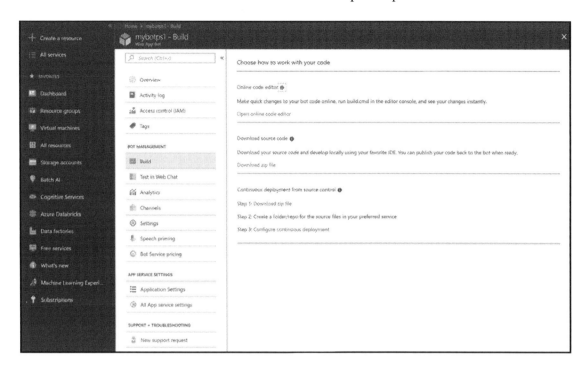

12. Let's try editing the code in the online code editor:

13. The two most important files are `Controllers` and `Dialogs`:

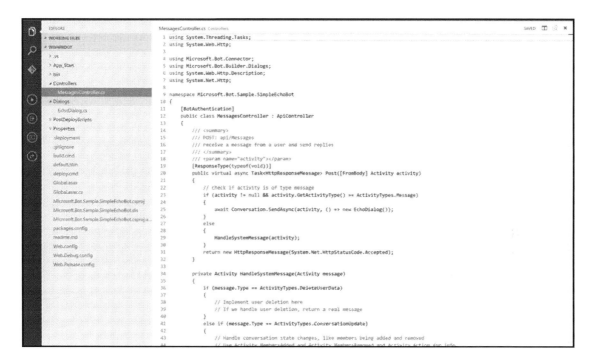

14. If we change something in the `Dialogs` file, this will be reflected in the deployed bot once we have rebuilt it and deployed it again.

In the following example, the bot will now say **Hi from v2!** before repeating the user's message.

15. Go to the console from the bar on the left-hand side and type `build.cmd` to rebuild and redeploy our model:

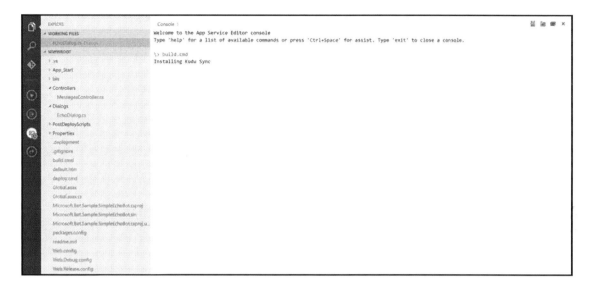

16. Once the build has finished, go back to the portal and test the changes made:

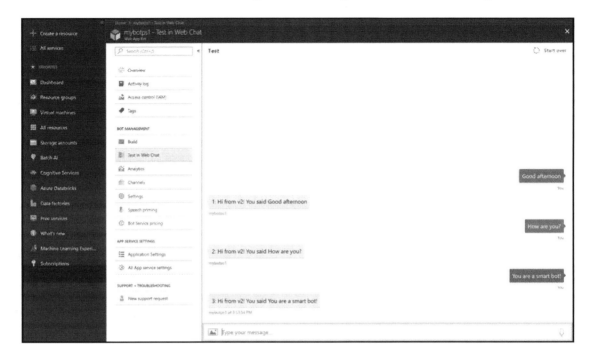

17. Let's now connect to a channel. To do this, click on **Channels** in the bar on the left-hand side, choose a channel, and then add it:

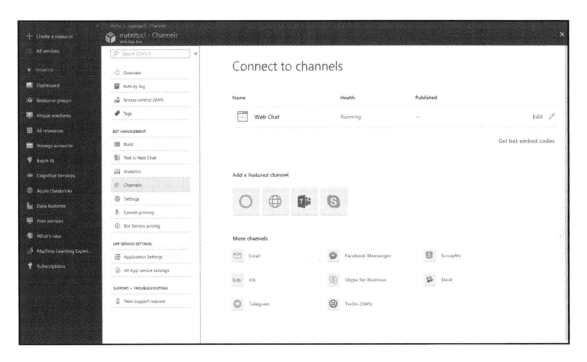

18. Each channel will have its own configuration. Skype and Web chat are pre-configured. To use the other channels, we need to provide the necessary details and the rest will be taken care of by the Bot Framework. The interaction will be similar to that which we saw earlier in the web chat, but the UI will automatically adapt to the channel that is being used.

In the following screenshot, we can see the details that are needed to enable our Bot in Facebook Messenger:

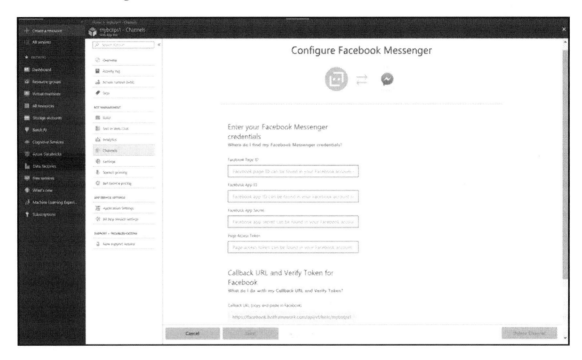

LUIS application

Our bot can also take in audio as an input, and the portal allows us to integrate an LUIS application. If you already have an LUIS application, you can provide the information here:

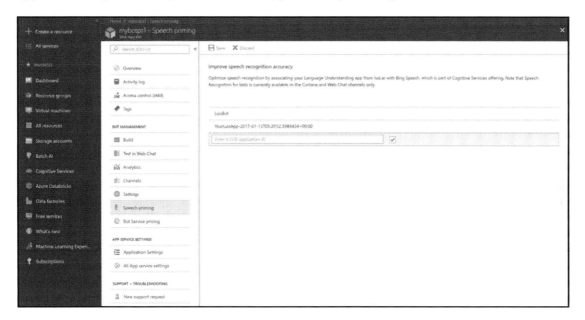

Summary

In this chapter, we have learned about using various Azure-based services that help us to create bots that can be integrated into different messenger services quickly and easily. In the next chapter, we will learn about Azure Machine Learning Studio, which we can use to create custom machine learning models.

5
Azure Machine Learning Studio

Azure Machine Learning Studio is an ML-as-a-Service platform for creating custom **machine learning** (**ML**) models. Azure ML Studio is a great tool for beginners who perhaps have some experience of consuming machine learning models and who would like to gain a deeper understanding of the training process. It offers more flexibility than the Cognitive Services APIs and an easy-to-learn development environment. The GUI does not require any programming and allows the user to concentrate on building ML models as efficiently as possible. Azure ML Studio is also a useful tool for more experienced AI developers who have a fairly simple problem at hand and need to get results quickly.

Azure ML Studio consists of two separate services: a Studio Workspace and Studio Web Services. Both of these services also include the backend computational resources needed for processing, so the user does not have to worry about the maintenance of the underlying operating system or hardware. The difference between the two services is clear: the Studio Workspace is used to train ML models and experiment with different configurations, while Studio Web Services provide a REST API interface for scoring examples, using the models published from the Workspace.

Azure ML Studio is designed for collaborative development. It integrates with Azure Active Directory, so users from the same organization can be added to the Workspace with a few clicks. All ML models in the ML Studio Workspace are visible to all members of the Workspace. Workspace members can also edit models created by others, so developers can try to improve each other's results iteratively. Therefore, it is a great tool when developers are following the **Team Data Science Process** (**TDSP**), for example.

ML models are developed inside *experiments*. An experiment contains all the steps required to produce an ML model, beginning with the input dataset. Experiments can be used to compare different ML models and parameter configurations. ML Studio provides a wide range of modules that can be added to an experiment to perform different tasks, such as preprocessing data or evaluating training results. By combining these modules, the experiment is built step by step, resulting in a training pipeline that can be run to produce a trained ML model. ML Studio also includes a wide experiment template collection, with ready-to-run examples from many different areas. In the next section, we will show how to deploy these templates to an ML Studio Workspace.

The pricing of Workspaces and web services is based on the use of computational resources. Workspace resources are consumed when new ML models are trained in ML Studio. Workspace billing is also based on the number of users, but using the ML Studio UI and building experiments does not incur any extra costs; only the experiment runtime is calculated.

When creating a new ML Studio Workspace, a new web service plan resource is created automatically. Web service resources are consumed when external applications call the ML Studio Web Services API. A web services pricing tier must be chosen when creating a web service resource in the Azure portal. The pricing tier determines the maximum amount of requests that can be handled in a month. If this limit is exceeded, each request is billed on top of the flat monthly price.

To use Azure ML Studio, you need a Workspace account. There are two types of Workspace accounts: *Free Tier* and *Standard T*ier. The Free Tier is an independent account that is not connected to an Azure subscription. It has more limitations in terms of use and does not include a production-scale web API, like the Standard Tier does. The Standard Tier requires an Azure subscription and the costs of the ML Studio resources are added to the subscription bill. The Workspace and web services appear as independent items in the resource group, and they can be managed in the Azure portal just like any other Azure resource.

To access the ML Studio UI, go to the **ML Studio Workspace** blade in the Azure portal and click on **Launch Machine Learning Studio**. You can also enter the portal address in the browser directly: `https://studio.azureml.net/`.

In this chapter, we will cover the following topics:

- Deploying an Azure AI Gallery template
- Building an experiment in Azure ML Studio
- Deploying a model as a web service in ML Studio

Deploying an Azure AI Gallery template

Developing models with ML Studio does not have to be done from scratch. Azure AI Gallery contains a wide selection of templates for many different scenarios. These scenarios include many common use cases for ML, such as credit risk prediction, demand estimation, and text sentiment analysis. Templates can be imported to an Azure ML Studio Workspace with a few clicks and they contain all the steps needed to produce a working ML model. Studying templates is a great way to learn about different use cases and the steps required to produce an ML model. Some templates are prepared by Microsoft, but users can also submit their own experiments to the gallery.

The template gallery can be accessed directly from ML Studio. Open the ML Studio UI (as described previously) and create a new experiment by clicking on the **+ New** in the bottom-left corner. This brings up the template collection, as follows:

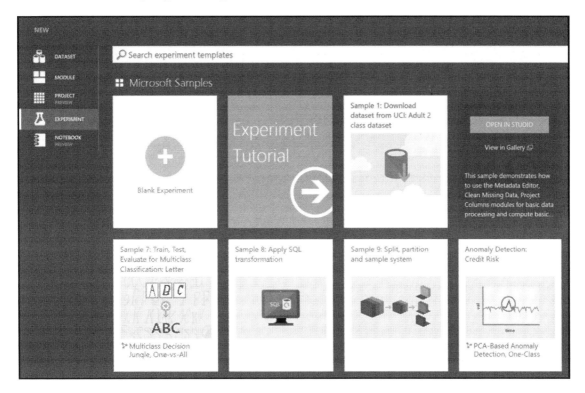

If you do not see the template collection, make sure that the **EXPERIMENT** tab is selected in the left-hand menu. Click on **OPEN IN STUDIO** to import the template to your Workspace. You can also view a description of the experiment in AI Gallery by clicking on **View in Gallery**.

Alternatively, you can browse AI Gallery at `https://gallery.azure.ai/`. AI Gallery contains templates for many other Azure AI services as well. The ML Studio examples can be viewed by filtering only the experiment type templates. Templates can be added to a Workspace from the AI Gallery website by clicking the **Open in Studio** button, demonstrated as follows:

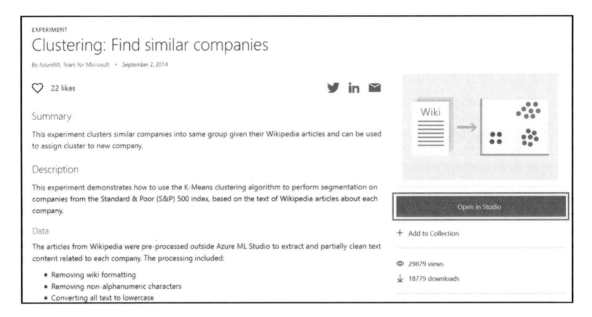

EXPERIMENT

Clustering: Find similar companies

By AzureML Team for Microsoft • September 2, 2014

♡ 22 likes 🐦 in ✉

Summary

This experiment clusters similar companies into same group given their Wikipedia articles and can be used to assign cluster to new company.

Description

This experiment demonstrates how to use the K-Means clustering algorithm to perform segmentation on companies from the Standard & Poor (S&P) 500 index, based on the text of Wikipedia articles about each company.

Data

The articles from Wikipedia were pre-processed outside Azure ML Studio to extract and partially clean text content related to each company. The processing included:

- Removing wiki formatting
- Removing non-alphanumeric characters
- Converting all text to lowercase

Open in Studio

+ Add to Collection

👁 29879 views

↓ 18779 downloads

This opens the ML Studio UI, imports the experiment to a Workspace (after the user has specified which Workspace the experiment should be imported to), and opens the experiment in the UI. You should see a training graph with some modules in it. The modules define the training process, consisting of data import, data preprocessing, choosing an ML algorithm, and training the model. The model is not yet trained, however. To train the model, click **Run** in the toolbar at the bottom, as follows:

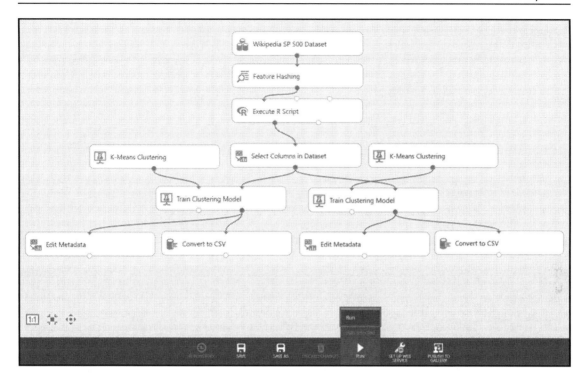

Training the model will take some time, depending on the chosen algorithm and the size of the input dataset. The model cannot be edited while the experiment is running. After the experiment has finished running, the model is trained and ready to be used for scoring. Alternatively, we could make some changes to the model and try to improve the results. In the following sections, we'll show how to use the modules in ML Studio to compare different models and parameters, and demonstrate how to deploy the trained model as a web service, so that external applications can use the model for scoring.

Building an experiment

In this section, we'll show how to build an experiment from scratch using a custom dataset. With the GUI, creating new experiments is very fast and results can be viewed immediately. Azure ML Studio contains modules for all common ML and data-processing tasks, so it is a great tool for testing ideas quickly and iteratively. If the built-in modules are not sufficient for the task at hand, the script modules can be used for improved extensibility, explained as follows.

Importing and preprocessing data

As already discussed, Azure ML Studio is a complete ML tool that takes care of every step in the ML model development process. The only input needed is a raw dataset in a format understood by ML Studio; if the original data format is not recognized, then a file conversion is required, using either an external tool or the custom script modules in ML Studio. For raw files, the data formats currently recognized by ML Studio are CSV, TSV, ARFF, SvmLight, and R objects. Datasets can also be saved in zipped format to save storage space and bandwidth.

Datasets can be imported to ML Studio in two ways: by uploading a local file from the user's computer, or using cloud storage in Azure. To import data from your local machine, click on the **+ New** button in the bottom-left corner, choose the **DATASET** tab on the left-hand panel, and click on **FROM LOCAL FILE**:

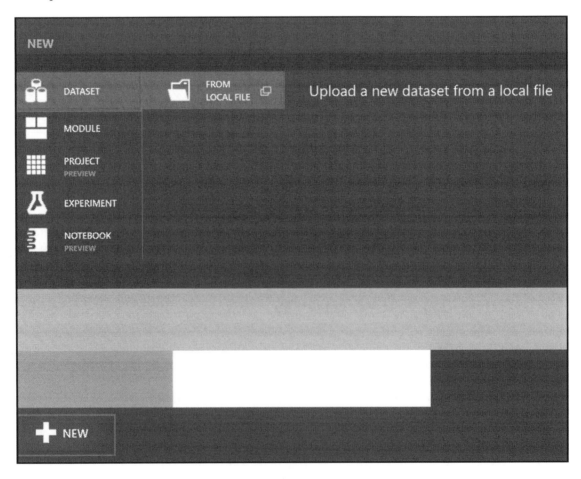

This brings up the new dataset panel where the file path and the file format must be specified. After the dataset has been configured, confirm the settings and the file upload process will begin. When the upload is finished, the dataset name is shown in the list of datasets and the content of the file is ready to be used in experiments.

Create a new experiment to start developing a new ML model. Choose the **Blank Experiment** template as a basis for the experiment, since we will add modules to the experiment one by one. If you uploaded your own dataset in the previous step, you can use this dataset as a starting point. Azure ML Studio also includes several built-in datasets that can be used for learning and experimenting if you do not have your own dataset at the moment. To add a dataset to the experiment, open the **Saved Datasets** menu on the left-hand toolbar. The datasets uploaded by the user will be shown under **My Datasets**. The built-in datasets are shown under **Samples**. Drag and drop your chosen dataset to the canvas to import it to the experiment.

Alternatively, the input data can also be imported from Azure cloud storage. The data can be stored as text files or in a relational database. Currently, ML Studio supports the following data sources:

- Azure Storage account v1 (Blob storage and Table storage)
- Azure SQL Database and SQL Server on-premises database
- Azure Cosmos DB
- Apache Hive query (HDInsight Hive tables)
- HTTP REST API
- OData feed provider

Unfortunately, Data Lake Storage and storage account v2 are not currently supported. To add a cloud store as a data source, use the **Import Data** module in the **Data Input and Output** menu. Configure the module by clicking on the module on the experiment canvas and choosing the data source in the configuration panel on the right-hand side of the experiment canvas. Also specify the location of the data source and the access credentials, if required.

To view the dataset, right-click on the output node of the dataset module and select **Visualize** (if using the import data module, the experiment must be run before the results can be viewed):

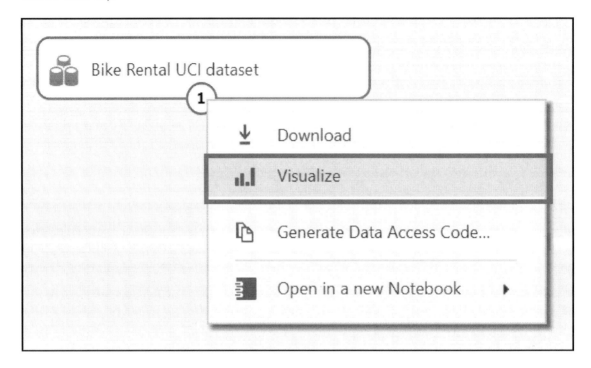

This shows the rows of the dataset in table format. By clicking on the `dataset` columns in the visualizer, we can get summary information and view a histogram of the column values on the right-hand side of the panel:

For testing purposes, it might sometimes be useful to enter data manually. The **Enter Data Manually** module can be used for this purpose.

Once the dataset has been imported to the experiment, it can be used as input for training ML models. However, raw input data might not always be suitable for training as such. The data might include invalid values or only a portion of the data may be needed, for example. Sometimes, data is stored in multiple locations and datasets must be joined from different sources. These preprocessing operations can be realized with the data manipulation modules.

The preprocessing modules are listed under the **Data Transformation** menu. The modules are grouped into five categories: filter, learning with counts, manipulation, sample and split, scale, and reduce. These modules transform the data into the final format, which can then be fed to the ML algorithm for training.

Perhaps the most commonly used modules are listed under the **Manipulation** menu:

- The **Select Columns in Dataset** module can be used to pick features for the model if the input data contains unused columns
- The **Clean Missing Data** module is used to specify what to do with rows that contain missing (null) values
- If you have two datasets with identical schemas, they can be appended using the **Add Rows** module

To join the columns of two datasets, there are two possible options. If the datasets have the same number of rows, the **Add Columns** module does the job. This module joins the rows in the same order as they are listed in the input datasets. If the rows have to be reordered before joining, this must be done in a separate module, for example, the **Apply SQL Transformation** module. If the number of rows is different in the two datasets, the **Add Columns** module can still be used, but the module will just add a blank (null) value for the elements that are not present in the smaller dataset. In this case, it would probably be more appropriate to use the **Join Data** module. It allows SQL-like joins based on a common value in key columns. This module supports both inner and outer join operations and also joining by multiple key columns.

Explore the **Data Transformation** menu to get an idea of what kind of transformations are possible with the native modules in ML Studio. The filter category contains modules for processing signal-like data, such as audio and visual data. **Learning with Counts** contains modules for producing counting statistics based on input variables. **Sample and Split** modules are used for taking subsets of data and the **Scale and Reduce** modules are useful for constraining values and reducing the dimensionality of the data. In the following subsections, we will give an example of how to split a dataset into a training dataset and a test dataset using the **Split Data** module.

In some cases, the native ML Studio modules are not sufficient to perform all the data preprocessing steps, but this does not necessarily mean that the data must be processed outside of ML Studio. The custom script modules in ML Studio can be used to perform arbitrary transformations using the SQL, Python, and R languages. For example, the **Apply SQL Transformation** module can be used to reorder datasets and create custom columns based on the existing columns. This module uses the SQLite syntax, which is similar to the Microsoft Transact-SQL syntax. As an example, suppose that we have two columns, Id and Name, that we wish to join by using the '_' character as the separator. This operation can be achieved by using SQLite's || concatenation operator as follows:

```
select Name||'_'||Id as Name_Id from t1;
```

The output dataset has one column named `Name_Id`, containing the values of the `Name` column appended with the values of the `Id` column. The `t1` table refers to the first input dataset of the **Apply SQL Transformation** module. The module accepts at most three input datasets and the last two datasets can be similarly referred to as `t2` and `t3`. By using more than one input dataset, it is possible to create more complex join operations than those available in the **Join Data** module.

In addition to SQL scripts, the **Execute Python Script** and **Execute R Script** modules provide extensibility for additional languages. The execution environments for these languages contain some of the most popular libraries by default. Users can also upload external libraries to the ML Studio service and import these to an experiment.

Finally, the **Text Analytics** menu contains a number of modules for processing free-form text documents. For example, the **Preprocess Text** module performs basic text preprocessing, such as converting text to lowercase, and removing stop words and punctuation. The **Feature Hashing** module can vectorize text via N-gram tokenization, which is used in text embedding.

Choosing and configuring algorithms

Choosing the right models and tuning the parameters for the model are at the core of AI application development. In most cases, there are several algorithms that are applicable to the task, and it may not be clear from the beginning which algorithm will perform best. For example, some algorithms might perform better for small datasets, while others excel on big data. Usually, there are also other constraints to think about, such as runtime or the amount of computational resources available. The best model is the one that achieves a sufficient level of accuracy with the minimum amount of computational resources.

The first step when solving an ML problem is to identify which family of algorithms should be used. The algorithm family depends mostly on the type of the *predicted* value, such as if predicting a number, the possible algorithms are different than when predicting a *categorical* value. A categorical value is one where the number of possible outcomes is finite. The simplest categorical value is a Boolean variable, which can take two values (true/false). The number of possible outcomes can also restrict which types of algorithms can be used for the problem, since not all algorithms handle very high-dimensional data well. One example of high-dimensional categorical data is encountered in text analysis, where each word might represent a different category and the number of categories is equal to the size of the dictionary. For such high-dimensional data, it is often best to use neural network models, which can handle a large number of output values.

Azure ML Studio contains a selection of the most commonly used ML algorithms that can be dragged and dropped to an experiment canvas. The algorithms are listed in the **Initialize model** section, under the **Machine Learning** menu. The algorithms are grouped into four categories. The anomaly detection modules are meant for detecting outliers in datasets where most of the values are similar to each other, but there are some exceptions that we want to identify. These models are widely used in predictive fault detection, for example, in the manufacturing and processing industries, where machines usually operate normally, but may sometimes produce anomalous values, indicating that the machine is about to break. The classification modules are used for training supervised algorithms that classify inputs to exclusive categories. The clustering modules provide unsupervised algorithms to find similar items in a dataset. Regression algorithms predict numerical values (but inputs can also be categorical variables). In addition to these ML algorithms, ML Studio provides modules for other common ML-related tasks, such as **Principal Component Analysis (PCA)** and text tokenization.

In this section, we'll show an example of how to train a regression model. The input dataset is a record of flight delay information from multiple airports, available as a built-in dataset in ML Studio. The dataset includes information on the time of the flight, its origin, and its destination airports, and the airline that operates the flight. The label column, the value that we want to predict, is the departure delay in minutes (column `DepDelay`). A positive value for `DepDelay` means that the flight has been delayed, and a negative value means that it has departed ahead of schedule. This is a fairly large dataset, containing over 2.7 million rows and 14 columns. To get more detailed information about the dataset, see the full description in the documentation available at `https://docs.microsoft.com/en-us/azure/machine-learning/studio/use-sample-datasets`.

The training process consists of the following steps:

1. Import data
2. Preprocess data (choose which columns are used)
3. Split data into training and test datasets
4. Pick an ML algorithm and train it using the training dataset
5. Use the trained model to create predictions for the test dataset
6. Compare the predicted values to the actual values in the test dataset

The input dataset contains mostly numerical data that does not require much preprocessing. The `Carrier` column contains categorical values in text format, but ML Studio converts these values into numeric values automatically. The only preprocessing step is choosing the columns to be used to train the model. In this example, the following columns are chosen as the features of the model:

Column	Description
Month	Month (categorical numeric, 1-12)
DayOfWeek	Day of week (categorical numeric, 1-7)
OriginAirportID	Airport—departure (categorical numeric, 70 unique values)
Carrier	Airline (categorical string, 16 unique values)
CRSDepTime	Time of day (categorical numeric, 1-2359, 1440 possible values)

Note that the time of departure is given in numeric format, where the number 101 corresponds to 01:01, for example. The **Select Columns in Dataset** module can be used to pick these columns and the label column (`DepDelay`) is to be used in the training process.

Before the model is trained, the data must be separated into training and test datasets. This is a crucial step in the training process: it is important that the accuracy of the model is measured with examples that the model has not seen during the training process. The **Split Data** module is meant for this purpose. By setting the **Fraction of rows in the first output dataset** property of the module to `0.75`, for example, the first output port of the module will contain 75% of the rows and the second output will contain 25%, selected randomly from the input dataset. We will use this splitting to divide the data into the training and test datasets, respectively.

Once the data has been processed and divided into training and test datasets, the model is trained with the training dataset. The **Train Model** module in ML Studio requires two inputs: an uninitialized ML model and the training dataset. The output of the module is the trained ML model that can be used to make predictions. In this example, the aim is to predict a numerical variable (the flight delay in minutes). As discussed previously, this type of problem requires a regression model. For simple testing, it is usually best to start with linear regression. This model does not often produce the best results, but it runs fast and gives a baseline for accuracy when evaluating more advanced models. Here is an example of a full training pipeline:

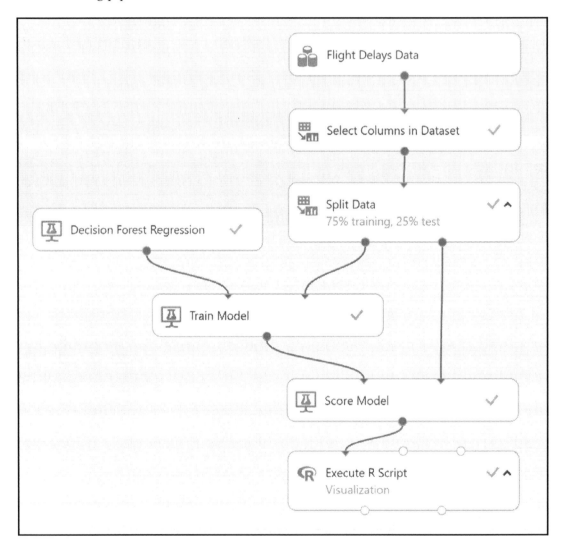

In this case, the **Decision Forest Regression** model was trained with 75% of the input data. This model can produce accurate results, but the training time can be long if the dataset contains many rows. Training this model with a little over 2 million rows took about 1 hour, while the linear regression model was trained in less than 1 minute. Although some algorithms may perform better in certain situations, it is usually difficult to predict beforehand which algorithm will produce the best results for a given problem. The best approach is to experiment with different algorithms and parameters to find the best model. We will show how this can be done in an organized manner using the modules in ML Studio, as follows.

To get more information about each module, click on the module so that the configuration panel appears on the right-hand side of the canvas. Follow the link at the bottom of the panel under **Quick Help**. The module documentation includes detailed information about each module and how to configure it.

After the **Train Model** module has been connected with an ML module and an input dataset, its output can be taken to the **Score Model** module to make predictions. To understand how well our model is performing, the test dataset is scored and the predictions for the model are compared to the true values (labels). The **Score Model** module will add a new column to the output data, containing the predicted values. The predicted values are then plotted against the actual values as a scatter plot to see how well they match up against each other.

Although ML Studio does not provide any native visualization modules, the **Execute R Script** module can produce R graphics as output. The `plot` command is suitable for simple figures and is supported natively in the R module. The `ggplot2` library is also available in the R module. This library is widely used and produces high quality pictures. Here is an example of how to plot the `DepDelay` (actual values) on the *x* axis and the `Scored Label Mean` (predicted value) on the *y* axis:

```
# Import ggplot2 library
library(ggplot2)

# Map the first input port to data frame
input1 <- maml.mapInputPort(1)

# Create a graph with ggplot
graph <- ggplot(input1, aes(x=DepDelay, y=`Scored Label Mean`))
graph <- graph + labs(x="Departure delay (actual)",
                      y="Departure delay (predicted)")
graph + geom_point(color="blue");

# Pass the data frame to the output port
maml.mapOutputPort("input1");
```

Note that if the linear regression model was used, the predicted values would be in a different column (Scored Labels).

These are all the steps needed to train the model and analyze the results in a single pipeline. The model can now be trained by clicking the **Run** button in the toolbar at the bottom in ML Studio. After the run has finished, the results can be viewed by right-clicking the second output (**R Device**) and choosing **Visualize**. The plotting output can be viewed under the **Graphics** section, as demonstrated in the following diagram:

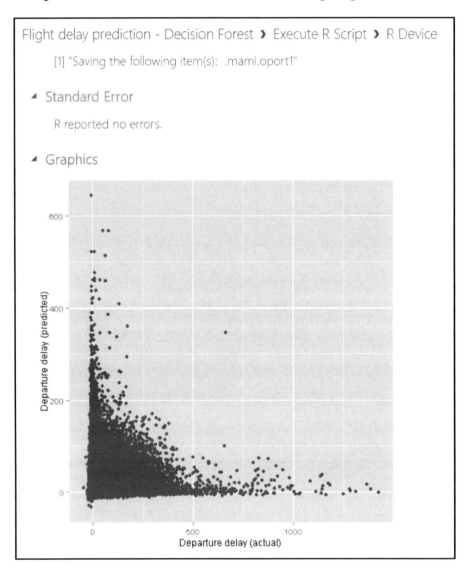

In an ideal scenario, each predicted value would be equal to the actual value and there would be a straight line from the bottom-left corner to the upper-right corner. The preceding screenshot is therefore far from ideal. It seems that the model predicts some high values when the actual values are low, and vice versa; it is not able to predict high values when it should. We can already see from this screenshot that the *variance* of the results is high. The conclusion is that the features that were given to the model are not conclusive enough to predict delays accurately. The selected features (see the preceding list) do not contain sufficient information to explain the variation in the label variable.

Since the initial results do not seem convincing, what should the next step be? Instead of continuing to experiment with different configurations, it might be more productive to take a step back and consider whether there is some additional data that gives more information about when delays might occur. For example, weather conditions might correlate well with flight delays, so it could be a good idea to include weather data in the model. To see an example of this, navigate to Azure AI Gallery and search for the `Binary Classification: Flight delay prediction` template.

In the following subsections, we'll examine how different feature variables contribute to the variation in the label variable. We'll also show how to use ML Studio modules to evaluate different models and explore different parameter configurations.

To a beginner, the wide selection of different ML algorithms may feel overwhelming. Which algorithm gives quick results, and which is good for large datasets? To help answer these and other questions, Microsoft has published an Azure ML algorithm cheat sheet: `https://docs.microsoft.com/en-us/azure/machine-learning/studio/algorithm-cheat-sheet`. The cheat sheet shows the pros and cons of each algorithm at a quick glance.

More advanced users will know that the algorithms in ML Studio are just a small portion of all of the available models. The algorithm selection can be extended with R libraries by using the **Create R Model** module. This is a code-based alternative for developing ML models in ML Studio.

Feature selection

A common problem when developing ML models is deciding which features should be used when training a model. For a supervised learning algorithm, the best features are those that are highly correlated with the label variable. This means, broadly speaking, that changing one of the variables induces a change in the other variable as well. An example of highly correlated variables could be the time of day and the amount of road traffic: traffic jams usually occur during the rush hour, while the amount of traffic during the night is particularly low.

The general aim of feature selection is to discover the variables that have the largest impact on the target variable. If the input dataset contains a large amount of columns, it might sometimes be beneficial to select only a subset of the columns. If the dataset contains columns that are not correlated with the target variable, including those columns in the model can decrease the level of accuracy, because the algorithm will have more parameters to fit, while the parameters do not include any additional information. Feature selection is particularly important when data is very high-dimensional, for example, in text analysis. In this case, it might be necessary to decrease the number of dimensions so that the model can be trained in a reasonable amount of time.

The **Feature Selection** menu in ML Studio contains a few modules that can be used for selecting features. Here, we'll demonstrate how to use the **Filter-Based Feature Selection** module to determine which variables in the flight delay dataset are correlated with the delay time. See the previous subsection for a description of the dataset.

The **Filter-Based Feature Selection** module can be used to compute various correlation metrics between the target variable and the feature variables and to choose the *n* most important columns according to the metrics. The module contains various correlation metrics to choose from, each with their own properties. The best metric depends on the input data and the problem. For details about each metric, refer to the module documentation. Here is an example of how to compare three different metrics in ML Studio:

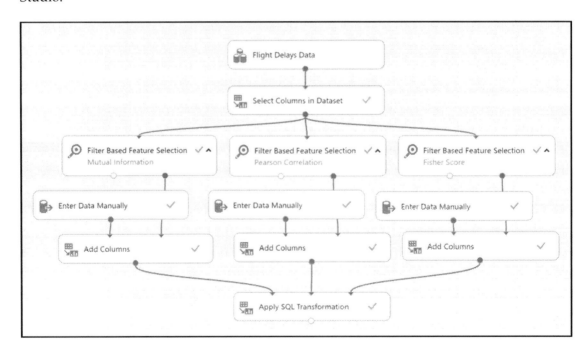

The selected columns are the same that were used to create a prediction model in the previous subsection. Similarly, the DepDelay column is selected as the target column in the feature selection module. This means that we examine the impact of each feature variable on the target variable and calculate the correlation metric between those variables, feature by feature.

The first output of the **Filter-Based Feature Selection** module contains the n most significant columns of the input dataset and the target column. The second output contains the values of the correlation metric for each column. The correlation metric is returned for all columns, not just the n most significant ones. Since we are only interested in the second output in this example, the value of n can be left to the default value (*1*).

The **Enter Data Manually** and **Add Columns** modules are added just to annotate which metric was used on each row. The **Apply SQL transformation** module is used to collect the results in a single table. Note that the **Filter-Based Feature Selection** returns the columns in the order of significance, so the order of columns might vary for different metrics. If the **Add Rows** module was used, an error would be thrown if the order of the columns was different, it is necessary to use the SQL module. To combine the results of each input, the union statement can be used as follows:

```
select CorrelationMetric, Carrier, OriginAirportID,
       Month, DayOfWeek, CRSDepTime, DepDelay
    from t1
union
select CorrelationMetric, Carrier, OriginAirportID,
       Month, DayOfWeek, CRSDepTime, DepDelay
    from t2
union
select CorrelationMetric, Carrier, OriginAirportID,
      Month, DayOfWeek, CRSDepTime, DepDelay
    from t3;
```

If more than three metrics were compared simultaneously, it would be necessary to use more than one SQL module and combine the results using the **Add Rows** module.

After running the experiment, the results can be viewed by visualizing the output of the SQL module, as follows:

Feature selection ❯ Apply SQL Transformation ❯ Results dataset

rows   columns
3   7

CorrelationMetric	Carrier	OriginAirportID	Month	DayOfWeek	CRSDepTime	DepDelay
Fisher Score	0	0.003502	0.004169	0.000445	0.066668	1
Mutual Information	0.065922	0.005257	0.007605	0.002801	0.036812	1
Pearson Correlation	0	0.018913	0.051139	0.00586	0.155088	1

For each metric, a higher value indicates a stronger correlation between the feature column and the target variable. A value of *1* corresponds to a perfect correlation: if we know the value of one of the variables, we can predict the other variable with 100% certainty. Therefore, it makes sense that the correlation value of DepDelay with itself is *1*. A value of *0* means that the variables contain absolutely no information about each other, and the guess is totally random, even if the value of the other variable is known.

Interestingly, the results do not agree on the most important columns. The **Fisher Score** and the **Pearson Correlation** indicate that the most significant column is CRSDepTime, the time of day of departure. **Mutual Information** states that the Carrier column is most significant, CRSDepTime being the second most important column. It is surprising how differently the **Fisher Score** and **Pearson Correlation** see the importance of the Carrier column, with respect to **Mutual Information**. According to the former's metrics, the Carrier column is totally insignificant, meaning that all airlines have the same amount of delays, while **Mutual Information** states that the airline is the biggest factor in delays. However, all of the metrics agree that DayOfWeek is the least significant of the five features.

So, could we make our prediction model more accurate by leaving out some of the columns and keeping only the most significant ones? Based on these results, the answer is probably not. The results are not conclusive regarding the most significant columns, so it might be better to keep all of them to get the maximum amount of information. On the other hand, all the variables yield correlation scores that are closer to *0* than *1*. This can be interpreted such that none of the features are strongly correlated with the label variable. Constructing a prediction model based on this data is therefore very challenging, since the features do not contain enough information to deduce the value of the label variable. This analysis confirms the poor initial results obtained in the previous subsection. As mentioned earlier, it could be better to add more features that might correlate with flight delays, for example, weather information.

Comparing models and parameters

One of the core tasks in developing ML models is choosing the ML algorithm and configuring the parameters of the algorithm. ML Studio provides modules for both of these tasks, allowing you to compare multiple models, or parameter values in a single run.

To train multiple models in one experiment, the training and test datasets can be reused by directing the datasets to multiple training branches as follows:

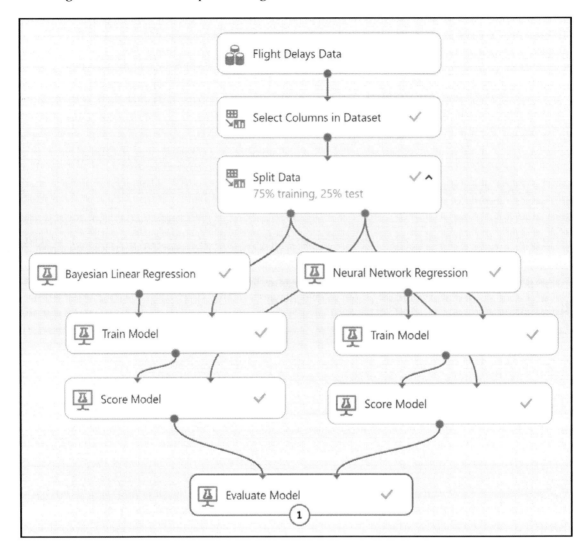

The preceding experiment is similar to the earlier training experiment, except that there are two **Train Model** modules with different algorithms as inputs. The results of the **Score Model** module are also directed to the **Evaluate Model** module, instead of visualizing the raw prediction results, as was done earlier. The evaluation module takes two datasets as inputs, each dataset containing the original labels and the predicted values from the scoring module.

The output of the evaluation module contains the summary statistics of the predicted values (the first input dataset is shown on the first row):

Flight delay prediction - Compare ❯ Evaluate Model ❯ Evaluation results

	Negative Log Likelihood	Mean Absolute Error	Root Mean Squared Error	Relative Absolute Error	Relative Squared Error	Coefficient of Determination
rows 2 / columns 6						
	5492524.863344	18.180083	35.405725	0.949358	0.963773	0.036227
	Infinity	18.831896	35.370147	0.983395	0.961837	0.038163

The columns of the evaluation results depend on the nature of the algorithms. The accuracy metrics that are used to evaluate regression models are different than those used for the evaluation of classification models, for example. As seen in the preceding screenshot, the evaluation module calculates several different metrics for a regression model. The different accuracy metrics capture different aspects of the errors. The **Root Mean Squared Error** is probably the most widely used metric for regression models. This metric indicates the confidence interval containing 95% of the examples in the test dataset.

Sometimes, different metrics can give contradicting results. In the preceding example, the second model has a lower **Root Mean Squared Error**, while other metrics, such as the **Mean Absolute Error**, are better in the first model. Therefore, it is important to choose the accuracy metric carefully when comparing results for different models. Different metrics emphasize different aspects of the error distribution, so the best metric depends on the problem and the input data. The properties of each metric is beyond the scope of this book, and we refer the reader to the ML Studio documentation and general statistics literature for details about the accuracy metrics.

As already mentioned, ML algorithms include parameters that affect how the model is trained. These parameters are often called **hyperparameters**. While the default values of the hyperparameters are chosen to work well in most cases, sometimes the accuracy of a model can be improved by choosing different values for the parameters. The **Tune Model Hyperparameters** module enables you to train a model multiple times in a single run using different parameter values. This module can be used instead of the **Train Model** module to create a trained model, as in the following experiment:

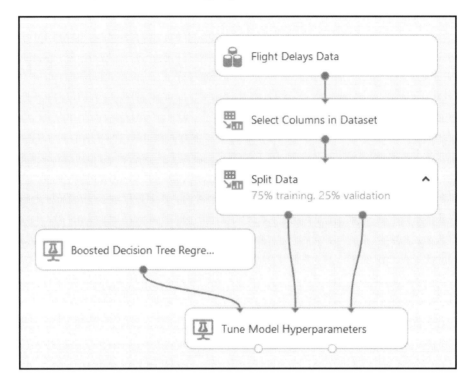

The inputs to **Tune Model Hyperparameters** are the same as for **Train Model**, except that the former accepts a validation dataset as a third optional input. Using the validation dataset means that the accuracy between different parameter values is evaluated with examples that were not used for training the model.

Each algorithm has its own set of parameters and the parameters used for training must be specified in the algorithm module. To enable multiple values for the parameters, switch the **Create trainer mode** option of the algorithm module to **Parameter Range**. Note that some algorithms, such as linear regression, do not allow hyperparameter tuning. The possible values of the parameters can be given as a comma-separated list or by specifying a range using the range builder, as follows:

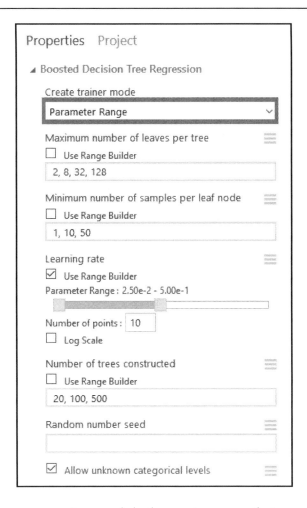

The **Tune Model Hyperparameters** module does not necessarily try out all of the possible combinations of the parameters. The module supports the following parameter sweep modes: entire grid, random grid, and random sweep. If entire grid mode is selected, all combinations will be tried. The random grid mode uses only a subset of all possible combinations, selected randomly. The total amount of runs in a random grid sweep can be controlled by setting the maximum number of runs on random sweep to a suitable value. This is particularly useful if there is a large number of combinations and it would take a very long time to sweep over the whole parameter space. Similarly, the random sweep mode can be used to run a subset of all possible combinations. The difference between the random grid and the random sweep modes is that the latter chooses the parameter values randomly within the specified range, while the former uses only the exact values defined in the algorithm module.

Before running the example, set the label column similarly, as for **Train Model**. The accuracy metric must also be defined, depending on the nature of the model (classification or regression). The accuracy metric determines which measure is used when selecting the best model. As already discussed, different metrics can disagree about the best model, so it is important to decide which metric is used to evaluate the performance of the model.

After the experiment has finished running, the results of the evaluation can be viewed in the first output of the **Tune Model Hyperparameters** module, as follows:

Flight delay prediction - Parameter tuning ❯ Tune Model Hyperparameters ❯ Sweep results

rows: 10 columns: 9

Number of leaves	Minimum leaf instances	Learning rate	Number of trees	Mean Absolute Error	Root Mean Squared Error	Relative Absolute Error	Relative Squared Error	Coefficient of Determination
2	50	0.31	20	18.227407	35.403769	0.951829	0.963666	0.036334
8	1	0.2625	20	17.749433	35.018912	0.926869	0.942829	0.057171
32	1	0.405	20	17.501632	34.767904	0.913929	0.929361	0.070639
8	50	0.215	500	17.389526	34.64951	0.908075	0.923043	0.076957
128	1	0.405	500	17.382583	35.592165	0.907712	0.973949	0.026051
32	1	0.405	100	17.351234	34.671923	0.906075	0.924237	0.075763

Each row in the results corresponds to an independent model, trained with different parameters. The columns show which parameter values were used in each case and the corresponding values of the accuracy metrics. The results are organized in decreasing order of accuracy, as defined by the metric chosen (here: **Mean Absolute Error**). The second output of **Tune Model Hyperparameters** contains the best trained model, also defined by the metric. This model can be used for scoring, similar to the output of the **Train Model** module.

In conclusion, Azure ML Studio includes many built-in modules to evaluate the accuracy of ML models, and to test different models and configurations. It must, however, be borne in mind that even the best models cannot perform well on poor data. If the values to be predicted are not correlated with the feature variables, the algorithm will not be able to make good predictions. Moreover, the algorithm that produces the best accuracy is not always the best model in practice. Particularly with large datasets, it is often necessary to consider the runtime of the training process. If the complexity of the training process grows uncontrollably as the amount of data grows, training the algorithm can become impossible in practice. These aspects must also be taken into account when choosing ML algorithms for any given problem.

Deploying a model as a web service

One of the biggest strengths of Azure ML Studio is the ease with which you can deploy models to the cloud, to be consumed by other applications. Once an ML model is trained, as demonstrated in the previous section, it can be exported to ML Studio Web Services with just a few clicks. Deployment creates a web API for the model, which can be called from any internet-connected application. The model takes the features as input data and produces a predicted value as output. By deploying models to the ML Studio Web Service, there is no need to worry about the underlying server infrastructure. The computing resources and maintenance are handled entirely by Azure.

The following subsections show how to deploy an already trained model to the web service and how to test a model with user input. In the final subsection, we'll show how to import and export experiments between environments. This can be useful when moving experiments across subscriptions, or if the experiment definitions need to be maintained in a version-control system.

Creating a predictive experiment

Before a trained model can be exported to the web service, the training experiment that created the model must be converted into a predictive experiment. A predictive experiment defines the scoring pipeline for creating predictions based on web service input. It does not contain any training modules, since the model is already trained. Instead, the model is just loaded from the list of trained models and imported as input to the **Score Model** module.

To create a predictive experiment, open a training experiment that has been previously run, or run the training experiment once to create a trained model. The experiment does not need to include a **Score Model** module—this will be added to the predictive experiment automatically. Click on **Set up Web Service | Create Predictive experiment**. This leads to a new view that shows the new predictive experiment, as follows:

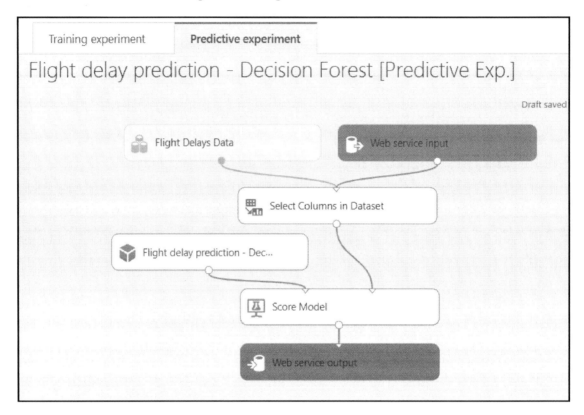

This example uses the same flight delay prediction experiment that was trained earlier. Note that the **Split Data** module has been removed from the predictive experiment and the training modules have now been replaced with the trained model. The **Split Data** module was only used to divide the data into training and test datasets, so ML Studio has inferred that it can be removed from the predictive experiment along with the training modules.

Run the experiment once before deploying it. The predictive experiment cannot be deployed as a web service before it has been run at least once. For instructions on how to deploy the model, skip to the next subsection.

In some cases, it might be useful to provide some of the module parameters as input from the web service. For example, the data preprocessing steps might depend on the input data. For this purpose, most of the module configurations can be parameterized so that the configuration values are supplied in the request as input. To parameterize a certain module parameter, go back to the training experiment and click on the module to be configured. In the configuration panel on the right-hand side of the canvas, click on the menu next to the field to be configured and select **Set as web service parameter**, as follows:

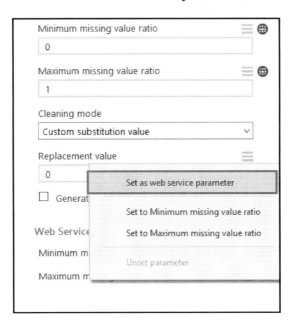

This will add the parameter to the list of **Web Services** parameters for the module. It is also possible to set a default value for the parameter, in case there is no value supplied in the request. Not all module parameters can be set as **Web Service** parameters, however. Those parameters that cannot be set do not have the context menu next to the field (see, for example, **Cleaning mode** in the preceding screenshot).

Sometimes, the deployed models might give poor predictions and we may wish to revert back to a previous version of the model. The previous runs can always be viewed from the **Run History**, which is found in the bottom panel of the experiment. The **Run History** shows every execution of the experiment, and clicking a version of the experiment will open it with the respective configuration and results. This version of the experiment will be locked and cannot be edited or deployed any more, but it can be saved as a new training experiment and retrained to create a new predictive experiment. This is useful if the model has been retrained several times and the optimal parameters for the model have been forgotten.

Deploying and testing a web service

The final step after creating the predictive experiment is to deploy the model to the cloud. Open the predictive experiment and make sure that it has been run successfully at least once, as discussed previously. From the bottom panel, choose **Deploy Web Service** | **Deploy Web Service [New]**. This brings up the deployment configuration view. Choose a name and the price plan for the web service. The price plan determines how many requests the service can handle in a month. The price plan is created at the same time as when a new ML Studio Web Service is created in the Azure portal. If there is no existing price plan, a new one can also be created by choosing **Create new...** from the menu.

When the configuration of the web service is ready, it can be deployed by pressing the **Deploy** button. This will deploy the model to ML Studio Web Services. If the deployment is successful, the user is directed to the ML Studio Web Services Management Portal (`https:/ /services.azureml.net/`). The management portal shows lots of useful information about the web service: how many times the API has been called, how many requests have failed, and how to call the web API from external applications, for example.

To verify that the API is working as expected, open the **Test** tab from the top menu. The web API has two operating modes: request-response, and batch mode. The request-response mode takes a single example as input and returns a single predicted value, while the Batch mode allows you to process multiple examples in a single request. To test the request-response mode, enter the values for the required parameters and press test request-response. To test the batch mode, a local file that contains multiple values for the input parameters must be supplied:

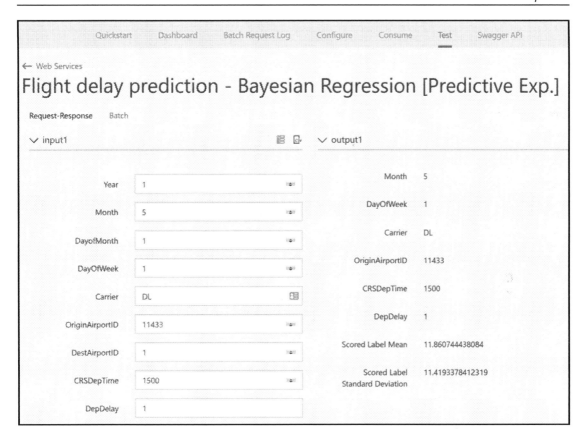

The output of the request-response test shows the features that were used to predict the target variable (`DepDelay`), and the predicted value (**Scored Label Mean**). Depending on the model, the predicted value might also be returned in the scored labels field. The **Scored Label Standard Deviation** field is also returned for the Bayesian Regression model, as shown in the example. Note that the input fields include all the columns that were present in the original input dataset. These fields will not, however, be used for the predictions, and they can be ignored when calling the web API.

The information needed to call the API from external applications can be found under the **Consume** tab. This includes the web URLs of the request-response and batch endpoints and the authorization keys that must be supplied in the header of the request. There are also code samples for multiple programming languages for calling the web API. These samples can be incorporated into an existing code base for quick integration with ML Studio Web Services.

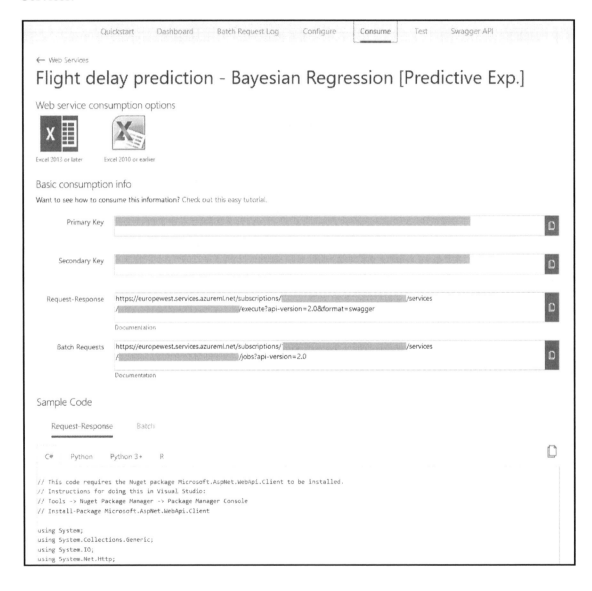

The **Swagger API** tab contains format definitions for the expected input and output data. These definitions can be useful when developing custom code for calling the web services API.

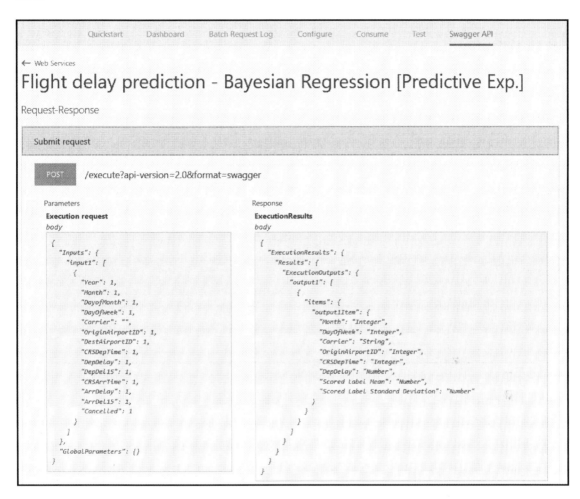

The web services API makes it possible to use custom ML models in almost any kind of application. The web services API also integrates natively with many Azure services. For example, the Logic Apps and Data Factory services include built-in connectors for ML Studio web services. Using web services with these services requires less configuration than with custom applications. These services also do not require any programming and so provide an easier interface for utilizing ML Studio models from external applications.

Summary

Azure Machine Learning Studio is a fully managed platform for developing machine learning models, enabling the user to concentrate on the essential tasks and problems in machine learning development. The graphical user interface is easy to learn and its usage requires no programming skills. Even users who have no prior experience in programming or machine learning can learn to use it, and the Experiment template collection contains many real-world examples of ML models to start with. ML Studio is a great way to start learning to develop ML models, and the sample datasets in ML Studio make it possible to develop your own models, even if you don't have your own data to start with.

Machine Learning Studio contains modules for all the most common ML-related tasks, such as data preprocessing, tuning hyperparameters, and evaluating the performance of ML algorithms. If the module collection is not sufficient for the task at hand, the R and Python script modules can be used to customize tasks and visualize the results, for example.

Machine Learning Studio is a complete environment for developing ML models, including all the steps from data ingestion to serving models in the cloud. Once the models have been trained in ML Studio Workspace, they can be converted to Predictive Experiments and deployed to the ML Studio Web Services for serving with a few clicks. The user does not need to worry about managing the underlying infrastructure behind the web services API, as this is managed entirely by the service. The web services portal contains comprehensive documentation and examples for integrating with the service, making it very easy to begin consuming the ML models from external applications. In the next chapter we will see how to use Azure in data science.

6
Scalable Computing for Data Science

In this chapter, we will learn how to use Azure in data science. We are going to look at how to prepare data, which includes cleaning and transforming it, creating engineering features, creating and training a machine learning model, and finally, making predictions using the machine learning model.

To build a machine learning algorithm with big data, we need to process a lot of data to train it. To do this, we need a lot of computing power. We also need the compute to be able to scale dynamically based on the load to serve these machine learning models at scale so that they can perform predictions.

In the era before public clouds, we had to buy all of our hardware beforehand. We had to pay for it all, whether or not we actually ended up using it. With Azure and other public clouds, we can now have different types of on-demand compute, based on our requirements. By scaling the compute based on our needs, we can save money, and still have sufficient compute power when required.

In this chapter, we will learn about the different compute types available in Azure, in order to train and deploy our machine learning model.

First, we are going to look at the compute types that are available for training, which include the following:

- **Data Science Virtual Machine (DSVM)**
- **Deep Learning Virtual Machine (DLVM)**
- Batch AI service

After that, we'll look at the compute types that are available for deployment, which include the following:

- **Azure Container Instance (ACI)**
- **Azure Kubernetes Service (AKS)**

Different scalable compute options in Azure

There are two types of scaling possible in Azure to help us scale our CPUs and/or GPUs:

- **Vertical scaling**: Increasing the number of CPU cores and the memory of the VM.
- **Horizontal scaling**: Increasing the number of VMs in the cluster, while keeping the CPU cores and the memory the same in each virtual machine. When we use horizontal scaling, we may have to write additional code to perform parallel or distributed computing using a supported framework.

Introduction to DSVMs

A DSVM is a Linux or Windows container that is made up of popular data science tools and frameworks. It can help us quickly get started with data analytics and data science. It supports a number of OSes; currently, we can create a DSVM with Windows 2012, Windows 2016, Ubuntu Linux, and CentOS Linux. The idea behind DSVMs is to decrease the time it takes to create a working environment.

A DSVM has preconfigured libraries that are tested for compatibility. It is updated every few months so that it uses the latest compatible version of tools, libraries, and frameworks. It supports GPU VMs and comes pre-installed with the necessary drivers. A DSVM also includes tutorials and guides on how to get started.

A DSVM is likely to come pre-installed with the following components:

- Programming languages, such as C#, Julia, Java, R, Python, and JavaScript
- Deep learning frameworks, such as Keras, PyTorch, TensorFlow, CNTK, and MXNet
- ML and AI tools, such as Azure Machine Learning, Microsoft ML, H2O, XGBoost, LightGBM, and Anaconda Python
- Data exploration and visualization tools, such as Power BI, SQL Server, and Apache Drill
- Data platform and ingestion tools, such as Apache Spark, Azure Data Factory, and ML Server
- Development tools, such as Jupyter, R Studio, Visual Studio, VS Code, and PyCharm

To find out more about the tools and libraries available, check out the following website: `https://azure.microsoft.com/en-us/services/virtual-machines/data-science-virtual-machines/`.

Provisioning a DSVM

Let's now go through the steps required to create a DSVM. In this example, we will create a Windows 2016 DSVM, but the steps are similar if you want to create a Linux DSVM:

1. Go to the Azure portal at `https://portal.azure.com`.

2. Click on **Create a resource**, and then go to **AI + Machine Learning** and click on **Data Science Virtual Machine – Windows 2016**:

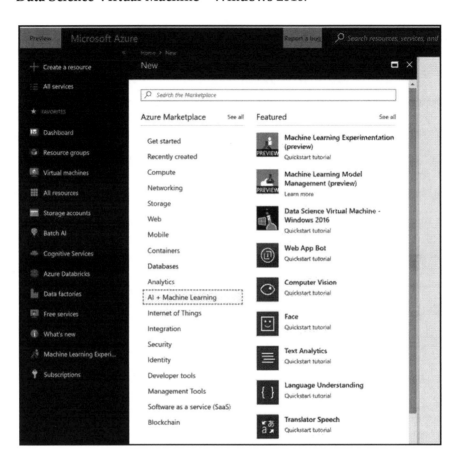

3. Alternatively, we can search for `data science virtual machine` in the Azure portal:

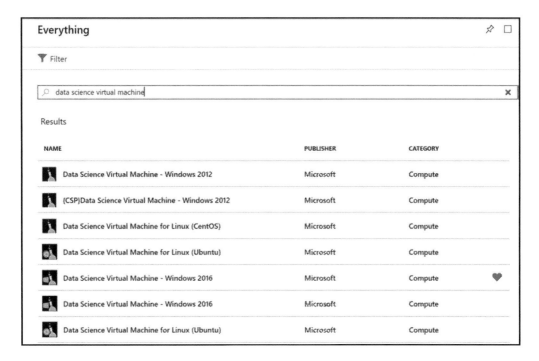

4. A window will appear that will show you some of the key characteristics of the DSVM that you choose:

5. We can create a DSVM quickly by providing the necessary information. This includes the **Resource group**, the **Region**, a **Username**, and a **Password**:

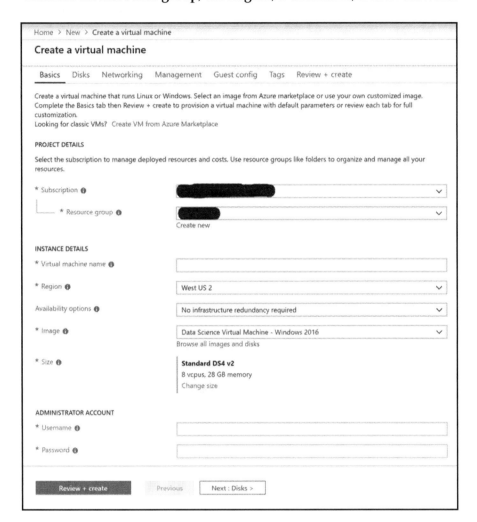

6. An important parameter that we need to consider is the **VM SIZE**. Here, we have the option of selecting a CPU- and/or a GPU-based VM. We have lots of options based on our CPU, our memory, and our networking requirements. A sample screenshot of different types of VMs is shown as follows:

VM SIZE	OFFERING	FAMILY	VCPUS	RAM (GB)	DATA DISKS	MAX IOPS	TEMPORARY STOR...	PREMIUM DISK SU...
D16_v3	Standard	General purpose	16	64	32	32x500	400 GB	No
D16s_v3	Standard	General purpose	16	64	32	25600	128 GB	Yes
D2_v3	Standard	General purpose	2	8	4	4x500	50 GB	No
D2s_v3	Standard	General purpose	2	8	4	3200	16 GB	Yes
D32_v3	Standard	General purpose	32	128	32	32x500	800 GB	No
D32s_v3	Standard	General purpose	32	128	32	51200	256 GB	Yes
D4_v3	Standard	General purpose	4	16	8	8x500	100 GB	No
D4s_v3	Standard	General purpose	4	16	8	6400	32 GB	Yes
D64_v3	Standard	General purpose	64	256	32	32x500	1600 GB	No
D64s_v3	Standard	General purpose	64	256	32	80000	512 GB	Yes
D8_v3	Standard	General purpose	8	32	16	16x500	200 GB	No
D8s_v3	Standard	General purpose	8	32	16	12800	64 GB	Yes
E16_v3	Standard	Memory optimized	16	128	32	32x500	400 GB	No
E16-4s_v3	Standard	Memory optimized	4	128	32	25600	256 GB	Yes
E16-8s_v3	Standard	Memory optimized	8	128	32	25600	256 GB	Yes

Wait for a few minutes while Azure creates our virtual machine. Once it is ready, we will get a notification in the portal.

After our VM has been created, we can access it using RDP or SSH, depending on the OS. From the overview window, we can look at different metrics when our VM is running, such as CPU usage or disk operations. These metrics can help us to decide whether we need to resize our VM:

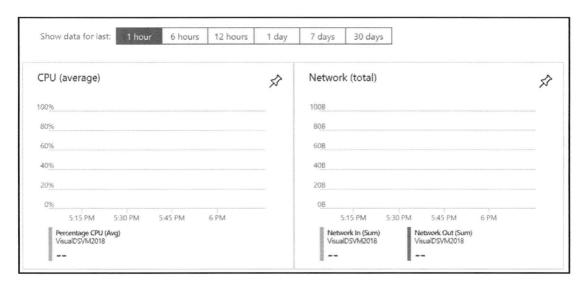

We can also configure the VM to shut down automatically using the **Auto-shutdown** option from the portal:

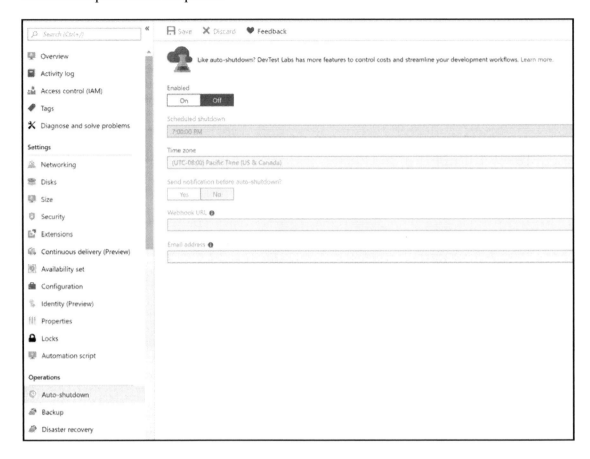

After we log in to our DSVM, we can start using its tools as if it were our local machine. For more information about each of the tools, please refer to the following website: `https://docs.microsoft.com/en-us/azure/machine-learning/data-science-virtual-machine/provision-vm#important-directories-on-the-vm`.

After using the VM, we can stop it from the portal to avoid paying for it unnecessarily. When we want to use it in the future, we can start it again without having to recreate it.

Let's now move on to look at a variant of a DSVM – a DLVM.

DLVM

A DLVM is a special type of DSVM that has a base image that is customized for deep learning. We can use either Windows 2016 or Ubuntu Linux as the OS. It has pre-installed frameworks, tools, and tutorials to get you started quickly with deep learning.

Provisioning a DLVM is similar to provisioning a DSVM. We need to select a GPU-based VM for a DLVM:

1. Go to the Azure portal and search for `deep learning virtual machine`. We can create a DLVM in the same way as we created a DSVM.

2. A window will pop up, asking us to provide a name and select an OS, username, password, resource group, location, and so on. The next window requires us to select a GPU-based VM. As shown in the following screenshot, the VM sizes that are not available in your region or with your current subscription will be grayed out:

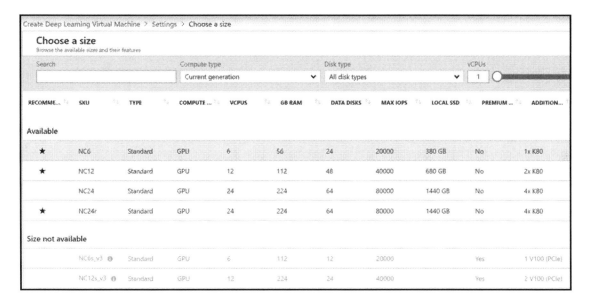

A DLVM requires a GPU-based VM. It comes with all GPU drivers, deep learning frameworks, and deep learning tutorials pre-installed.

Depending on the type of OS (Windows or Linux), we can access our VM using either SSH or RDP. After we log in to our DLVM, we can start using the tools installed on it as if it were our local machine. For more information about the frameworks that are available in a DLVM and a DSVM, please head to the following website: `https://docs.microsoft.com/en-us/azure/machine-learning/data-science-virtual-machine/dsvm-deep-learning-ai-frameworks`.

After using the VM, we can stop it from the portal to avoid paying for it unnecessarily. When we want to use it in the future, we can just start it again without having to recreate it.

Batch AI service

DSVMs and DLVMs are good at carrying out single node-based computing. In scenarios where we need to distribute training, however, we can use the Batch AI service, which allows us to focus on training instead of having to worry about managing the cluster. A Batch AI service has VMs that use the same base image as the DSVM, meaning that all the libraries, tools, and frameworks that are available in a DSVM are available in the Batch AI service as well. The Batch AI service allows us to use parallel training and GPU-based VMs for deep learning, and we can also deploy a Docker container to a Batch AI node. When using the Batch AI service, we can mount our Azure Blob or Azure Data Lake Storage with our cluster. This means that we can train with a huge amount of data without having to copy the data to the cluster because it can be streamed instead.

At the time of writing, the Batch AI service is only available as a preview, so there may be new features when the service is available generally.

Provisioning a Batch AI service

Let's now proceed to create a Batch AI service:

1. Go to the Azure portal at `https://portal.azure.com`. Go to **Create a resource** and search for `batch ai`:

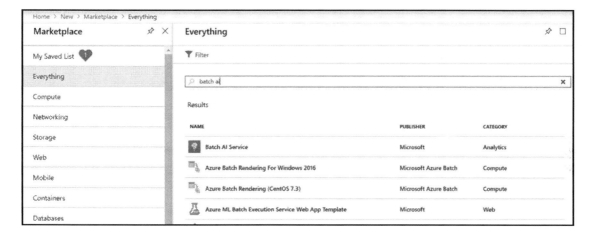

2. In the next screen, we can create our Batch AI service.
3. The screen after that asks for the name, the subscription, the resource group, and the location for our Batch AI service workspace. The workspace is where the cluster, experiments, and file server can be added.

4. The **Batch AI Cluster** will provide the computing power for running your experiments. We can provide basic information, such as the number of VMs, the VM type, the user account details, and the network configuration:

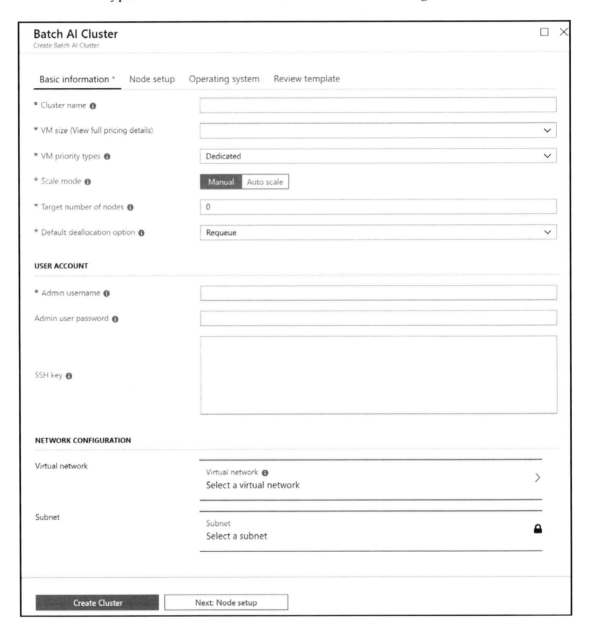

5. We can pick from various sizes for our VM. All GPU-based VM types are supported, whereas only a few CPU-based VM types are supported. This is because GPU-based VMs in Batch AI are more effective when they are used for machine learning, especially for deep learning:

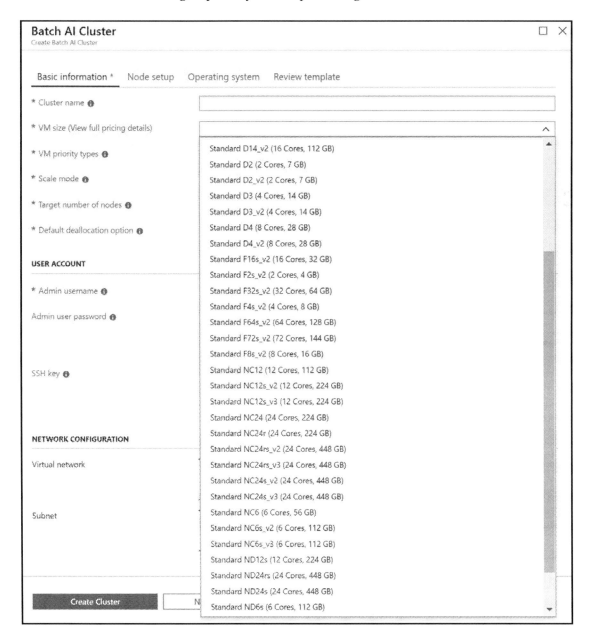

6. We can select either **Low-Priority** or **Dedicated** as the **VM priority types**. Low priority VMs can be preempted and can help us save money. We can enable either **Manual** or **Auto scale** as the **Scale mode** for our cluster:

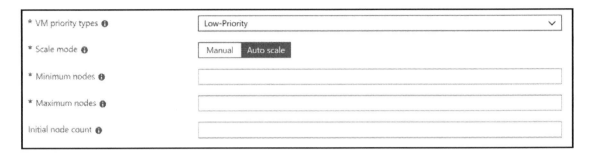

7. We can create a file server that can be accessed by our compute cluster to store our data. Both standard and premium storage can be selected:

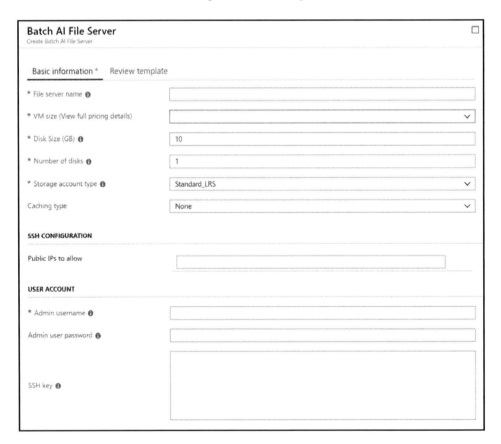

8. We can create an experiment and submit jobs to the Batch AI cluster. Our Batch AI jobs can use one of the pre-installed frameworks or tools, or we can use a custom tool:

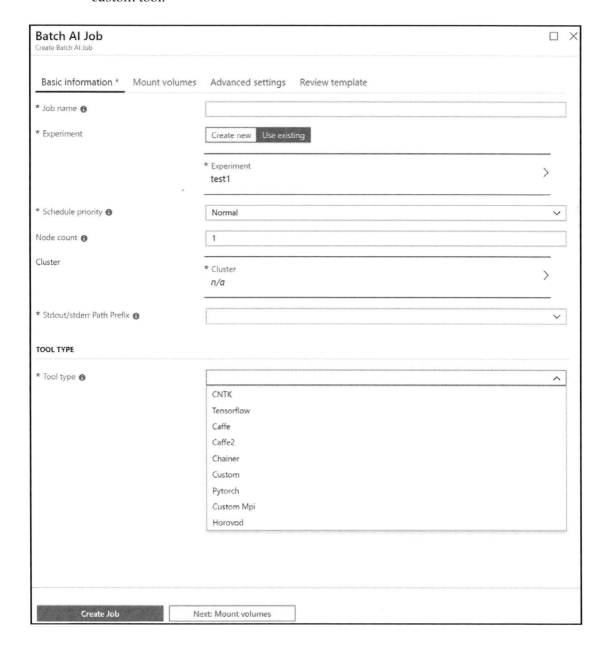

9. We can also mount different storage types for our jobs:

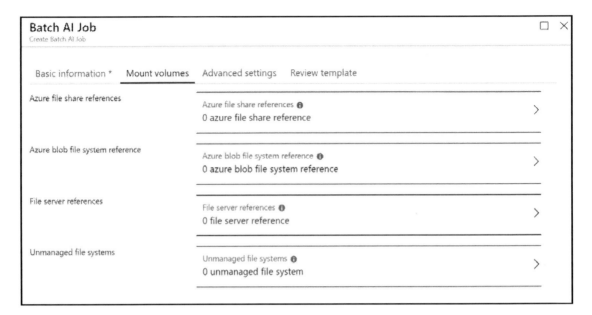

After our experiments have run, we can delete the cluster or set auto scale to zero so that we don't have to pay for the cluster when it is not in use. For more details on the Batch AI service, visit the following
website: `https://docs.microsoft.com/en-us/azure/batch-ai/overview`.

ACI

As a data scientist, after we have trained our machine learning model, we may want to deploy the model as a web service for real-time or batch scoring. When we train our machine learning model, we use a certain framework and libraries. In most cases, the same environment should be available in our deployment environment. Containers are a fast and simple way to create such an environment, in which we can host our model and dependencies. Containers can be created easily with ACI. As data scientists, we can use AML to deploy our machine learning model as a web service to an ACI. This way, we can development test our model and then deploy it in production. For more details on ACI, refer to the following website: `https://docs.microsoft.com/en-us/azure/container-instances/container-instances-overview`.

AKS

Kubernetes is an open source project for managing applications that are hosted in containers. AKS is a managed Kubernetes service that makes it easy to use Kubernetes. Once you test your machine learning model, you can deploy it to a scalable cluster with AKS. You can then have a scalable web service for your machine learning model. You can use AML to deploy your model to AKS. For more details on AKS, refer to the following website: https://docs.microsoft.com/en-us/azure/aks/intro-kubernetes.

Summary

In this chapter, we have learned about the different types of compute options that are available for you to scale your machine learning training and deployment. We learned about the vertical and horizontal scaling compute options that can be used to provide you with a large amount of compute power for your machine learning projects.

In the next chapter, we will learn about the machine learning server, which can be used for on-premise deployments.

7
Machine Learning Server

Microsoft ML Server and its capabilities in SQL Server and HDInsight are the subject of this chapter. In addition, the chapter will provide a walk-through on ML Server's use in order to demonstrate optimal situations in which to use it and how to deploy a solution with it.

Classified algorithms are supervised learning algorithms, which means that they make predictions based on a set of examples.

Often, it is useful to use data to predict a category, and this is known as classification. Take, for example, Andrew Ng's work on the classification of YouTube content as a cat video, or a video of something that is not a cat. As in the famous work by Andrew Ng, when there are only two choices, it is called **two-class** or **binomial classification**. When there are more categories, this problem is known as **multi-class classification**. Multi-class classification is useful for creating models that predict three or more possible outcomes.

Data needs to be intelligible. People need to interact with their data in order to understand it better. Using Microsoft tools such as Azure HDInsight, and Microsoft ML Server, allows us to achieve more with our data than simply storing it; we can use it to provide insights and drive actions for our organizations.

In this chapter, we will focus on Microsoft ML Server, and we will look at R and Python as key parts of this architecture for scalable machine learning using open source software.

In this chapter, we will cover the following topics:

- The basics regarding Microsoft ML server
- Setting up the Python environment in Visual studio
- Analysing results in ML models

What is Microsoft ML Server?

Microsoft ML Server brings machine learning and artificial intelligence to your data. It makes it possible for you to have data underlying intelligence apps in an enterprise environment that provides the opportunities of open source, with the security and reliance of Microsoft software. Microsoft ML Server offers an enterprise-ready platform for cleaning, modelling, and analyzing data at scale. It allows organizations to become insight-driven, allowing you to analyze data in SQL, as well as offering full enterprise support for Python and R.

ML Server meets the needs of everyone involved in analyzing data, from business users to data engineers and data scientists. With SQL, Python, and R, businesses can be assured of having the opportunity to analyze their data using the most commonly-known and adopted languages in the world, offering businesses the opportunity to have data-based innovation. With Microsoft ML Server, the availability of R, SQL, and Python amalgamates the best of the open source and proprietary worlds together to bring true data science.

Microsoft ML Server used to be known as Microsoft R Server. In continuation of this effort to democratize data, R support is built on a legacy of previous versions of Microsoft R Server, and Revolution R Enterprise products.

With the advent of Microsoft ML Server, significant machine learning and AI capabilities enhancements are made in every release. Python support was added in the most recent release. ML Server supports the full data science life cycle of your Python-based analytics.

Additionally, ML Server enables operationalization support so that you can deploy your models to a scalable grid for both batch and real-time scoring. This means that you can go through the machine learning process, and then set your model for use by everyone in the organization. This is the true democratization of data for everyone!

What problems does Microsoft ML Server solve? Microsoft ML Server can help solve many different, real-life business problems. It can take care of data in an end-to-end process. For example, it can clean and preprocess larger sets of data so that downstream systems can work with the data in order to produce insights. There are different examples for which HDInsight is useful, such as:

- Sentiment analysis
- Website traffic patterns
- Weather correlation effects

- Sales analysis
- Customer analysis
- **Internet of Things (IoT)** projects

Next, we will look at getting started with Microsoft ML Server.

How to get started with Microsoft ML Server

To get started with Microsoft ML Server, it is recommended that the Microsoft **Data Science Virtual Machine (DSVM)** is used.

The DSVM is a specially-built custom virtual machine that is hosted on Microsoft's Azure cloud. It is designed specifically for data science, and for giving learners a jump start in learning this new technology. It has Microsoft ML Server pre-installed and preconfigured so you can get started right away with data science projects.

You can use languages such as R and Python to do your data analytics right on the Microsoft DSVM. It is great for prototyping, and is a useful learning tool so that learners are set up for success early in the process.

Configuring the DSVM

The wizard that creates the Microsoft DSVM needs to be configured. The options are listed as follows:

- **Name**: Give the DSVM a name.
- **VM disk type**: Choose SSD or HDD.
- **Username**: Specify the admin account ID to sign in.
- **Password**: Specify the admin account password.
- **Subscription**: If you have more than one subscription, select the one on which the machine is to be created and billed.
- **Resource group**: You can create a new resource group or use an existing group.
- **Location**: Select the data center that is most appropriate. For the fastest network access, it is the data center that has most of your data or is closest to your actual location.
- **Size**: Select one of the server types that meets your functional requirements and cost constraints. For more choices of VM sizes, select **View All**.

- **Settings**:
  - Use managed disks. Choose **Managed** if you want Azure to manage the disks for the VM. If not, you need to specify a new or existing storage account.
  - Other parameters. You can use the default values. If you want to use non-default values, hover over the informational link for help on the specific fields.
  - Once the settings have been configured, the next step is to check and verify that all the information you entered is correct. Then, select **Create** and the DSVM will be set up in Azure.

Now that the DSVM is set up, let's look at the opportunities to use Python in Microsoft ML Server.

Machine learning with Python

Python has a lot of machine learning functionality. One of the most commonly used machine learning libraries in Python is the scikit-learn library. It is used for creating, training, and evaluating models. In this hands-on book, the Python scikit-learn library is used in the code to train and evaluate the model.

Getting started with Python

Python is a popular programming language that is rapidly gaining worldwide acceptance. Python has many strengths; it is reliable, flexible, easy to learn and use, and is free to use on all operating systems. It has been widely adopted among the open source community, and is supported by a strong developer community. Python has many free libraries for you to download and use in your data science work.

Python meets developers where they are; it supports all different types of development, including web applications, iterative development, web services, desktop apps, scripting, scientific, and mathematical computing. Python is used by businesses as well as many universities, scientists, casual developers, and professional developers alike.

Throughout this chapter, the Python coding will be completed using Microsoft Visual Studio, which incorporates a powerful Python IDE on Windows. Visual Studio provides open source support for the Python language through the Python development and data science workloads (Visual Studio 2017) and the free **Python Tools for Visual Studio (PTVS)** (Visual Studio 2015 and earlier).

Using the DSVM, we can clean, model, analyze, and visualize our data and develop models using Microsoft ML Server with Python.

For Python, there are many common development studios. Since the chapter will use R and Python, we will use Visual Studio Community edition because it has both R and Python IDEs in place. For the hands-on part of the chapter, the DSVM already has the PTVS extension and R extensions pre-installed, so there is no need for us to take time to install and configure these additional items.

Set up your Python environment in Visual Studio

Visual Studio needs to be configured so that it is using Python with Microsoft ML Server. This is the first step, and it only needs to be conducted once.

In Visual Studio, select the **View** | **Other Windows** | **Python Environments** menu command.

We are going to create a `cookiecutter` Python project. To do this, firstly, we need to install `cookiecutter`.

Open Command Prompt, and type in the following command:

```
easy_install --user cookiecutter
```

Then, we can proceed to use the `cookiecutter` functionality in Visual Studio to get off to a great start with Python and Visual Studio.

In this exercise, the code will come from a Microsoft repository, which is stored on GitHub.

1. In Visual Studio, choose **File | New | Repository**.
2. The next step is to clone a repository from GitHub. Open **Team Explorer**:

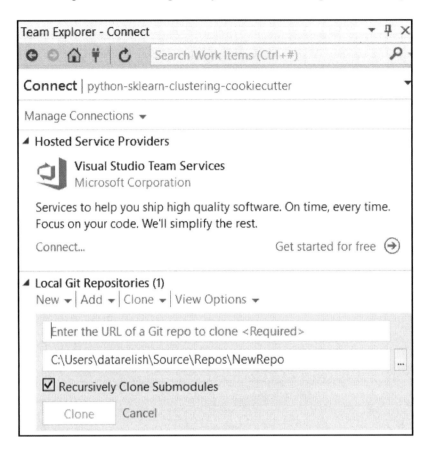

3. Click on the **Clone** option under the **Local Git Repositories** heading.
4. After clicking the **Clone** button, enter the URL for your Git repo—this will be provided by your team or Git hosting provider. You can place the URL in the box highlighted in yellow, which states `Enter the URL of a Git repo to clone <Required>`

5. Then, click the **Clone** button, and the repository will appear in your local Git repository. A completed example is shown in the following screenshot:

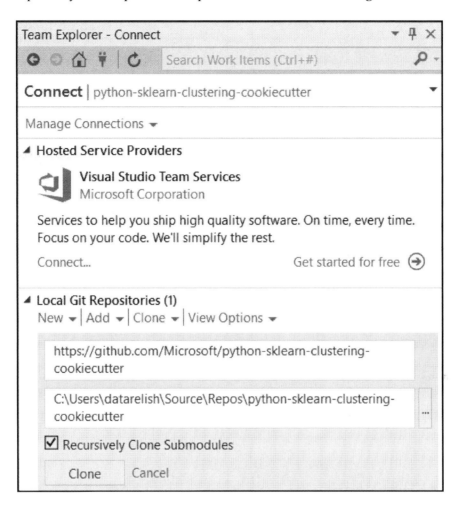

6. The next step is to move from the **Team Explorer** view to the **Solution Explorer** view. In the **Team Explorer** view, select the **Show Folder View** option.

7. The Visual Studio solution will be shown in **Solution Explorer**. For the purposes of this example, the Python code is stored in the `clustering.py` file. This is shown in **Solution Explorer**. Double-click on this file so that it appears in the main Visual Studio canvas. Ensure that the `clustering.py` file remains selected:

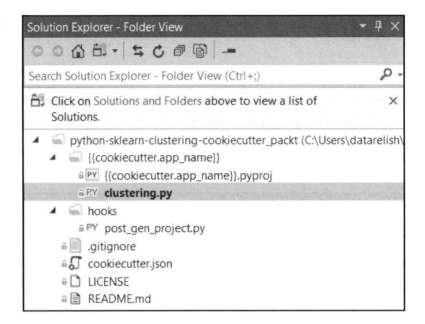

8. It is important to view the results so that the Python code is understood better. Ensuring that the file is selected, execute the code by clicking on the button with the green arrow. The button should show the name of the current file. An example is shown in the following screenshot:

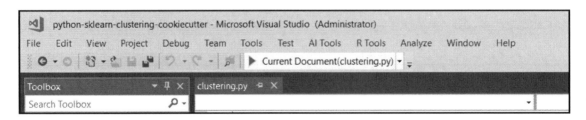

9. The Python code will execute. The first item to appear is Command Prompt, which will provide a progress update:

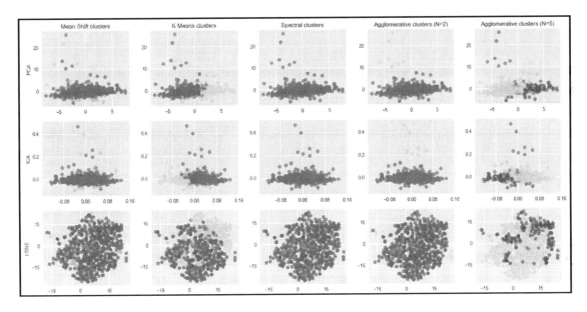

10. The final chart will also appear. An example is provided here:

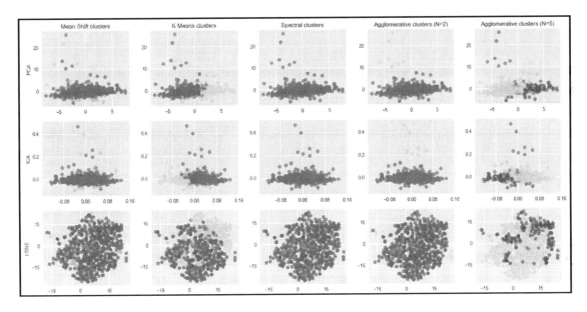

In this exercise, Python has been used to conduct machine learning using a number of Python libraries, such as scikit-learn, NumPy, and Pandas. Visual Studio has been used in order to create and run Python scripts.

Writing your own code with Python in Microsoft ML Server

In the last section, there was an end-to-end example that demonstrated the ability to use machine learning with Python in Microsoft ML Server. In this hands-on walk-through, there will be an exploration of writing Python code from scratch using Microsoft ML Server.

Walk-through: reading data in and out in Microsoft ML Server

In this hands-on walk-through, the same Iris dataset will be used to provide further examples using a familiar dataset. The purpose of the code is to show one of the in-built datasets, and read it out to the Python output screen.

In this walk-through, we will read data in and out of Microsoft ML Server. Initially, the code imports the Iris dataset from the scikit-learn library. The initial code will print out the data in the Iris dataset. The data is assigned to the df variable , which is set to a dataframe.

Here is the sequence of steps, in summary, of how we will proceed at a high level:

- It imports the Iris dataset from the scikit-learn library
- The Pandas library is imported, and is assigned to the pd variable
- The iris variable is used to hold the Iris dataset
- Finally, a dataframe is created using the Iris data, and this is assigned to the df variable

The code is as follows:

```
from sklearn
import datasets
import pandas as pd
iris = datasets.load_iris()
df = pd.DataFrame(iris.data, columns=iris.feature_names)
```

As before, Microsoft Visual Studio with Python extensions will be used, with Python provided by Microsoft ML Server.

1. To start a new Python Project in Visual Studio, go to **File** | **New** | **Project**. Here is a screenshot:

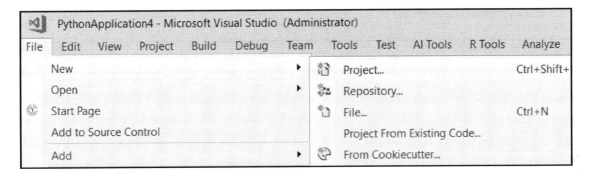

2. Give the project a name. For the purposes of this example, the project will be called `Python Packt Example`. The package will appear in the **Solution Explorer**. Here is a screenshot:

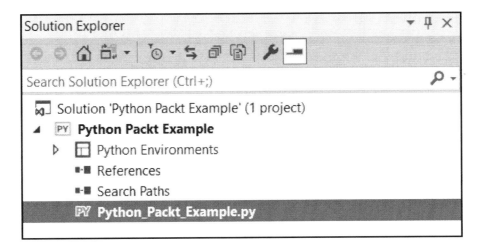

3. Copy the following code into the `.py` file:

```
from sklearn import datasets import pandas as pd iris =
datasets.load_iris() df = pd.DataFrame(iris.data,
columns=iris.feature_names)
```

4. On the main canvas, paste the code. The screen will now appear as follows:

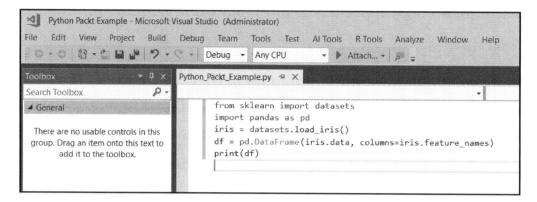

5. When the code is pasted into the file, we can execute it by clicking on the file in the **Solution Explorer** window, and then clicking the **Start** button in the middle of the menu bar.

6. When the code is executed, the output will appear in a Python window as follows:

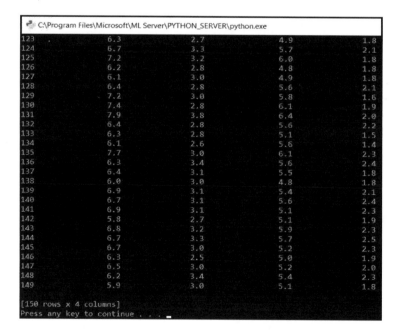

This code provides an example of the basic process for working with a small sample dataset using Python.

At a high level, the steps are matched to the data science team process as follows. In the data acquisition and understanding phase, one of the activities is to access data. The code downloads a dataset using the Pandas Python library. Another part of the data acquisition and understanding phase is to process clean the data, and the sample code uses NumPy to build out this contribution. The scikit-learn library is an impressive Python library that is used for creating, training, and evaluating models. It is used in the code here to train and evaluate the model. This is a key part of the data science team process, and is categorized under the modelling phase.

Introducing regression with Python in Microsoft ML Server

In this example, the Iris dataset is used again, since it is already available as part of the Python installation. In this segment of Python code, the Python Seaborn library is used to produce charts and graphs. Seaborn is a Python package that allows us to produce interesting results that can help our machine learning work.

In this next demo, the code will be changed in order to produce more charts, and save them to the Git repository on the DSVM.

At a high level, the code uses the Iris dataset, and produces charts based on the data. In the last plot, the linear regression line is added for clarity.

The chart shows the relationship between the length of the sepal, and the length of the petals, in three species of Iris. The data is grouped by color, and it is clear to see that the linear regression line fits through each of the three species.

In the simplest invocation, the Seaborn `lmplot` function draws a scatterplot of two variables, x and y, and then fits the regression model y ~ x. It plots the resulting regression line and a 95% confidence interval for that regression. In the example here, it has been conducted for each of the species.

The code is commented at a low level as follows:

The first step is to load the Iris dataset:

```
iris = sns.load_dataset("iris")
```

Then, the colour scheme is set:

```
colours = ['#066082', '#b12acf', '#808080']
```

This code will generate a joint plot using the Iris dataset:

```
sns_pairplot = sns.pairplot(iris, hue='species', size=2.5,palette=colours)
```

The next step is to save the output to an image, and then produce a plot:

```
sns_pairplot.savefig("Packtpairplotoutput.png")
print("Produced Pairplot Image")
```

This code will generate a `jointplot` using the Iris dataset:

```
sns_jointplot = sns.jointplot(x="sepal_length", y="petal_length",
data=iris);
```

Next, we save the output to an image:

```
sns_jointplot.savefig("Packtjointplotoutput.png")
```

Then, we feed back success to the user:

```
print("Produced Jointplot Image")
```

This code will generate a linear regression plot using the Iris dataset:

```
sns_lmplot = sns.lmplot(x='sepal_length', # X-axis name y='petal_length', #
Y-axis name data=iris, fit_reg=True, hue='species', # one colour per iris
species scatter_kws={"s":100}, size=8, palette=colours)
```

The output is then saved to an image:

```
sns_lmplot.savefig('PacktLinearRegression.jpeg', bbox_inches='tight')
```

Then, we feed back success to the user via the console:

```
print("Produced Linear Regression Image")
```

When the script is executed, the image files can be found in the Visual Studio repository folder. This is an example of where the images might be found in a repository folder: `C:\Users\myusername\source\repos\Python Packt Example\Python Packt Example.`

More data visualization charts in Python and the Microsoft Machine Learning service

The code will also produce two more charts: a pairplot and a jointplot.

A pairplot sets out to plot pairwise relationships in a dataset. The pairplot takes variables such as petal width, petal length, sepal width, and sepal length, and correlates them with one another. The output is generated very quickly using Python in Microsoft ML Server. The visualization allows the patterns in the data to be seen very quickly. For example, there is an interesting relationship between petal length and petal width, which can be viewed from the lower row of the pairplot.

In Seaborn, a jointplot draws a plot of two variables with bivariate and univariate graphs. This is produced easily with Python and Microsoft Machine Learning service. The walk-through code produces a jointplot using the Iris dataset.

An example jointplot produced by the Python code is shown here:

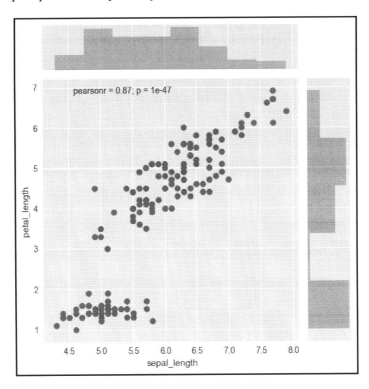

In this screenshot, the jointplot shows the relationships between the sepal length and the petal length. The central scattergram is supplemented by histograms on either side of the chart. The length of the bars represents the density of points for the petal length and sepal length.

Regression code walk-through with Python and Microsoft ML Server

We will change the file by commenting out the existing Python code, and we can add our new code to the same file. It is important to know how to comment out code, so that the code is readable and maintainable:

1. Comment out the existing Python code by inserting a hash sign, # , at the start of each line.

2. The code should appear as follows:

```
# from sklearn import datasets
# import pandas as pd
# iris = datasets.load_iris()
# df = pd.DataFrame(iris.data, columns=iris.feature_names)
```

3. Copy the code given previously into the file. The file should appear as illustrated in the next screenshot, which only shows some of the code for the purposes of clarity:

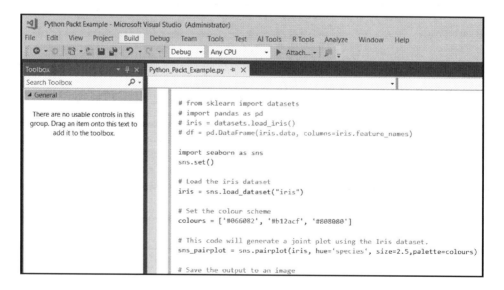

4. To run the code, click on the file in **Solution Explorer** so that it is highlighted.
5. Click the **Start** button.
6. The code will execute, and the Python interpreter will appear. Here is an example:

```
C:\Program Files\Microsoft\ML Server\PYTHON_SERVER\python.exe
Produced Pairplot Image
Produced Jointplot Image
Produced Linear Regression Image
Press any key to continue . . . ▄
```

7. Once the code finishes execution, press any key to continue, as instructed.
8. Search for the repository folder on the DSVM to look for the images produced by the Python code. If you are unclear about the repository location, search for `*.png` and you will find the completed files.
9. Save your work by going to **File | Save All** in the Visual Studio menu bar.

Analyzing results in machine learning models

No data has meaning apart from in its context. Machine learning is the way forward to understand data, but it needs to be interpreted as well. At a very high level, this process can be depicted as follows:

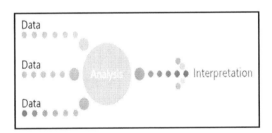

Data needs to be understood; data goes through an analysis process. There can be trade-offs between accuracy and performance. Sometimes it is better to select an algorithm that is less accurate in order to have better performance. Another advantage of choosing more approximate methods is that they naturally tend to avoid overfitting.

There is no one single best method for interpreting statistics or selecting models. This is one of the most difficult parts of machine learning, and some of the concepts for understanding statistics are presented here.

Measuring the fit of the model

How well do the model's predictions actually match the observed data? It is crucial to understand the extent to which the predicted response value for a given observation is close to the actual response value for that observation.

In regression, the most common measure is the **mean squared error (MSE)**, which is the average squared difference between the estimated values and the actual value that is estimated. If the MSE is small, then the predicted responses are very close to the true responses. If the MSE is large, then the predicted and true responses differ substantially. This is the first step in showing that the model is not a good fit.

Note that the analysis focuses on the MSE test data, not the MSE for the training data. The most interesting results use test data that the model has not seen previously, and this is where we focus our analysis on MSE results.

Cross validation

As we test and train our model, the MSE can vary widely across different sets of data. For this reason, cross-validation is important in order to understand the true results. Cross validation seeks to show how the model works in practice. The question is: Will our model generalize to an independent dataset?

To conduct cross validation, the model is continually trained and then it is given a series of test sets of data. Cross validation combines the measures of fitness and averages them in order to derive model prediction performance.

Variance and bias

What do we mean by the variance and bias of the results? Variance refers to the amount by which the predicted values would change if it was estimated using a different set of training data. Throughout the training process, different training datasets will result in different predictions, but it is hoped that the predictions will not vary too much between training sets.

Bias refers to the error that is introduced by simplifying a real-life problem to a dataset. By simplifying data into a simpler model, bias may be introduced. When we look at the complexities of real life, this is a common issue that needs to be understood and taken into account when interpreting results.

Summary

In this chapter, we have investigated Visual Studio for Python and run through some interesting walk-throughs. We have learned about the modelling process using the **Team Data Science Process** (**TDSP**). As part of this process, we have looked at modeling and analyzing our results, as well as conducting data visualization to evangelize our work.

8
HDInsight

HDInsight is a type of implementation of Hadoop that runs on the Microsoft Azure platform. HDInsight builds on the **Hortonworks Data Platform (HDP)**, and is completely compatible with Apache Hadoop.

HDInsight can be perceived as Microsoft's **Hadoop-as-a-Service (Haas)**. You can quickly deploy the system from a portal or through Windows PowerShell scripting, without having to create any physical or virtual machines.

The following are features of HDInsights:

- You can implement a small or large number of nodes in a cluster
- You pay only for what you use
- When your job is complete, you can deprovision the cluster and, of course, stop paying for it
- You can use Microsoft Azure Storage so that even when the cluster is deprovisioned, you can retain the data
- The HDInsight service works with input-output technologies from Microsoft and other vendors

As mentioned, the HDInsight service runs on Microsoft Azure, and that requires a little explaining before we proceed further.

Data is described as 'big data' to indicate that it is being collected in ever-escalating volumes, at increasingly high velocities, and for a widening variety of unstructured formats and variable semantic contexts. Big data collection does not provide value to an enterprise on its own. For big data to provide value in the form of actionable intelligence or insight, it must be accessible, cleaned, analyzed, and then presented in a useful way, often in combination with data from various other sources.

Apache Hadoop is a software framework that facilitates big data management and analysis. The core of Apache Hadoop provides reliable data storage with the **Hadoop Distributed File System (HDFS)**, and a simple MapReduce programming model to process and analyze the data stored in this distributed system in parallel. HDFS uses data replication to address hardware failure issues that arise when deploying such highly distributed systems.

Windows Azure HDInsight makes Apache Hadoop available as a service in the cloud. It makes the HDFS or MapReduce software framework and related projects available in a simpler, more scalable, and cost-efficient environment. To simplify configuring and running Hadoop jobs, and managing the deployed clusters, Microsoft provides JavaScript, and Hive interactive consoles. This simplified JavaScript approach enables IT professionals and a wider group of developers to deal with big data management and analysis by providing a more accessible path into the Hadoop framework for them.

For data scientists who already use R, HDInsight offers a route into the cloud to empower big data analytics. For IT professionals and system administrators, it allows the administration of big data with straightforward management.

As in the previous chapters, we will use Microsoft's TDSP as a backdrop for producing machine learning models with HDInsight. Now, we will use R and HDInsight to analyze and model a sample dataset.

R with HDInsight

What are the main features of HDInsight? It is a Microsoft proprietary solution, but it is a 100% Apache Hadoop solution in the Microsoft Azure cloud. Azure HDInsight is a service that deploys and provisions Apache Hadoop clusters in the cloud for big data analytics.

HDInsight provides a software framework designed to manage, analyze, and report on big data. You can use HDInsight to perform interactive queries at petabyte scales over structured or unstructured data in any format. You can also build models, connecting them to BI tools. HDInsight is aimed at providing big data analytics and insights through Excel and Power BI. Azure's HDInsight service makes Apache Hadoop available as a service in the cloud, providing a software framework designed to manage, analyze, and report on big data. As a cloud-based service, it makes these resources available in a simpler, more scalable, and cost-efficient environment.

HDInsight is aimed at production environments, with enterprise security, and manageability. For this purpose, it is easy to deploy and develop solutions quickly on the cloud. It is built on HDP technology in a joint effort with Microsoft and Hortonworks engineers.

This means that it is possible to derive new insights from data of any type or size, whether structured or unstructured, through HDInsight, available as a Windows Azure service.

It is recommended that you ensure that HDInsight is torn down when you have stopped using it. HDInsight is charged by the minute and it will cost you money to leave it running.

If you are simply wanting to run code and learn how to use Microsoft ML services, the following code samples will also work on Microsoft ML Server in Visual Studio on the DSVM.

Getting started with Azure HDInsight and ML services

HDInsight has a number of cluster types, which include Hadoop (Hive), HBase, Storm, Spark, Kafka, Interactive Hive (LLAP), and ML Services (R Server) (with R Studio, R 9.1). Here is the ML **Cluster configuration**, which is established during setup:

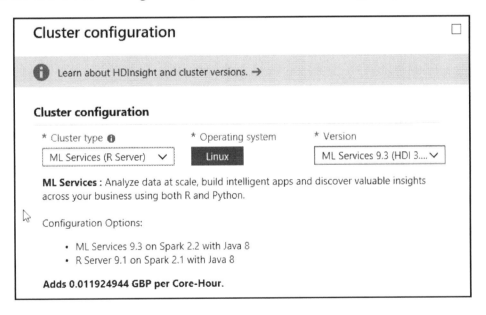

Setup and configuration of HDInsight

In this section, we will set up and configure HDInsight. To set up and configure HDInsight, carry out the following steps:

1. Ensure that you have an Azure account
2. Log into the Azure portal at `portal.azure.com`
3. When you are logged into the Azure portal, click on the button to add a new resource
4. In the search query box, type in `HDInsight` and you will be given a number of options
5. Select the option that simply says **HDInsight**

Next, we will set up a basic configuration of HDInsight.

Basic configuration of HDInsight

On the basic configuration item, you will need to enter in the name you wish to use for your Azure HDInsight, along with the storage options. Here is an example configuration:

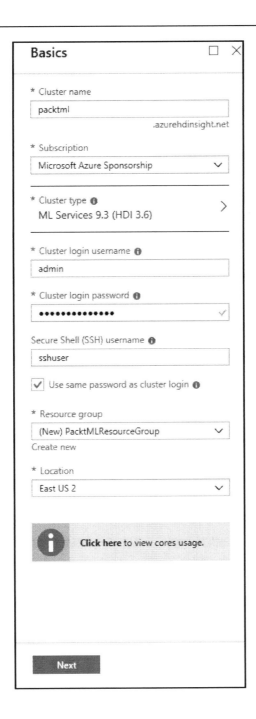

For **Cluster type**, ensure that you select the **ML Services** option. Here is an example:

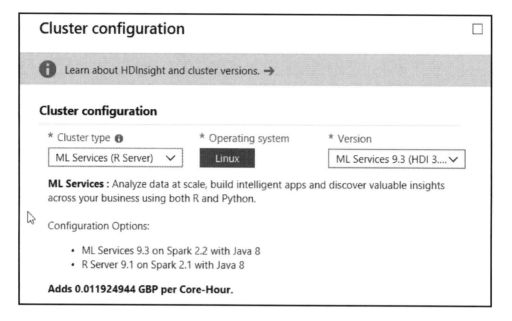

Storage options for Azure HDInsight

Once the cluster type has been selected, the next step is to consider the storage. At the time of writing, there are two types of storage: default Azure Storage, and Azure Data Lake Storage Generation 1. For this walk-through, the default **Azure Storage** will be used:

To finalize the creation of the HDInsight cluster, click on **Next**. Then check through the settings and click **Create**.

The HDInsight cluster will take approximately twenty minutes to set up.

When setup is complete, click on the **Azure HDInsight** cluster in the portal. Here is a screenshot of the portal:

Here is a screenshot of the Azure HDInsight storage account that was set up:

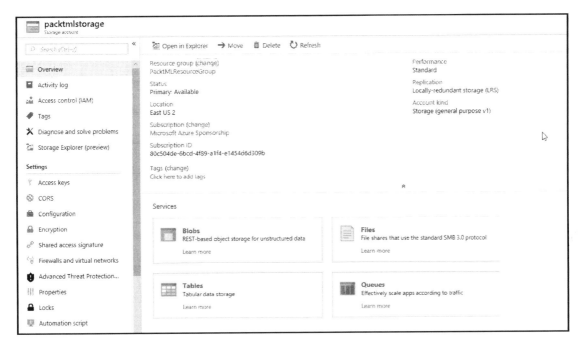

Connect to the HDInsight cluster using SSH

The Azure Cloud Shell permits data scientists to access the HDInsight clusters using SSH. The Azure Cloud Shell can be found at the top navigation of the Azure portal, and it is denoted with an arrow sign. Here is a screenshot:

1. Click on the Azure Cloud Shell icon in the Azure portal.
2. Select a subscription to create a storage account and Microsoft Azure Files share.
3. Select **Create storage**.
4. Check that the environment dropdown on the left-hand side of the shell window says **Bash**. Now, you can log in using the `ssh` command. Here is a screenshot:

Once you have logged in, you can then access Microsoft ML Services on the Azure HDInsight cluster.

Accessing Microsoft ML Services on Azure HDInsight

In the bash prompt, simply type in R to access Microsoft ML Services. Here is a screenshot:

```
Bash          v    ⏻  ?  ⚙  ⎘  ⎗  {}

See "man sudo_root" for details.

sshuser@hn0-packtm:~$ R

R version 3.4.3 (2017-11-30) -- "Kite-Eating Tree"
Copyright (C) 2017 The R Foundation for Statistical Computing
Platform: x86_64-pc-linux-gnu (64-bit)

R is free software and comes with ABSOLUTELY NO WARRANTY.
You are welcome to redistribute it under certain conditions.
Type 'license()' or 'licence()' for distribution details.

  Natural language support but running in an English locale

R is a collaborative project with many contributors.
Type 'contributors()' for more information and
'citation()' on how to cite R or R packages in publications.

Type 'demo()' for some demos, 'help()' for on-line help, or
'help.start()' for an HTML browser interface to help.
Type 'q()' to quit R.

Microsoft R Open 3.4.3
The enhanced R distribution from Microsoft
Microsoft packages Copyright (C) 2018 Microsoft

Loading Microsoft R Server packages, version 9.3.0.
Type 'readme()' for release notes, privacy() for privacy policy, or
'RevoLicense()' for licensing information.

Using the Intel MKL for parallel mathematical computing(using 4 cores).
Default CRAN mirror snapshot taken on 2018-01-01.
See: https://mran.microsoft.com/.
```

To see the files on the HDInsight cluster, use the following RevoScaleR command:

```
rxHadoopListFiles
```

The files are then read into the DOS prompt box. Here is an example:

```
> rxHadoopListFiles("/")
 [1] "Found 16 items"
 [2] "drwxr-xr-x   - root    supergroup          0 2018-09-27 12:55 /HdiNotebooks"
 [3] "drwxr-xr-x   - root    supergroup          0 2018-09-27 13:08 /HdiSamples"
 [4] "drwxr-xr-x   - hdfs    supergroup          0 2018-09-27 12:47 /ams"
 [5] "drwxr-xr-x   - hdfs    supergroup          0 2018-09-27 12:47 /amshbase"
 [6] "drwxrwxrwx   - yarn    hadoop              0 2018-09-27 12:47 /app-logs"
 [7] "drwxr-xr-x   - hdfs    supergroup          0 2018-09-27 12:47 /apps"
 [8] "drwxr-xr-x   - yarn    hadoop              0 2018-09-27 12:47 /atshistory"
 [9] "drwxr-xr-x   - root    supergroup          0 2018-09-27 13:00 /custom-scriptaction-logs"
[10] "drwxr-xr-x   - root    supergroup          0 2018-09-27 13:07 /example"
[11] "drwxr-xr-x   - hbase   supergroup          0 2018-09-27 12:47 /hbase"
[12] "drwxr-xr-x   - hdfs    supergroup          0 2018-09-27 12:47 /hdp"
[13] "drwxr-xr-x   - hdfs    supergroup          0 2018-09-27 12:47 /hive"
[14] "drwxr-xr-x   - mapred  supergroup          0 2018-09-27 12:47 /mapred"
[15] "drwxrwxrwx   - mapred  hadoop              0 2018-09-27 12:47 /mr-history"
[16] "drwxrwxrwx   - hdfs    supergroup          0 2018-09-27 12:47 /tmp"
[17] "drwxr-xr-x   - hdfs    supergroup          0 2018-09-27 12:47 /user"
[1] TRUE
```

Once the files are read out, we can start to work with some sample datasets in R. The Iris dataset will be used to explain the use of R in Microsoft ML Services in HDInsight.

Typing in the following command will reassure the data scientist that R is installed and working properly:

```
iris
```

By typing in the `iris` variable, the command will return the dataset. The `iris` command will give us the following result:

```
Bash          ∨    ⏻  ?  ⚙  ▸  ⮐  {}

> iris
   Sepal.Length Sepal.Width Petal.Length Petal.Width  Species
1           5.1         3.5          1.4         0.2    setosa
2           4.9         3.0          1.4         0.2    setosa
3           4.7         3.2          1.3         0.2    setosa
4           4.6         3.1          1.5         0.2    setosa
5           5.0         3.6          1.4         0.2    setosa
6           5.4         3.9          1.7         0.4    setosa
7           4.6         3.4          1.4         0.3    setosa
8           5.0         3.4          1.5         0.2    setosa
9           4.4         2.9          1.4         0.2    setosa
10          4.9         3.1          1.5         0.1    setosa
11          5.4         3.7          1.5         0.2    setosa
12          4.8         3.4          1.6         0.2    setosa
13          4.8         3.0          1.4         0.1    setosa
14          4.3         3.0          1.1         0.1    setosa
15          5.8         4.0          1.2         0.2    setosa
16          5.7         4.4          1.5         0.4    setosa
17          5.4         3.9          1.3         0.4    setosa
18          5.1         3.5          1.4         0.3    setosa
19          5.7         3.8          1.7         0.3    setosa
20          5.1         3.8          1.5         0.3    setosa
21          5.4         3.4          1.7         0.2    setosa
22          5.1         3.7          1.5         0.4    setosa
```

Once the data has been retrieved, we can conduct a number of analyzes on the data. If you are familiar with the Iris dataset, you will know that petal length and petal width are highly correlated over all species of Iris. This can be shown by running linear regression. When we use the least squares fit `lsfit` function, we get the following result:

```
> lsfit(iris$Petal.Length, iris$Petal.Width)$coefficients
  Intercept           X
 -0.3630755   0.4157554
```

We could also use a linear model, which provides a similar result for the intercept value:

```
> summary(lm(Sepal.Length ~ Sepal.Width, data=iris))

Call:
lm(formula = Sepal.Length ~ Sepal.Width, data = iris)

Residuals:
    Min      1Q  Median      3Q     Max
-1.5561 -0.6333 -0.1120  0.5579  2.2226

Coefficients:
            Estimate Std. Error t value Pr(>|t|)
(Intercept)   6.5262     0.4789   13.63   <2e-16 ***
Sepal.Width  -0.2234     0.1551   -1.44    0.152
---
Signif. codes:  0 '***' 0.001 '**' 0.01 '*' 0.05 '.' 0.1 ' ' 1

Residual standard error: 0.8251 on 148 degrees of freedom
Multiple R-squared:  0.01382,   Adjusted R-squared:  0.007159
F-statistic: 2.074 on 1 and 148 DF,  p-value: 0.1519
```

The `p-value` is extremely low, suggesting that this model is a good fit for the data.

Let's take a look at the relationship between the sepal length and the sepal width using linear modelling:

```
summary(lm(Sepal.Length ~ Sepal.Width, data=iris))
```

This gives us the following result:

```
> summary(lm(Sepal.Length ~ Sepal.Width, data=iris))

Call:
lm(formula = Sepal.Length ~ Sepal.Width, data = iris)

Residuals:
    Min      1Q  Median      3Q     Max
-1.5561 -0.6333 -0.1120  0.5579  2.2226

Coefficients:
            Estimate Std. Error t value Pr(>|t|)
(Intercept)   6.5262     0.4789   13.63   <2e-16 ***
Sepal.Width  -0.2234     0.1551   -1.44    0.152
---
Signif. codes:  0 '***' 0.001 '**' 0.01 '*' 0.05 '.' 0.1 ' ' 1

Residual standard error: 0.8251 on 148 degrees of freedom
Multiple R-squared:  0.01382,   Adjusted R-squared:  0.007159
F-statistic: 2.074 on 1 and 148 DF,  p-value: 0.1519
```

When we examine p-values here, the p-value is much larger.

We could add more to the data by adding in further iterations from the sepal and the petals.

HDInsight and data analytics with R

Firstly, we need to get our data into Azure so that HDInsight can see it. We can upload data directly to Azure Storage, or we can use functionality in **SQL Server Integration Services** (**SSIS**). SSIS has the capability of connecting to Azure Blob Storage and Azure HDInsight. It enables you to create integration service packages that transfer data between an Azure Blob Storage and the on-premise data source. Then, the Azure HDInsight process can conduct processing on the data.

In order to get the data into HDInsight using SSIS, it's necessary to install the Azure Feature Pack. The Microsoft SSIS Feature Pack for Azure provides SQL Server Integration Services with the capability to connect to many Azure services, such as Azure Blob Storage, Azure Data Lake Store, Azure SQL Data Warehouse, and Azure HDInsight. It is a separate install, and you will need to ensure that the SQL server is installed before installing the Azure Feature Pack on a server. Otherwise, the components in the Feature Pack may not be available when you deploy packages to the SSIS catalog database.

To install the Microsoft SQL Server 2017 Integration Services Feature Pack for Azure, search for the Microsoft download page by using the term `Microsoft SQL Server 2017 Integration Services Feature Pack for Azure`. Then, download the file and run through the wizard.

How do Azure Data Factory and HDInsight interact?

It is possible to move files or read and write data to Azure Blob storage. The benefit of using Azure Data Factory means that it is possible to extend existing ETL pipelines with cloud storage, or cloud-based SSIS execution through Azure VMs. It is possible to deploy SSIS packages in Azure Data Factory Version 2, which went to general availability release in July 2018. It provides powerful functionality that facilitates data preparation for cloud compute services such as HDInsight and Microsoft ML Server. It can do a range of tasks, including data archival to cloud storage, and straightforward enumeration of files in blob storage.

There are specific HDInsight processing tasks in the Azure Data Factory suite. Here is an illustrated summary:

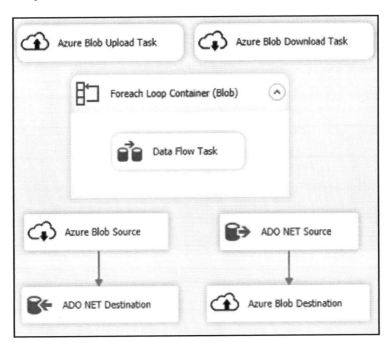

For example, it is now possible to trigger HDInsight jobs and manage your HDInsight cluster lifecycle directly from SSIS. This provides HDInsight users with a number of benefits. Now it is possible to integrate big data processing into your existing ETL flows. This means that your big data projects are easily incorporated into the existing technical estate.

It is important to clean data as early in the process as possible. The ADF functionality for HDInsight includes the ability to filter and process raw cloud-born data using HDI before moving it to your data warehouse. It is also possible to dynamically create your HDI cluster on demand, and tear it down once processing is complete. For large enterprise environments, it can work with Azure Storage connectors to extend your ETL environments to the cloud.

How do we do these tasks? There are many designer improvements in SSDT, including multi-version support in SSDT.

Running queries on Azure HDInsight with ML Services

In ML Services on HDInsight, the compute context specifies the physical location of the computational engine handling a given workload. The default is local, which means that it is running on your local machine. In order to make the most of running in the cloud, you will need to switch from local to remote.

R script runs within the R interpreter on that node, if it is run in the ML Services cluster on the edge node. If it calls a RevoScaleR function, then it is executed in a compute environment that is determined by how you set the RevoScaleR compute context. In this case, when you run your R script from an edge node, the possible values of the compute context are as follows:

- local sequential (*local*)
- local parallel (*localpar*)
- MapReduce
- Spark

Parallel offers the best performance. The local and localpar options both execute other `rx` function calls in a parallel manner across all available cores unless specified otherwise. To do this, the `rxOptions numCoresToUse` setting is used, and here is an example:

```
rxOptions(numCoresToUse=6)
```

If the amount of data to analyze is small, and is a one-off or infrequent analysis, then it is recommended that you stream it directly into the analysis routine using local or localpar. If the amount of data to analyze is on a small or medium scale, and requires repeated or iterative analysis, then copy it to the local filesystem, import it to XDF, and analyze it via local or localpar.

RevoScaleR in Azure

RevoScaleR is a set of powerful Microsoft proprietary functions that are used for practicing data science at scale. RevoScaleR gives extra power when conducting big data analyzes using R, such as data-related functions for import, transformation, manipulation, summarization, visualization, and analysis. Using R and HDInsight provides you with the capability to perform these tasks against very large datasets, in parallel and on distributed file systems. RevoScaleR uses external memory algorithms that allow it to work on one chunk of data at a time, updating results, and proceeding through all available data.

RevoScaleR functions are provided through the RevoScaleR package, which is available in Azure HDInsight ML Services. RevoScaleR is compatible with the open source R language, and your scripts may use a combination of base R and RevoScaleR functions. In order to distinguish them from base R, RevoScaleR functions are denoted with an `rx` or `Rx` prefix so it is clear what functions use the RevoScaleR package.

How can we read data into HDInsight using ML Services?

Using RevoScaleR R default commands, we can read data with ML Services on HDInsight. These data types include the following:

- Reading data through **Open Database Connectivity (ODBC)** data sources
- Reading in files from other file systems, such as SAS, SPSS, ODBC, Teradata, delimited, and fixed format text
- Using an internal dataframe as a data source
- Processing data from sources that cannot be read natively by R Server

RevoScaleR is also embedded in Azure HDInsight, Azure DSVMs, and SQL Server. RevoScaleR also includes an extensible framework for writing your own analyzes for big datasets.

The preferred data format is an XDF format. From there, we can do a number of analyzes with HDInsight and ML Services, using R.

What kind of analyzes can we do with R in ML Services on HDinsight?

We can do summaries, cross-tabs, and create cubes, and conduct modelling such as decision trees and forests, as well as standard R work. To execute code, we will execute the Microsoft R server commands using RStudio. RStudio makes R easier to use. It includes a code editor, as well as debugging and visualization tools. In the following examples, the code exercises and images will be executed using RStudio. We will also use R Notebooks as a tidy way to execute code. An R Notebook is a document with code chunks that can be executed independently and interactively. As we will see throughout the exercises, the output is visible immediately beneath the input. We can visualize our results with the data with `ggplot2` in R, or we can use Power BI.

Here are some sample code snippets to help you to understand how to use R to access data.

Reading data from files into Azure HDInsight ML Services

ML Services can read almost all flat text files, such as SPSS, CSV, and TXT files. Here is an example where we provide the path direction and read file directory from the given path to R:

```
filename <- read.csv ( file = "Filename.csv" )
```

We can also import the text file into R and then view the file to read it:

```
filename <- rxImport ( "full file path")
```

It is crucial to start by checking the location of the working directory in R. It is good practice to confirm your path. The command is executed using the following command: getwd()

In our example, the working directory is on the D drive, and it is the Demo folder.

To read in a CSV file, we provide the path, and then we read the file path, which is directed toward a variable name. In this example here, the file will be stored in the variable called SalesRecordsFile:

```
SalesRecordsFile <- read.csv ( "D:/Demo/SalesRecordsFile.csv" , header =
TRUE )
```

Next, we will take the SalesRecordsFilevariable and we will set it to a command to read in a CSV file.

Once we execute the SalesRecordsFile command, then Microsoft ML Server will read in the SalesRecordsFile.csv file.

Converting text and CSV files to the preferred XDF format

An XDF file is small in size and is compressed, as compared to CSV files. This means that an XDF file can be read and processed much faster than a CSV file. The flat file contains records that have no structured inter-relationship. XDF file formats can only be read by Microsoft ML Server. It is a very efficient way of storing, and querying data stored in flat files. These files are very small in size compared to other files, so they are analyzed quickly, and easily. RStudio can easily handle the task of converting our source text or CSV files into XDF format.

To convert the file, we can use the `rxImport` function, which loads data held in a flat file, such as a text file, to the preferred XDF file. The `rxImport` function can load the data into memory as a dataframe.

In this example, we will focus on converting a CSV file to an internal Microsoft R file called an XDF file. We will also look at XDF files in more detail, since they are a core item for ML Services on HDinsight. Note that XDF files are only readable in Microsoft R format.

We can convert data to an XDF file format by changing the `rxImport` command so that it includes an `OutFile` variable, which holds the location of the newly generated XDF file. Here is some sample code, which takes a `.csv` file called `SalesRecords.csv` and outputs a file called `SalesRecordsFile.xdf`. It assigns the file to a variable called `SalesRecordsXDF`:

```
inFile <- file.path(rxGetOption("sampleDataDir"), "SalesRecordsFile.csv")
SalesRecordsXDF <- rxImport(inData=inFile, outFile =
"SalesRecordsFile.xdf", stringsAsFactors = TRUE, rowsPerRead = 200000)
```

Next, we will look at using the new `SalesRecordsXDF` XDF file in Microsoft ML Services.

Using the new XDF file in Microsoft ML Services

We set the `SalesRecordsXDF` variable to hold the path of the inbound data, and to specify where the XDF file has to be written.

We can use the `print` command to find out more about the contents in the variable called `SalesRecordsXDF`. When we run the code, we can see the output, which details the number of rows processed and the location. If we want to see the content of the file, we can use the `rxGetInfo` command to provide us with some information. In this example, we are going to obtain the first five rows of data.

XDF versus flat text files

Now that we have looked at a CSV file and an XDF file, which one is better? XDF files can be read and processed so they are stored on the local disk. Microsoft R Server, with a call to `rxImport()`, will read an XDF file and decompress it, and then insert it into memory as a dataframe.

The XDF file format is a Microsoft file format. This means it is important to check output and export functionality, because other programs will not be able to read it. The XDF file is aimed at supporting the set of analytical and data processing functions in the RevoScaleR package.

What is the advantage of the file size? For big data, this means the data can be as large as the available disk on the machine without putting any strains on R. An XDF file is stored on the disk and does not sit in memory, but the XDF format can help R to read the data quickly.

In order to make a decision about the file format, we need to understand the I/O trade-offs involved. Converting the file from CSV to XDF is itself a cost in terms of runtime. On the other hand, when the original CSVs are converted to XDFs, the runtime of processing both the reading and writing of the XDF files will be lower.

Reading data from SQL Server

To connect to SQL Server, there is a sequence of events that should be followed:

1. Connect to Microsoft SQL Server
2. Retrieve data from Microsoft SQL Server

Connecting to a SQL Server database

Microsoft ML Services can also read data through **Open Database Connectivity (ODBC)**, which is a well-known and commonly accepted database access method. Initially, the connection string is set up, and it is assigned to a variable. In this example, the variable name holds the connection string. Here is the example code:

```
sqlServerConnectionString <-
"SERVER=<IP Address goes here>;
DATABASE=<database name goes here>;
UID=<User Name goes here>;
PWD=<Your Password Goes Here>"
```

Extracting data from a table retrieving data from Microsoft SQL Server

Once we have set up the connection string information, the next step is to set up a variable to hold the SQL command to retrieve the data. Here is an example piece of code:

```
sqlServerDataSource <- RxSqlServerData(sqlQuery = "SELECT * FROM <view name
goes here>",connectionString = sqlServerConnectionString)
```

Installing R packages on Microsoft ML Services

It is possible to use the same R code in Azure ML Studio, Microsoft ML Server, and in SQL Server machine learning services.

In this example, the `rjson` package allows users to import the data using the `fromJSON()` function. If the `rjson` package is not installed on Microsoft ML Server, then you will need to install it. The instructions are as follows:

1. Navigate to the folder where the R tools are installed.
2. Right-click `RGui.exe`, and select **Run as administrator**. If you do not have the required permissions, contact the database administrator and provide a list of the packages you need.
3. From the command line, if you know the package name, type: `install.packages("rjson")`.
4. Note that double quotation marks are required for the package name.
5. When asked for a mirror site, select any site that is closest to your location.

If the target package depends on additional packages, the R installer automatically downloads the dependencies and installs them for you, in addition to the required `rjson` package. Here is a sample command to download and install the `rjson` package. Once the `rjson` package is installed, it is possible to work with JSON data:

```
install.packages("rjson")
```

In this example, Microsoft ML Services will go and download the required `rjson` packages. The next step is to call the `rjson` package, which is done by using the `library` command:

```
library("rjson")
```

In this example, now that we have invoked the library command, we can work with JSON data. To demonstrate this concept, let's work through an example. Here, we will plot the `cars` dataset, using the `plot` command:

```
plot(cars, pch=1)
```

This command will produce the following chart:

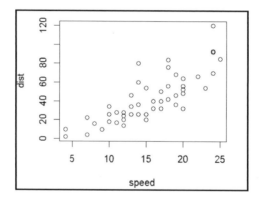

Once the data has been visualized, we can convert the `cars` dataset to JSON format. Here is the command to make the conversion:

```
json_cars <- toJSON(as.list(cars))
```

We can now see the data by typing in the `json_cars` variable name. Here is the output:

```
> json_cars
[1] "{\"speed\":[4,4,7,7,8,9,10,10,10,11,11,12,12,12,12,13,13,13,13,14,14,14,14,15,15,15,16
>|
```

Let's plot the JSON data so that we can see the difference. Using the `plot` command, we can add in some extra details in order to make the data clearer. The following command will replot the chart with the new data:

```
points(data.frame(fromJSON(json_cars)), col = "red", pch = 4)
```

When we execute the command, the following plot appears:

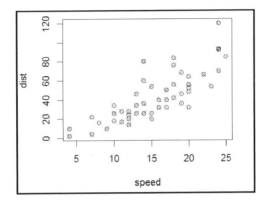

The redrawn plot includes the initial car data, and it is overlaid with the new JSON data, which is highlighted with red crosses.

Analyzing and summarizing data in Microsoft ML Services

We can analyze and summarize our data using different types of statistics. Some statistics are more basic, and we start from using simple crosstabs. Then, we can move onto more complex statistics.

Cross tabs and univariate statistics

Cross tabs offer a function that aids the exploration of survey data through simple tabulations of respondent counts and proportions, including the ability to specify the following:

- A frequency count or a row/column/joint/total table proportion
- Multiple row and column variables
- All margins, only grand margins, or no margins

To create crosstabs, the rxCrossTabs() function is used. rxCrossTabs() is also used to compute sums according to combinations of different variables:

```
rxCrossTabs(formula, data, ...)
```

The rxCrossTabs function uses a formula containing the variables that you want to cross tabulate. It also has a reference to the data, which refers to the dataset in which you want to look for variables specified in the formula.

Some sample code to clarify the use of rxCrossTabs is as follows:

```
IrisDataCrossTabs <- rxCrossTabs
(
 Petal.Width ~ Species,
 data = Iris
 )
```

The following shows example output from the rxCrossTabs function:

```
> IrisDataCrossTabs <- rxCrossTabs(
+       Petal.Width ~ Species,
+       data = iris
+ )
Rows Read: 150, Total Rows Processed: 150, Total Chunk Time: 0.056 seconds
Computation time: 0.080 seconds.
> IrisDataCrossTabs
Call:
rxCrossTabs(formula = Petal.Width ~ Species, data = iris)

Cross Tabulation Results for: Petal.Width ~ Species
Data: iris
Dependent variable(s): Petal.Width
Number of valid observations: 150
Number of missing observations: 0
Statistic: sums

Petal.Width (sums):

setosa       12.3
versicolor   66.3
virginica    101.3
>
```

It is also possible to add in additional arguments to the rxCrossTabs() function in order to make it more flexible.

Working with cubes of data

One important feature of analysis is the aggregation of data. In Microsoft ML Server, the rxCube() function is used when we want to aggregate data for further analysis within R.

rxCube() performs a very similar function to rxCrossTabs(). rxCube() helps with the analysis by computing metrics such as tabulated sums or means. rxCube() produces the sums or means in long format rather than a table. Example syntax for rxCube is as follows:

```
rxCube(formula, data, ...)
```

The code shows that rxCube requires a formula containing the variables to cross-tabulate. It differs from rxCrossTabs() in the default value of the means argument (true for rxCube(); false for rxCrossTabs()). As with rxCrossTabs, the data item refers to the dataset in which you want to look for variables specified in the formula. Here is an example piece of code, using the Iris dataset, as before:

```
IrisDataCube <- rxCube(Petal.Width ~ Species, data = iris)
```

In order to clarify its use, the following demonstrates a sample output:

```
> IrisDataCube
Call:
rxCube(formula = Petal.Width ~ Species, data = iris)

Cube Results for: Petal.Width ~ Species
Data: iris
Dependent variable(s): Petal.Width
Number of valid observations: 150
Number of missing observations: 0
Statistic: Petal.Width means

  Species    Petal.Width Counts
1 setosa     0.246          50
2 versicolor 1.326          50
3 virginica  2.026          50
>
```

Now that we have seen how to do some preliminary analysis, we can further investigate the data by doing some grouping.

Grouping data using Microsoft ML Server and R

In Business Intelligence and analytics, many data operations are completed on grouped data, defined by variables. In Microsoft ML Services, there is an additional enhanced R formula, called rxSummary, which summarizes data, which is a good starting point when investigating data. rxSummary works by computing summary statistics that include a variable mean.

Here is an example of the output using rxSummary and the Iris dataset:

```
> rxSummary(~Petal.Length, data = iris)
Call:
rxSummary(formula = ~Petal.Length, data = iris)

Summary Statistics Results for: ~Petal.Length
Data: iris
Number of valid observations: 150

 Name          Mean  StdDev   Min Max ValidObs MissingObs
 Petal.Length 3.758 1.765298 1   6.9 150       0
```

The summary focuses on one of the columns, Petal.Length. It produces the same information that we expect from the summary command in R.

Computing quantiles with R in Microsoft ML Server

In Microsoft ML Server, the rxQuantile function is used to quickly compute approximate quantiles. Note that this computation doesn't include any type of sorting. The following piece of code uses rxQuantile on the petal length of the Iris dataset:

```
> rxQuantile("Petal.Length", iris)
   0%    25%    50%   75%   100%
1.000 1.507 4.300 5.056 6.900
```

The quantile calculation provides the quantiles for the data and prints it out.

Logistic regression in Microsoft ML Services

Logistic regression is a standard tool for modeling data with a binary response variable. In R, you fit a logistic regression using the `glm` function, specifying a binomial family and the logit link function. In Microsoft ML Services, `rxGlm` is used for the same purpose, and in the same way:

```
irisGLM <- rxGlm(Petal.Width~ Species,family = Gamma,dropFirst = TRUE,data
= iris)
```

Then, we can type in the variable name in order to see the result. Here is a screenshot:

```
> irisGLM
Generalized Linear Model Results for: Petal.Width ~ Species
Data: iris
Dependent variable(s): Petal.Width
Total independent variables: 4 (Including number dropped: 1)
Number of valid observations: 150
Number of missing observations: 0
Family-link: Gamma-inverse


Coefficients:
                    Petal.Width
(Intercept)            4.065041
Species=setosa          Dropped
Species=versicolor    -3.310893
Species=virginica     -3.571457
```

To interpret the coefficients better, we can transform them back to the original scale of the dependent variable. To do this, we execute the following command:

```
exp(coef(irisGLM))
```

This command gives us the following output:

```
> exp(coef(irisGLM))
      (Intercept)     Species=setosa Species=versicolor  Species=virginica
      58.26727706                 NA         0.03648359         0.02811485
```

A common method for checking for overdispersion is to calculate the ratio of the residual deviance with the degrees of freedom, which should be about fitting the assumptions of the model. In this case, the code would appear as follows:

```
irisGLM$deviance / irisGLM$df
```

Overdispersion is the presence of greater variability in a dataset than would be expected based on a given model. If the variance of the residual deviance is greater than the residual degrees of freedom, then this means that there is overdispersion and unexplained variation. This could be a sign that the model does not fit the data very well. In this case, we can see that the ratio is preceding one.

Predicting values with the model

If the input dataset is the same as the dataset used to fit the rxLinMod object, the resulting predictions are the fitted values for the model. If the input dataset is a different dataset, the resulting predictions are true predictions of the response for the new data from the original model. As you can see from the following example, the residuals for the predicted values can be obtained by setting the computeResiduals flag to TRUE:

```
rxPredict(irisGLM, data = iris, writeModelVars = TRUE, computeResiduals =
TRUE, overwrite = TRUE)
```

Next, we use rxPredict to obtain the fitted values, prediction standard errors, and confidence intervals. By setting writeModelVars to TRUE, the variables used in the model will also be included in the output dataset. Sample output is as follows:

```
> rxPredict(irisGLM, data = iris, writeModelVars = TRUE, computeResiduals = TRUE, overwrite = TRUE)
Rows Read: 150, Total Rows Processed: 150, Total Chunk Time: 0.005 seconds
     Petal.Width_Pred Petal.Width_Resid Petal.Width    Species
1             0.246            -0.046          0.2      setosa
2             0.246            -0.046          0.2      setosa
3             0.246            -0.046          0.2      setosa
4             0.246            -0.046          0.2      setosa
5             0.246            -0.046          0.2      setosa
6             0.246             0.154          0.4      setosa
7             0.246             0.054          0.3      setosa
8             0.246            -0.046          0.2      setosa
9             0.246            -0.046          0.2      setosa
10            0.246            -0.146          0.1      setosa
11            0.246            -0.046          0.2      setosa
12            0.246            -0.046          0.2      setosa
13            0.246            -0.146          0.1      setosa
14            0.246            -0.146          0.1      setosa
15            0.246            -0.046          0.2      setosa
```

We can view the summary of the `irisGLM` model here:

```
> summary(irisGLM)
Call:
rxGlm(formula = Petal.Width ~ Species, data = iris, family = Gamma,
    dropFirst = TRUE)

Generalized Linear Model Results for: Petal.Width ~ Species
Data: iris
Dependent variable(s): Petal.Width
Total independent variables: 4 (Including number dropped: 1)
Number of valid observations: 150
Number of missing observations: 0
Family-link: Gamma-inverse

Residual deviance: 10.2775 (on 147 degrees of freedom)

Coefficients:
                    Estimate Std. Error t value Pr(>|t|)
(Intercept)           4.0650     0.1571   25.87 2.22e-16 ***
Species=setosa       Dropped    Dropped Dropped  Dropped
Species=versicolor   -3.3109     0.1598  -20.72 2.22e-16 ***
Species=virginica    -3.5715     0.1583  -22.56 2.22e-16 ***
---
Signif. codes:  0 '***' 0.001 '**' 0.01 '*' 0.05 '.' 0.1 ' ' 1

(Dispersion parameter for Gamma family taken to be 0.07471402)

Condition number of final variance-covariance matrix: 82.5219
Number of iterations: 5
> |
```

The output shows that these are highly significant p-values, which means that the model looks like a good fit.

However, we can check that the model is sound by looking at the ratio between the residual deviance and the residual degrees of freedom, which is 10.2/147, giving us a result of 0.06. This means that the model is quite under-dispersed. Another option is to redo the `irisGLM` model using a binomial instead of a gamma family.

In order to understand the data better, it is possible to visualize it using default R and custom functionality in Microsoft ML Services.

Visualizing data

Microsoft ML Services has facilities for producing graphs using R as the visualization engine. It is possible for you to provide a variety of charts and dashboards that represent both univariate and multivariate numerical and categorical data in a straightforward manner.

Creating histograms

`rxHistogram()` is used to create a histogram for the data. Here is an example of the syntax for the Iris dataset:

```
rxHistogram(~Petal.Width, data = iris)
```

You can see in the formula that the simplest case is a formula with only a single variable to the right-hand side of the ~.

As before, the Iris dataset is the data used here, and this is the part of the formula in which you want to specify the dataset you are using. Here is an example of the output:

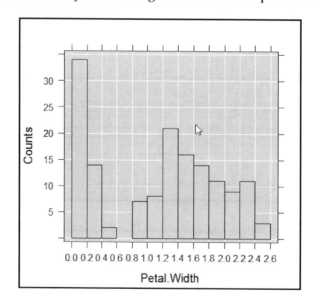

It is very simple to create a histogram with a single line of code.

Creating line plots

A histogram is only one way of visualizing the data. Another example is the `rxLinePlot` example, which creates the line of a scatter plot using data. For this function, this formula should have one variable on the left-hand side of the ~ that reflects the *y* axis, and one variable on the right-hand side of the ~ that reflects the *x* axis. Here is an example of the line plot:

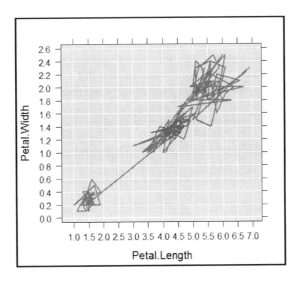

We can also transform subsets of data using other features and functionality in Microsoft ML Services, and then revisualize the data.

Once we can see and understand our data, we can enrich it further by using additional Microsoft ML Services functionalities.

Enriching data for analysis

With big data solutions, sometimes the data needs to be transformed and processed into smaller chunks due to its sheer size. In order to deal with this problem, Microsoft have introduced some functionality to help. This section will cover the features that are designed to assist with big data issues.

rxDataSteps

The `rxDataStep` function can be used to process data in chunks. It is one of the important data transformation functions in Microsoft ML Services.

The `rxDataStep` function can be used to create and transform subsets of data. The `rxDataStep` function processes data one chunk at a time, reading from one data source and writing to another. `rxDataStep` allows you to modify existing columns or add new columns to the data. It can also enrich analysis by working with your columns and rows, and by filtering and excluding them before working with the data further.

A common use of `rxDataStep` is to create a new dataset with a subset of rows and variables, as follows:

```
rxDataStep(inData = iris, outFile = "myIrisXDF.xdf")
```

In the previous piece of code, the Iris dataset is converted to an XDF file called `myIrisXDF`. This means that it can make use of the XDF file functionality.

Summary

In this chapter, we have examined the machine learning process for Microsoft ML Services on HDInsight. We have reviewed how to ingest data, how to clean it, how to model it, and how to visualize it.

The final step is to ensure that HDInsight is torn down when you have stopped using it. HDInsight is charged by the minute and it will cost you money to leave it running. It is recommended that you save code and tear everything down when you no longer need it.

If you are simply wanting to run code and learn how to use Microsoft ML Services, the previous code samples will also work on Microsoft ML Server in Visual Studio on the DSVM.

Machine Learning with Spark 9

This chapter covers the use of Spark on the Microsoft platform and will also provide a walk-through on how to train ML models using Spark, along with the options available in Azure to perform Spark-based ML training.

We will be covering the following topics:

- ML with Azure Databricks
- Azure HDInsight with Spark
- Walkthroughs of some labs so that you can see exciting technologies in action

Machine learning with Azure Databricks

By adopting ML, enterprises are looking to improve their business, or even radically transform it by using data as the lifeblood for digital transformation. Databricks empowers companies to develop their data science competency quickly, and turn that into a competitive advantage by providing a fully integrated unified analytics platform in Azure.

Enterprises want to leverage the treasure trove of data they have collected historically. Organizations have begun to collect more data recently. This includes data in a variety of forms, including new customer data in the form of clickstreams, web logs, and sensor data from Internet of Things devices and machines, as well as audio, images, and videos.

Using insights from this data, enterprises across various verticals can improve business outcomes in many different ways that impact our daily lives. These include medical diagnosis, fraud detection, detecting cyber attacks, optimizing manufacturing pipelines, customer engagement, and so forth.

Databricks offers a unified analytics platform that brings data engineers, data scientists, and businesses together to collaborate across the data life cycle, starting from ETL programs, through to building analytic applications for production environments.

Data engineers can use Databricks' ETL capability to create new datasets from various sources, including structured, semi-structured, and unstructured data. Data scientists can choose from a variety of programming languages, such as SQL, R, Python, Scala, and Java, and **Machine Learning** (**ML**) frameworks and libraries including Scikit-learn, Apache Spark ML, TensorFlow, and Keras.

Databricks allows enterprises to explore data, and create and test their models in a collaborative way, using Databricks' notebook and visualization capacities. Time-to-delivery is quick and the process of sending ML pipelines to production is also quick.

What challenges is Databricks trying to solve?

Integrating data is always difficult. However, integration challenges are even more difficult in ML because of the various frameworks and libraries that need to be integrated.

Databricks has a focus enterprise readiness of data science platforms in terms of security and manageability.

How do we get started with Apache Spark and Azure Databricks? The first step is to get the Azure Databricks software set up in Azure.

Getting started with Apache Spark and Azure Databricks

In this walk-through, we will start to explore Azure Databricks. A key step in the process is to set up an instance of Azure Databricks, and this is covered here:

1. Log in to the Azure portal (`https://portal.azure.com/`).
2. Select **+ Create a resource** | **Analytics** | **Azure Databricks**.
3. In the Azure Databricks Service dialog, provide the workspace configuration.
4. **Workspace name**:
    * Enter a name for your Azure Databricks workspace
5. **Subscription**:
    * Select your **Azure subscription**
6. **Resource group**:
    * Create a new resource group (`https://docs.microsoft.com/en-us/azure/azure-resource-manager/resource-group-overview`) or use an existing one

7. **Location**:
   - Select a **geographical region** (`https://docs.azuredatabricks.net/administration-guide/cloud-configurations/regions.html`)

8. **Pricing Tier**:
   - Select a **pricing tier** (`https://azure.microsoft.com/en-us/pricing/details/databricks/`). If you select **Trial (Premium - 14-Days Free DBUs)**, the workspace has access to free Premium Azure Databricks DBUs for 14 days.

9. Select **Pin to dashboard** and then click **Create**. The portal will display **Deployment in progress**. After a few minutes, the Azure Databricks service page displays, as can be seen in the following screenshot:

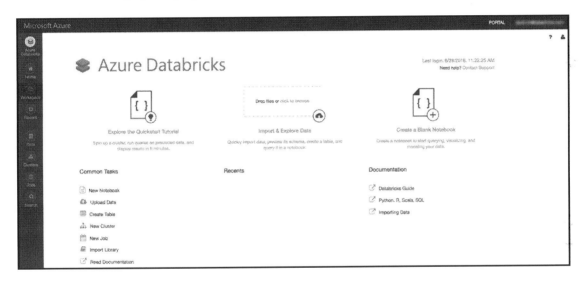

On the left-hand side, you can access fundamental Azure Databricks entities: workspace, clusters, tables, notebooks, jobs, and libraries.

The workspace is the special root folder that stores your Azure Databricks assets, such as notebooks and libraries, and the data that you import:

Creating a cluster

A cluster is a collection of Azure Databricks computation resources:

1. To create a cluster, click the **Clusters** button in the sidebar and click **Create Cluster**:

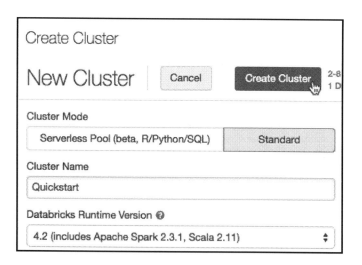

2. On the **New Cluster** page, specify the cluster name.
3. Select **4.2 (includes Apache Spark 2.3.1, Scala 11)** in the Databricks Runtime Version dropdown.
4. Click **Create Cluster.**

Create a Databricks Notebook

A Notebook is a collection of cells that run computations on a Spark cluster. To create a Notebook in the Workspace, follow these steps:

1. In the sidebar, click the **Workspace** button.
2. In the `Workspace` folder, select **Create Notebook**:

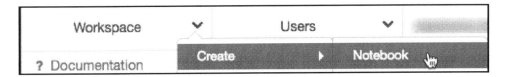

3. On the **Create Notebook** dialog, enter a name and select **SQL** in the **Language** dropdown.
4. Click **Create**. The Notebook opens with an empty cell at the top.

Using SQL in Azure Databricks

In this section, you can run a SQL statement to create a **table** and work with data using SQL Statements:

1. Copy and paste this code snippet into the notebook cell to see a list of the Azure Databricks datasets:

```
display(dbutils.fs.ls("/databricks-datasets"))
```

2. The code appears as follows:

```
DROPTABLEIFEXISTS diamonds;
CREATETABLE diamonds
USING csv
OPTIONS (path "/databricks-
datasets/Rdatasets/data-001/csv/ggplot2/diamonds.csv", header
"true")
```

3. Press *Shift + Enter*. The notebook automatically attaches to the cluster you created in *Step 2*, creates the table, loads the data, and returns OK:

```
1  DROP TABLE IF EXISTS diamonds;
2
3  CREATE TABLE diamonds
4    USING csv
5    OPTIONS (path "/databricks-datasets/Rdatasets/data-001/csv/ggplot2/diamonds.csv", header "true")

OK
```

4. Next, you can run a SQL statement to query the table for the average diamond price by color.

5. To add a cell to the Notebook, hover over the **cell bottom** and click the icon:

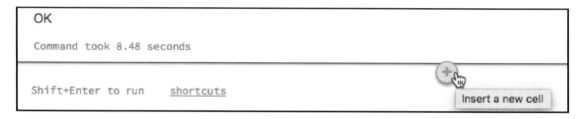

6. Copy this snippet and paste it into the cell:

```
SELECT color, avg(price) AS price FROM diamonds
GROUP BY color ORDER BY COLOR
```

7. Make sure that the cursor is in the cell and press *Shift + Enter* to execute the command.

8. The notebook displays a table of diamond colors and their average prices, as shown in the following screenshot:

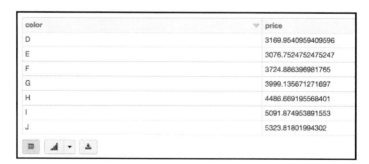

color	price
D	3169.9540959409596
E	3076.7524752475247
F	3724.886396981765
G	3999.135671271697
H	4486.669195568401
I	5091.874953891553
J	5323.81801994302

Displaying data

Display a chart of the average diamond price by color:

1. Click the **Bar chart** icon
2. Click **Plot** options
3. Drag **color** into the **Keys** box
4. Drag **price** into the **Values** box
5. In the **Aggregation** dropdown, select **AVG**:

6. Click **Apply** to display the bar chart:

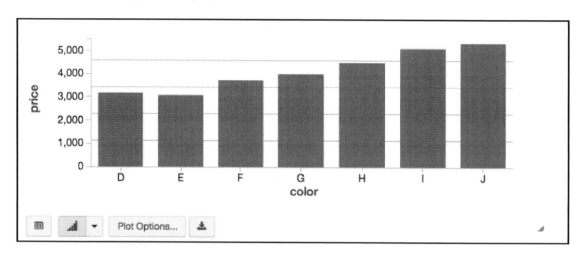

Machine Learning with HDInsight

Apache Spark is the largest open source process in data processing. Since its release, Apache Spark has seen rapid adoption by enterprises across a wide range of industries. Apache Spark is a fast, in-memory data processing engine, with elegant and expressive development APIs to allow data workers to efficiently execute streaming. In addition, Apache Spark facilitates ML and SQL workloads that require fast iterative access to datasets.

The focus of the current chapter is Apache Spark, which is an open source system for fast, large-scale data processing and ML.

The Data Science virtual machine provides you with a standalone (single node in-process) instance of the Apache Spark platform.

What is Spark?

Spark is designed as a high-performance, general-purpose computation engine for fast, large-scale big data processes. Spark works by distributing its workload across different nodes in a cluster. Spark scales out to process large volumes of data. Spark is aimed at big data batch processing, and is excellent for producing analytics using low-latency, high-performance data as a basis for operations.

Apache Spark consists of Spark Core and a set of libraries. Core is the distributed execution engine and the Java, Scala, and Python APIs offer a platform for distributed ETL application development. This allows developers to quickly achieve success by writing applications in Java, Scala, or Python.

Spark is built on the concept of a **Resilient Distributed Dataset (RDD)**, which has been a core Spark concept for working with data since the inception of Spark. RDDs are similar to dataframes in R. RDDs are high-level abstractions of the data that provide data scientists with a schema to retrieve and work with data. RDDs are immutable collections representing datasets and have the inbuilt capability of reliability and failure recovery. RDDs create new RDDs upon any operation, such as transformation or action. They also store the lineage, which is used to recover from failures. For example, it's possible to separate the data out into the appropriate field and columns in that dataset, which means that data scientists can work with them more intuitively.

The Spark process involves a number of steps, which can involve more than one RDD. So, it is possible to have more than one RDD during processing. Here is an example, which shows how RDDs can be the source and the output of different processing steps:

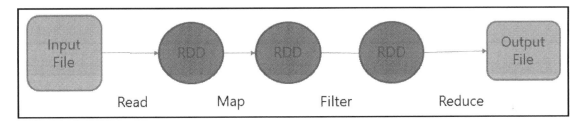

Apache Spark allows for complex data engineering, and it comes with a built-in set of over 80 high-level operators. As well as longer processing, it is possible to interactively query data within the shell. In addition to the Map and Reduce operations, it supports SQL queries, Streaming Data, ML, and Graph Data Processing.

Developers can use these capabilities standalone, or combine them to run in a single data pipeline use case.

Spark powers a stack of libraries, including SQL and DataFrames (https://spark.apache.org/sql/), MLlib (https://spark.apache.org/mllib/) for ML, GraphX (https://spark.apache.org/graphx/), and Spark Streaming (https://spark.apache.org/streaming/). You can combine these libraries seamlessly in the same application.

In this chapter, RDDs will be the focus of the ML exercises. We will be focusing on hands-on exercises using Jupyter Notebooks. Jupyter Notebooks are available on the Data Science Virtual Machine, and they are installed by default as a service with the Azure HDInsight deployment of Spark.

HDInsight and Spark

Apache Spark is an open source parallel processing framework that supports in-memory processing to boost the performance of big data analytic applications. The Apache Spark cluster on HDInsight is compatible with Azure Storage (WASB), as well as Azure Data Lake Store.

When the developer creates a Spark cluster on HDInsight, the Azure compute resources are already created with Spark installed and configured. It only takes about 10 minutes to create a Spark cluster in HDInsight. The data to be processed is stored in Azure Storage or Azure Data Lake Storage.

Apache Spark provides primitives for in-memory cluster computing, which means that it is the perfect partner for HDInsight. An Apache Spark job can load and cache data into memory and query it repeatedly, which means that it produces results much more quickly than disk-based systems. In addition to this, Apache Spark also integrates into the Scala programming language to facilitate developers to create and manipulate distributed datasets as if they were local collections of datasets.

Apache Spark uses the concept of RDD to transparently store data in memory. When RDD stores the value in memory, the data that does not fit in memory can undergo one of two options. The data can be recalculated in the RDD, or the excess data can be sent to disk. Therefore, Apache Spark persists the data to disk only if it is required to do so. This functionality helps to reduce most of the disk read and write, thereby circumventing the main time-consuming factors of data processing.

The YARN operation system in Apache Spark

YARN is one of the key features in the second-generation Hadoop 2 version of the Apache Software Foundation's open source distributed processing framework, and it is retained and progressed in Hadoop Version 3. YARN is implemented on Azure HDInsight to facilitate large-scale, distributed operating systems for big data applications and predictive analytics.

YARN is efficient because it decouples MapReduce's resource management and scheduling capabilities from the data processing component. Since Apache Spark uses this methodology, it empowers Hadoop to support more varied processing approaches and a broader array of applications.

How can we use Spark to conduct predictive analytics? ML focuses on taking data and applying a process to that data to produce a predicted output. There are many different types of ML algorithms that we can create and use with Spark. One of the most common methods is supervised ML, which works by taking in some data that consists of a vector of what we call features and a label. What do we mean by this?

A vector is a set of information that we use in order to make a prediction. A label is a characteristic that is used to make the prediction.

We will take an example. Let's say that we have a set of information about people, and we would like to predict something about this group of people: whether they are likely to become homeless or not. The characteristics of these people might include their age, education level, earnings, military service, and so on. The characteristics of the people would be called the features, and the thing that we would like to predict is known as the **label**.

In this case, the data scientist would take some data where they know that they have already become homeless, and therefore the label value would be known to the researchers at that point.

Using Spark, we would then process the data and fit the data to the model to see how successful it is. The model would tell us what we need to see in the characteristics in order to see the likelihood of homelessness occurring for these individuals.

The model is essentially a function that specifies what we expect to see in the vector features to see the outcome, or prediction.

The next step is to take previously unseen, new data that doesn't contain a known label to see how it fits the model. This dataset just has the features because the actual label, or outcome, isn't known. In this supervised learning example, data with a known label is used to train the model to predict data with the known label, and then the model is faced with data that does not have the known label.

In unsupervised learning, the label is not known. Unsupervised learning takes a similar approach, where the data scientist will ingest data and feed it, which simply has the vector of features, and no label is present. With this type of data science methodology, I may simply be looking at the similarities that are found in the vector features in order to see whether there are any clusters or commonalities in the data.

Working with data in a Spark environment

When data scientists work with data in an Apache Spark environment, they typically work with either RDDs or DataFrames. In our examples so far, the data may be stored in the RDD format, and it is fed into the model by building a predictive feed into the model.

In these exercises, the Spark library is called `spark.mllib`. The MLlib library is the original ML library that comes with Spark. The newer library is called **Spark ML**.

Using Jupyter Notebooks

The Jupyter Notebook is an incredibly powerful tool for collaboratively developing and producing data science projects. It integrates code, comments, and code output into a single document that combines code, data visualizations, narrative text, mathematical equations, and other data science artefacts. Notebooks are increasingly popular in today's data science workflows because they encourage iterative and rapid development for data science teams. Jupyter project is the successor to the earlier IPython Notebook. It is possible to use many different programming languages within Jupyter Notebooks, but this chapter will focus on Apache Spark.

Jupyter is free, open source, and browser-based. It can be used to create notebooks for working with your code in normal ways, such as writing and commenting code. One key feature of Jupyter Notebooks is that they are very useful for collaboration with other team members, thereby enabling productivity. The Jupyter Notebook supports a number of different engines, also known as kernels. The Jupyter Notebook can be used to run code on Python or Scala.

In this walk-through, the Spark ML tutorial will be used in order to introduce the concepts of Spark and ML.

Configuring the data science virtual machine

If you are using the Ubuntu Linux DSVM edition, there is a requirement to do a one-time setup step to enable a local single node Hadoop HDFS and YARN instance. By default, Hadoop services are installed but disabled on the DSVM. In order to enable it, it is necessary to run the following commands as root the first time:

```
echo -e 'y\n' | ssh-keygen -t rsa -P '' -f ~hadoop/.ssh/id_rsa
cat ~hadoop/.ssh/id_rsa.pub >> ~hadoop/.ssh/authorized_keys
chmod 0600 ~hadoop/.ssh/authorized_keys
chown hadoop:hadoop ~hadoop/.ssh/id_rsa
chown hadoop:hadoop ~hadoop/.ssh/id_rsa.pub
chown hadoop:hadoop ~hadoop/.ssh/authorized_keys
systemctl start hadoop-namenode hadoop-datanode hadoop-yarn
```

You can stop the Hadoop-related services when you do not need them by executing the following command:

```
systemctl stop hadoop-namenode hadoop-datanode hadoop-yarn
```

This requirement is not necessary in the Windows version of the data science virtual machine.

Now, we will start a Jupyter Notebook using the data science virtual machine:

1. On the Data Science Virtual Machine, double-click the Jupyter icon.
2. The Jupyter command window will appear, as shown in the following screenshot:

3. The Jupyter Notebook will launch in a browser, displaying the Jupyter home page, as follows:

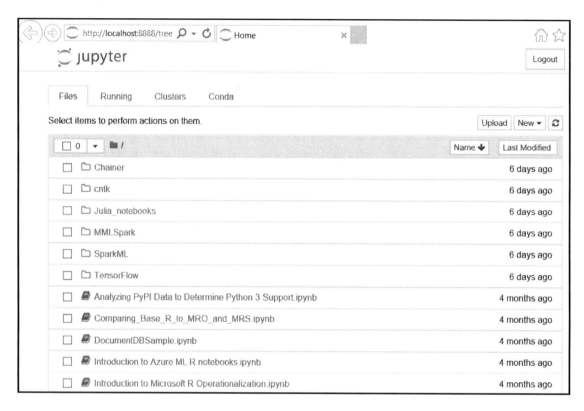

4. In the Jupyter homepage, click on the **SparkML** link.
5. Click on the **PsySpark** link.

6. Click on the **pySpark 2.0 modeling.ipynb** link.
7. The first time that Spark runs, it may be necessary to set the kernel if it is not already set. Hence, the following message may appear in the browser:

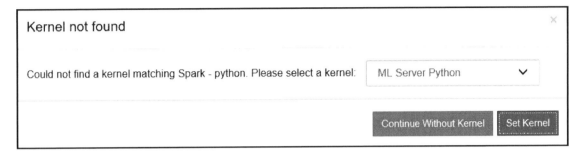

8. Click **Set Kernel** and select the kernel called **Python 3 Spark - local.**
9. The kernel will restart.
10. Select the **Trust** option so that the Notebook is trusted.

Running Spark MLib commands in Jupyter

The default Jupyter lab will demonstrate features and capabilities of Spark's MLlib toolkit for ML problems. The walk-through uses a sample dataset, which holds data from real trips of NYC taxis. The data holds the NYC taxi trip and fare dataset to show MLlib's modeling features for binary classification and regression problems.

In this lab, many different Spark MLib functions will be used, including data ingestion, data exploration, data preparation (featurizing and transformation), modeling, prediction, model persistence, and model evaluation on an independent validation dataset. Data visualization will also be used in order to demonstrate the results.

The lab will focus on two types of learning: classification offers the opportunity to try out supervised and unsupervised Learning. The first sample will use binary classification to predict whether a tip will be given. In the second sample, regression will be used to predict the level of tip given.

In Jupyter, the code is executed in the cell. The cell structure is a simple way of enabling the data scientist to query the RDD dataframe, and interactively display information in the Jupyter Notebook, including data visualization. It's a very flexible, intuitive, and powerful way to work with our data to use ML using Spark.

Data ingestion

The first activity is to set the appropriate directory paths.

1. Set the location of training data:

```
taxi_train_file_loc =
"../Data/JoinedTaxiTripFare.Point1Pct.Train.csv"
taxi_valid_file_loc =
"../Data/JoinedTaxiTripFare.Point1Pct.Valid.csv"
```

2. Set the model storage directory path. This is where models will be saved:

```
modelDir = "../Outputs/"; # The last backslash is needed;
```

3. In the Jupyter menu, put the cursor in **cell** and select the **Run** option from the menu. This will assign the training and test sets to the `taxi_train_file_loc` and `taxi_valid_file_loc` variables.

4. Next, the data will be set into a new dataframe, and it will be cleaned. Data ingestion was completed using the `spark.read.csv` function, which assigns the data to a new dataframe called `taxi_train_df`. The data undergoes some cleaning to remove unnecessary columns, and removes unnecessary outlier values. The code appears as follows:

```
## READ IN DATA AND CREATE SPARK DATAFRAME FROM A CSV
taxi_train_df = spark.read.csv(path=taxi_train_file_loc,
header=True, inferSchema=True)
```

5. Next, we can create a cleaned dataframe by removing columns that we do not need. Also, we can filter the data to remove outliers, or data that is badly formatted:

```
taxi_df_train_cleaned =
taxi_train_df.drop('medallion').drop('hack_license').drop('store_an
d_fwd_flag').drop('pickup_datetime')\
.drop('dropoff_datetime').drop('pickup_longitude').drop('pickup_lat
itude').drop('dropoff_latitude')\
.drop('dropoff_longitude').drop('tip_class').drop('total_amount').d
rop('tolls_amount').drop('mta_tax')\
.drop('direct_distance').drop('surcharge')\
```

```
.filter("passenger_count > 0 and passenger_count < 8 AND
payment_type in ('CSH', 'CRD') \
AND tip_amount >= 0 AND tip_amount < 30 AND fare_amount >= 1 AND
fare_amount < 200 \
AND trip_distance > 0 AND trip_distance < 100 AND trip_time_in_secs
> 30 AND trip_time_in_secs < 7200" )
```

6. Then, the dataframe holding the clean data is registered as a temporary table in SQL:

```
taxi_df_train_cleaned.createOrReplaceTempView("taxi_train")
```

Data exploration

In the next step, it's important to explore the data. It's easy to visualize the data right in the Jupyter interface by plotting the target variables and features. The data is summarized using SQL. Then, the data is plotted using `matplotlib`. To plot the data, the dataframe will first have to be converted to a pandas dataframe. At that point, matplotlib can use it to generate plots.

Since Spark is designed to work with large big data datasets, if the Spark dataframe is large, a sample of the data can be used for data visualization purposes.

In the following example, 50% of the data was sampled prior to converting the data into the dataframe format, and then it was incorporated into a pandas dataframe.

The code is provided in the following snippet:

```
%%sql -q -o sqlResults
SELECT fare_amount, passenger_count, tip_amount, tipped FROM taxi_train

sqlResultsPD = spark.sql(sqlStatement).sample(False, 0.5,
seed=1234).toPandas();
%matplotlib inline

# This query will show the tip by payment

ax1 = sqlResultsPD[['tip_amount']].plot(kind='hist', bins=25,
facecolor='lightblue')
ax1.set_title('Tip amount distribution')
ax1.set_xlabel('Tip Amount ($)'); ax1.set_ylabel('Counts');
plt.figure(figsize=(4,4)); plt.suptitle(''); plt.show()

# TIP AMOUNT BY FARE AMOUNT, POINTS ARE SCALED BY PASSENGER COUNT

ax = sqlResultsPD.plot(kind='scatter', x= 'fare_amount', y = 'tip_amount',
```

```
c='blue', alpha = 0.10, s=2.5*(sqlResultsPD.passenger_count))
ax.set_title('Tip amount by Fare amount')
ax.set_xlabel('Fare Amount ($)'); ax.set_ylabel('Tip Amount ($)');
plt.axis([-2, 80, -2, 20])
plt.figure(figsize=(4,4)); plt.suptitle(''); plt.show()
```

This will produce a histogram of the results.

The relationship between the fare amount and the tip amount is shown in the following chart:

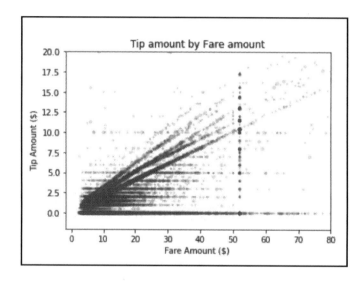

Feature engineering in Spark

In feature engineering, we can take care of numerous data engineering tasks, such as creating new features and grouping, transforming, and cleaning up data. The data can undergo further indexing and be enriched by additional classification, grouping, and the encoding of categorical features.

In the following example code, we create a new feature by binning hours into traffic time buckets using Spark SQL:

```
sqlStatement = """ SELECT *, CASE
WHEN (pickup_hour <= 6 OR pickup_hour >= 20) THEN "Night"
WHEN (pickup_hour >= 7 AND pickup_hour <= 10) THEN "AMRush"
WHEN (pickup_hour >= 11 AND pickup_hour <= 15) THEN "Afternoon"
WHEN (pickup_hour >= 16 AND pickup_hour <= 19) THEN "PMRush"
END as TrafficTimeBins
```

```
FROM taxi_train
"""
taxi_df_train_with_newFeatures = spark.sql(sqlStatement)
```

Here, we only transform a few variables to show examples, which are character strings. Other variables that are represented by numerical values, such as week-day, can also be indexed as categorical variables. In this piece of code, the dataset sample is split into a training and a test set, and the data is placed in memory. The code is as follows:

```
trainingFraction = 0.5; testingFraction = (1-trainingFraction);
seed = 1234;
encodedFinalSampled = encodedFinal.sample(False, 0.5, seed=seed)
```

In the next step, it is important to split the data into two sets: a training dataset and a testing dataset. It's important to split data into training and testing sets as it is an important part of evaluating data science models. Generally, when a dataset is split into a training set and a testing set, it means that most of the data is used for training, and a smaller portion of the data is used for testing:

```
trainData, testData = encodedFinalSampled.randomSplit([trainingFraction,
testingFraction], seed=seed);
```

Next, we need to cache the dataframes in memory:

```
trainData.cache(); trainData.count();
testData.cache(); testData.count();
```

Caching is one of the many optimization techniques for Apache Spark computations. We can use this functionality to save data as a series of intermediate results, thereby encouraging reuse later on in the analysis.

Using Spark for prediction

In this part of the chapter, the exercise is to use the Spark sample code to create a logistic regression model, save the model, and evaluate the performance of the model on a test dataset. For modeling, the features and class labels are specified using the RFormula function. In this example, we will train the model using the pipeline formula and a logistic regression estimator. This can be seen from the following code snippet:

```
logReg = LogisticRegression(maxIter=10, regParam=0.3, elasticNetParam=0.8)
```

The following code block sets up the training formula and assigns it to the `classFormula` variable, which can be seen from the following code:

```
classFormula = RFormula(formula="tipped ~ pickup_hour + weekday +
passenger_count + trip_time_in_secs + trip_distance + fare_amount +
vendorVec + rateVec + paymentVec + TrafficTimeBinsVec")
```

The following code block trains the pipeline model:

```
model = Pipeline(stages=[classFormula, logReg]).fit(trainData)
```

The following code block saves the model that we have created:

```
datestamp = str(datetime.datetime.now()).replace(' ','').replace(':','_');
fileName = "logisticRegModel_" + datestamp;
logRegDirfilename = modelDir + fileName;
model.save(logRegDirfilename)
```

The following code block uses the model to predict results, using test data. The following code block helps to evaluate the model:

```
predictions = model.transform(testData)
predictionAndLabels = predictions.select("label","prediction").rdd
metrics = BinaryClassificationMetrics(predictionAndLabels)
print("Area under ROC = %s" % metrics.areaUnderROC)
```

Next, we plot the ROC curve:

```
%matplotlib inline
predictions_pddf = predictions.toPandas()
labels = predictions_pddf["label"]
prob = []
for dv in predictions_pddf["probability"]:
prob.append(dv.values[1])
fpr, tpr, thresholds = roc_curve(labels, prob, pos_label=1);
roc_auc = auc(fpr, tpr)
plt.figure(figsize=(5,5))
plt.plot(fpr, tpr, label='ROC curve (area = %0.2f)' % roc_auc)
plt.plot([0, 1], [0, 1], 'k--')
plt.xlim([0.0, 1.0]); plt.ylim([0.0, 1.05]);
plt.xlabel('False Positive Rate'); plt.ylabel('True Positive Rate');
plt.title('ROC Curve'); plt.legend(loc="lower right");
plt.show()
```

The regression output is shown next:

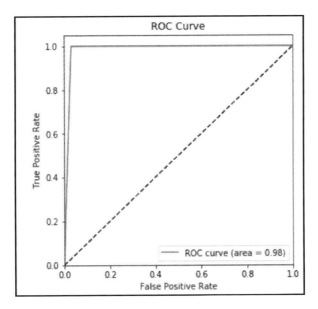

The ROC Curve is the blue curve, which sits very high at the top-left corner. The ROC result shows that the model is performing extremely well. As a heuristic, the closer the blue line is to the top of the upper-left side of the chart, the better the result.

In this section, the random forest model regression method will be used to predict how much of a tip will be given. In a standard classification tree, the data is split based on the homogeneity of the data. A decision tree is built top-down from a root node. The process involves partitioning data into subsets that contain instances that are homogeneous.

In a regression tree, the target variable is a real-value number. In this case, the data is fitted against a regression model to the target variable using each of the independent variables. For each independent variable, the data is split at several split points. We calculate the **Sum of Squared Error (SSE)** at each split boundary between the predicted value and the actual values. The variable resulting in the lowest SSE is selected for the node. Then, this process is recursively continued until all of the data is covered.

The code is as follows:

```
## DEFINE REGRESSION FORMULA
regFormula = RFormula(formula="tip_amount ~ paymentIndex + vendorIndex +
rateIndex + TrafficTimeBinsIndex + pickup_hour + weekday + passenger_count
+ trip_time_in_secs + trip_distance + fare_amount")
```

Then, we define the indexer for the categorical variables:

```
## DEFINE INDEXER FOR CATEGORIAL VARIABLES
featureIndexer = VectorIndexer(inputCol="features",
outputCol="indexedFeatures", maxCategories=32)
```

Then, we set up the random forest estimator. The value is set to the `randForest` variable:

```
## DEFINE RANDOM FOREST ESTIMATOR
randForest = RandomForestRegressor(featuresCol = 'indexedFeatures',
labelCol = 'label', numTrees=20,
featureSubsetStrategy="auto",impurity='variance', maxDepth=6, maxBins=100)
```

The next step is to fit the model using the defined formula and the relevant transformations:

```
## Fit model, with formula and other transformations
model = Pipeline(stages=[regFormula, featureIndexer,
randForest]).fit(trainData)
```

The next crucial step is to save the model:

```
## SAVE MODEL
datestamp = str(datetime.datetime.now()).replace(' ','').replace(':','_');
fileName = "RandomForestRegressionModel_" + datestamp;
andForestDirfilename = modelDir + fileName;
model.save(randForestDirfilename)
```

Then, we need to use the model to predict against the test data so that we can evaluate its success:

```
predictions = model.transform(testData)
predictionAndLabels = predictions.select("label","prediction").rdd
testMetrics = RegressionMetrics(predictionAndLabels)
print("RMSE = %s" % testMetrics.rootMeanSquaredError)
print("R-sqr = %s" % testMetrics.r2)
```

There's no substitute for visualizing the data. In the next code block, the data is visualized using a scattergram format. The end result is shown after the code block:

```
## PLOC ACTUALS VS. PREDICTIONS
predictionsPD = predictions.select("label","prediction").toPandas()ax =
predictionsPD.plot(kind='scatter', figsize = (5,5), x='label',
y='prediction', color='blue', alpha = 0.15, label='Actual vs. predicted');
fit = np.polyfit(predictionsPD['label'], predictionsPD['prediction'],
deg=1)
ax.set_title('Actual vs. Predicted Tip Amounts ($)')
ax.set_xlabel("Actual"); ax.set_ylabel("Predicted");
```

```
ax.plot(predictionsPD['label'], fit[0] * predictionsPD['label'] + fit[1],
color='magenta')
plt.axis([-1, 15, -1, 15])
plt.show(ax)
```

The resulting chart can be found next:

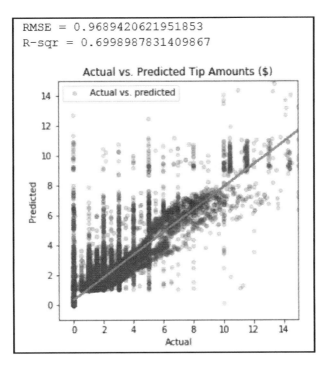

The lower the **Root Mean Square Error (RMSE)** value, the better the absolute fit. The RMSE is calculated as the square root of the variance of the residuals. It specifies the absolute fit of the model to the data. In other words, it denotes how close the observed actual data points are to the model's predicted values. As the square root of a variance, RMSE can be conceived as the standard deviation of the unexplained variance. The RMSE has the useful property of being in the same units as the response variable, so it intuitively makes sense. Lower RMSE values indicate a better fit. RMSE is a good measure of how accurately the model predicts the response. RMSE is the most important criterion for fit in this case, since the main purpose of the model is prediction.

R-sqr is intuitive. Its value ranges from zero to one, with zero indicating that the proposed model does not improve prediction over the mean model, and one indicating perfect prediction. Improvement in the regression model results in proportional increases in R-sqr.

Whereas R-sqr is a relative measure of fit, RMSE is an absolute measure of fit, and that's why it's shown here.

Loading a pipeline model and evaluating the test data

In this example, we will load a pipeline model and then evaluate the test data:

```
savedModel = PipelineModel.load(logRegDirfilename)
predictions = savedModel.transform(testData)
predictionAndLabels = predictions.select("label","prediction").rdd
metrics = BinaryClassificationMetrics(predictionAndLabels)
print("Area under ROC = %s" % metrics.areaUnderROC)
```

In the next step, we define random forest models:

```
randForest = RandomForestRegressor(featuresCol = 'indexedFeatures',
labelCol = 'label',
featureSubsetStrategy="auto",impurity='variance', maxBins=100)
```

Now, we will define a modeling pipeline that includes formulas, feature transformations, and an estimator:

```
pipeline = Pipeline(stages=[regFormula, featureIndexer, randForest])
```

Let's define a parameter grid for random forest:

```
paramGrid = ParamGridBuilder() \
.addGrid(randForest.numTrees, [10, 25, 50]) \
.addGrid(randForest.numTrees, [3, 5, 7]) \
.build()
```

Now, define cross-validation:

```
crossval = CrossValidator(estimator=pipeline,
estimatorParamMaps=paramGrid,
evaluator=RegressionEvaluator(metricName="rmse"),
numFolds=3)
```

After defining cross-validation, it's time to train the model using CV:

```
cvModel = crossval.fit(trainData)
```

Since the model is trained, it's important to predict and evaluate the test dataset:

```
predictions = cvModel.transform(testData)
evaluator = RegressionEvaluator(labelCol="label",
predictionCol="prediction", metricName="r2")
r2 = evaluator.evaluate(predictions)
print("R-squared on test data = %g" % r2)
```

Finally, let's save this best model:

```
fileName = "CV_RandomForestRegressionModel_" + datestamp;
CVDirfilename = modelDir + fileName;
cvModel.bestModel.save(CVDirfilename);
```

The next step is to ingest data from a `.csv`, and assign it to a dataframe. Then, a number of unnecessary columns are removed, and the data is filtered:

```
taxi_valid_df = spark.read.csv(path=taxi_valid_file_loc, header=True,
inferSchema=True)
taxi_df_valid_cleaned =
taxi_valid_df.drop('medallion').drop('hack_license').drop('store_and_fwd_fl
ag').drop('pickup_datetime')\
.drop('dropoff_datetime').drop('pickup_longitude').drop('pickup_latitude').
drop('dropoff_latitude')\
.drop('dropoff_longitude').drop('tip_class').drop('total_amount').drop('tol
ls_amount').drop('mta_tax')\
.drop('direct_distance').drop('surcharge')\
.filter("passenger_count > 0 and passenger_count < 8 AND payment_type in
('CSH', 'CRD') \
AND tip_amount >= 0 AND tip_amount < 30 AND fare_amount >= 1 AND
fare_amount < 200 \
AND trip_distance > 0 AND trip_distance < 100 AND trip_time_in_secs > 30
AND trip_time_in_secs < 7200")
```

The dataframe can be registered in the SQL database as a temporary table. Then, standard SQL is used to create four buckets of data, which are sliced according to the time that the taxi picked up the passenger:

```
taxi_df_valid_cleaned.createOrReplaceTempView("taxi_valid")
sqlStatement = """ SELECT *, CASE
WHEN (pickup_hour <= 6 OR pickup_hour >= 20) THEN "Night"
WHEN (pickup_hour >= 7 AND pickup_hour <= 10) THEN "AMRush"
WHEN (pickup_hour >= 11 AND pickup_hour <= 15) THEN "Afternoon"
WHEN (pickup_hour >= 16 AND pickup_hour <= 19) THEN "PMRush"
END as TrafficTimeBins
FROM taxi_valid
"""

taxi_df_valid_with_newFeatures = spark.sql(sqlStatement)
```

The data is then transformed so that the structure of the test data matches the original training data:

```
encodedFinalValid = Pipeline(stages=[sI1, en1, sI2, en2, sI3, en3, sI4,
en4]).fit(taxi_df_train_with_newFeatures).transform(taxi_df_valid_with_newF
eatures)
```

Once the test data structure matches the training data structure, the data is loaded into the model. The results are evaluated and printed:

```
savedModel = PipelineModel.load(CVDirfilename)
predictions = savedModel.transform(encodedFinalValid)
r2 = evaluator.evaluate(predictions)
print("R-squared on test data = %g" % r2)
```

We will add some code so that we can see the results of the testing:

1. Using the following code, we can put the test results on a chart in order to understand them better
2. Copy the following code into the cell at the bottom of the existing Jupyter Notebook:

```
predictionsPD = predictions.select("label","prediction").toPandas()
ax = predictionsPD.plot(kind='scatter', figsize = (5,5), x='label',
y='prediction', color='#066083', alpha = 0.15, label='Actual vs.
predicted');
fit = np.polyfit(predictionsPD['label'],
predictionsPD['prediction'], deg=1)
ax.set_title('Actual vs. Predicted Tip Amounts ($)')
ax.set_xlabel("Actual"); ax.set_ylabel("Predicted");
ax.plot(predictionsPD['label'], fit[0] * predictionsPD['label'] +
fit[1], color='#b4d11e')
```

```
plt.axis([-1, 15, -1, 15])
plt.show(ax)
```

3. In the cell, the code will appear as follows:

```
In [20]: predictionsPD = predictions.select("label","prediction").toPandas()

ax = predictionsPD.plot(kind='scatter', figsize = (5,5), x='label', y='prediction', color='#066083',
fit = np.polyfit(predictionsPD['label'], predictionsPD['prediction'], deg=1)
ax.set_title('Actual vs. Predicted Tip Amounts ($)')
ax.set_xlabel("Actual"); ax.set_ylabel("Predicted");
ax.plot(predictionsPD['label'], fit[0] * predictionsPD['label'] + fit[1], color='#b4d11e')
plt.axis([-1, 15, -1, 15])
plt.show(ax)
```

4. Click inside **cell**, and hit the **Run** button at the top of the page.

5. The resulting chart appears as follows:

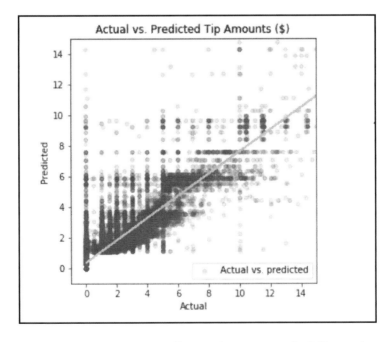

Now, the second chart appears slightly different, but not much different from the first. The colors have been changed so that the difference is noted.

Setting up an HDInsight cluster with Spark

It's crucial to provision an HDInsight Spark cluster in order to start the work.

Provisioning an HDInsight cluster

If you already have a Spark HDInsight cluster running, you can skip this procedure.

1. In a web browser, navigate to `http://portal.azure.com` and, if prompted, sign in using the Microsoft account that is associated with your Azure subscription.

2. In the Microsoft Azure portal, in the Hub Menu, click **New**. Then, in the **Data + Analytics** section, select **HDInsight** and create a **new HDInsight cluster** with the following settings:

   - **Cluster Name**: Enter a unique name (and make a note of it!)
   - **Subscription**: Select your Azure subscription
   - **Cluster Type**: Spark
   - **Cluster Operating System**: Linux
   - **HDInsight Version**: Choose the latest version of Spark
   - **Cluster Tier**: Standard
   - **Cluster Login Username**: Enter a username of your choice (and make a note of it!)
   - **Cluster Login Password**: Enter a strong password (and make a note of it!)
   - **Create a new resource group**: Enter a unique name (and make a note of it!)
   - **Location**: Choose any available data center location
   - **Storage**:
     - **Primary storage type**: Azure Storage
   - **Selection Method**: My Subscriptions
   - **Create a new storage account**: Enter a unique name consisting of lowercase letters and numbers only (and make a note of it!)
   - **Default Container**: Enter the cluster name you specified previously

- **Applications**: None
- **Number of Worker nodes**: 1
- **Worker node size**: Leave the default size selected
- **Head node size**: Leave the default size selected
- **Advanced Settings**: None

3. In the Azure portal, view notifications to verify that deployment has started. Then, wait for the cluster to be deployed (this can take a long time—often 30 minutes or more. Feel free to catch up on your social media networks while you wait!).

 As soon as an HDInsight cluster is running, the credit in your Azure subscription will start to be charged. Free-trial subscriptions include a limited amount of credit that you can spend over a period of 30 days, which should be enough to complete the labs in this course, as long as clusters are deleted when not in use. If you decide not to complete this lab, follow the instructions in the *Clean Up* procedure at the end of the lab to delete your cluster so as to avoid using your Azure credit unnecessarily.

View the HDInsight cluster in the Azure portal

- In the Azure portal, browse to the Spark cluster you just created.
- In the blade for your cluster, under Quick Links, click **Cluster Dashboards**.
- In the Cluster Dashboards blade, note the dashboards that are available. These include a Jupyter Notebook dashboard that you will use later in this course.

Summary

In this chapter, you were introduced to some of the latest big data analytics technologies in Microsoft Azure. The chapter has focused on two main technologies: Azure HDInsight with Spark, and Azure Databricks.

In the chapter, we have looked at the different ways of modelling data, and we have covered useful tips to help you to understand what the models actually mean. Often, this is not the end of the data science process, because this may throw up new questions as you get new insights. So, it is a process rather than a race—but that's what makes it interesting!

Further references

- Review the Spark Machine Learning Programming Guide at `https://spark.apache.org/docs/latest/ml-guide.html`
- Documentation for Microsoft Azure HDInsight, including Spark Clusters is at `https://azure.microsoft.com/en-us/documentation/services/hdinsight`
- Documentation and getting started guidance for Programming with Scala is at `http://www.scala-lang.org/documentation/`
- Documentation and getting started guidance for Programming with Python is at `https://www.python.org/doc/`
- You can view the Spark SQL and DataFrames Programming Guide at `https://spark.apache.org/docs/latest/sql-programming-guide.html`
- Classification and Regression: `https://spark.apache.org/docs/latest/ml-classification-regression.html`
- Pipelines: `https://spark.apache.org/docs/latest/ml-pipeline.html`

10
Building Deep Learning Solutions

Deep learning is a superset of machine learning incorporating algorithms influenced by the design and functionality of the human brain, known as the artificial intelligent neural network. It's represented in the form of supervised, semi-supervised, and unsupervised algorithms, where architectures profoundly concentrate on deep neural networks, deep belief networks, and recurrent neural networks. Deep learning today is widely accepted and utilized in industry as well as in R and D sectors in the field of computer vision, speech recognition, audio synthesis, image recognition, natural language processing, social media content moderation, and so on.

In this chapter, we will learn about the following topics:

- An overview of Microsoft CNTK and the MMLSpark framework, along with third-party deep learning tools
- TensorFlow and Keras, and the steps of deployment on Azure compute

What is deep learning?

Deep learning is a subclass of traditional machine learning algorithms that utilizes a series of non-linear processing layers for feature extraction, transformation, and, finally, analysis over the successive layers of output from the previous layers of input.

The first layer of the deep learning neural network consists of an input layer, an output layer (the outermost layer), and a hidden layer, which is a complex layer in-between the input and output layers:

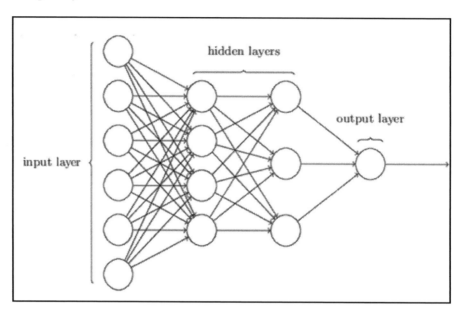

Differences between traditional machine learning and deep learning

The comparison between traditional machine learning and deep learning are as follows:

Traditional Machine learning	Deep learning
Traditional machine learning needs manual features of data extraction/engineering.	Deep learning learns automatically from the data features.
For unstructured data, feature extraction is difficult.	Deep learning updates learned network weights and bias in each layer.

Common Deep Learning Neural Networks (DNNs)

There are a diverse set of deep learning neural networks available that are used to solve deep learning problems in the data science platform. Some of them are as follows:

- **Deep Convolutional Neural Network (DCNN)**: Used for the extraction of images representation
- **Recurrent Neural Network (RNN)**: Used for the extraction of sequential data representation
- **Deep Belief Neural Network (DBN)**: Applied for the extraction of hierarchical dataset representation
- **Deep Reinforcement Learning (DRL)**: Prediction of agent behaviors to maximize the future cumulative reward

The traditional manner of working on various deep learning frameworks and tools comes with a lot of challenges as it consists of various dependencies like the execution of DL frameworks on GPU-based processors, the utilization of CUDA, cuDNN, and MKL drivers, and many other platform-based dependencies. Working on deep learning frameworks with Azure is made available with two options:

- Using Azure Notebook services
- Using Azure Deep Learning Virtual Machine toolkits

Overview of the Azure Notebook service

The Azure Notebook service is a managed service that basically provides easy access to Jupyter Notebooks by using the computational power of R, Python, and F#, and users can utilize its numerous visual libraries and share the notebooks both publicly and in a private manner with a shareable link.

Microsoft's **Cognitive Toolkit (CNTK)** has native support for Azure Notebook services so that Python-based Jupyter Notebooks can be executed with the CNTK framework. For execution in other DL frameworks like TensorFlow, Keras, or Theano, users need to install the respective framework components by using Miniconda or Pip/wheel.

The Azure Notebook services are available at `https://notebooks.azure.com/`, and leverage the features of free, cloud-based, web-based Jupyter Notebook environments, including facilities for the creation of libraries and numerous interactive graphics that are built using data science languages like Python 2, Python 3, R, and F#. You can create your own libraries and build interactive notebooks, and you can simply upload your existing Jupyter Notebooks as well:

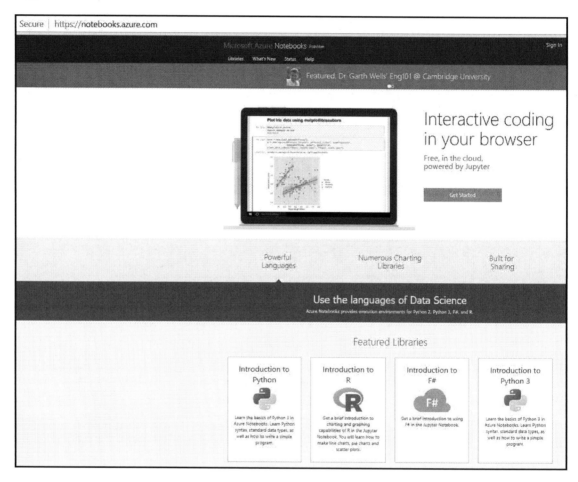

Microsoft CNTK notebooks have built-in support in Azure Notebooks. All of the notebooks in Azure Notebooks can be organized into individual groups known as libraries that are shareable but non-editable. Notebooks can be cloned from other repositories as well.

Data can be uploaded with ease to Azure Notebooks by using the **Data** menu and loading it into memory with function cells. It can also be downloaded, as demonstrated in the following screenshot:

Azure Notebook services provide the ability to implement interactive IPython notebooks by using libraries like matplotlib, scikit-learn, scipy, numpy, pandas, and so on. In the following demo, an interactive IPython notebook on the World's Population Growth rate analytics has been implemented:

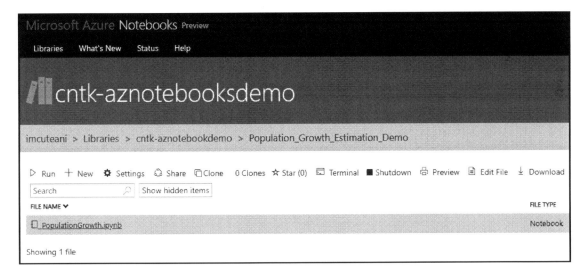

First, data exploration is performed by importing the raw data into a DataFrame:

```
import pandas as pd
 df_population_density =
pd.read_csv('/home/nbuser/library/World_Population_Growth.csv')
 df_population_density.head(10)
```

Then, we implement the filtering in order to build a more concise pivot table:

```
filtered_cells_df =
df_population_density[['Location','Time','Births','Deaths','GrowthRate']].d
ropna(how="any")
 filtered_cells_df
```

The output of the preceding code snippet is as follows:

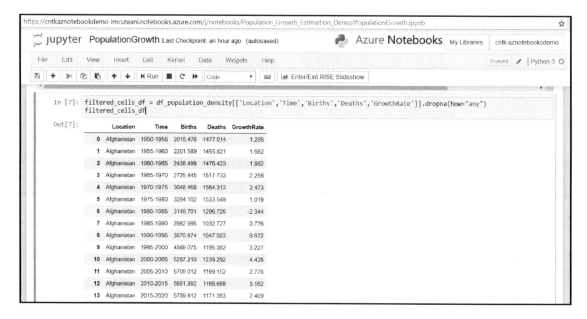

Pivot table formation with Azure Notebook

The Pivot table can be populated using function like `pivot_table()`:

```
df_population_pivot =
filtered_cells_df.pivot_table('GrowthRate','Location','Time')
 df_population_pivot.head(100)
```

Finally, we can build interactive Python-based visuals by using visualization libraries, such as `matplotlib`, `seaborn`, `pandas`, `folium` and so on:

```
import numpy as np
 import matplotlib.pyplot as plot
 plot.figure(figsize=(15,10),dpi = 80)
 plot.plot(df_population_pivot.ix[:,0:1], label="Net Growth rate, both
sexes males and females")
 plot.plot(df_population_pivot.ix[:,1:2], label="Net migration rate (per
1000 population distribution)")
 plot.plot(df_population_pivot.ix[:,2:3],label="Population growth rate
(%)")
 plot.xlabel('Location')
 plot.ylabel('GrowthRate')
 plot.title("Annual Population Growth")
 xvalues = list(df_population_pivot.index)
 x = np.array(range(0,len(xvalues)))
 plot.xticks(x,xvalues,rotation=70)
 plot.legend(bbox_to_anchor=(1.05,1),loc=2, borderaxespad=0.)
 plot.show()
```

The output of the Azure Notebook looks like as the following screenshot.

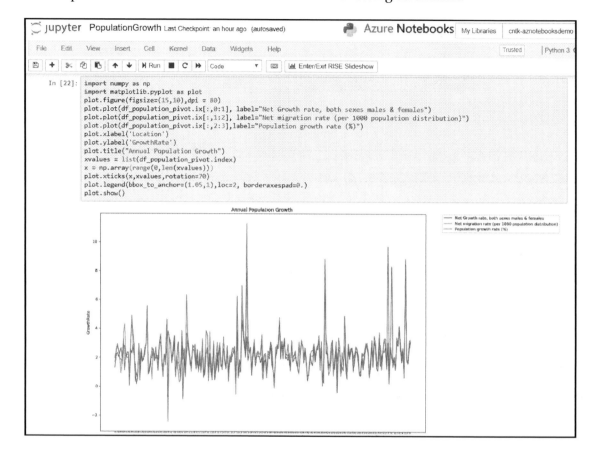

You can also utilize the feature of applying a slideshow of Jupyter Notebooks running on Azure Notebooks and share these for collaboration via social media/embedding in email, or by using a customized URL:

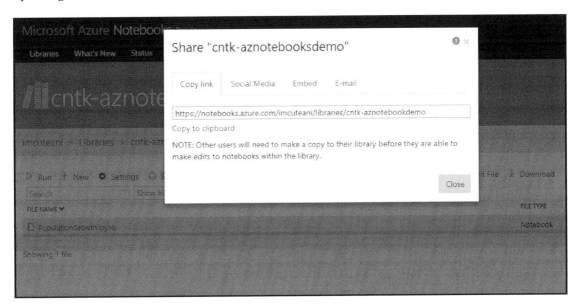

Overview of Azure Deep Learning Virtual Machine toolkits

The **Deep Learning Virtual Machine (DLVM)** is a superset variant of the traditional Azure data science VM which consists of pre-configured environments that are mainly used to develop and deploy deep learning models on top of GPU instances (for example, a Azure GPU NC series VM), and is available on two OSes—Windows Server 2016 and Ubuntu Linux edition.

The DSVM on Azure contains several AI tools that have been pre-built, including CNTK, Keras, Caffe2, and Chainer to pre-process and extract visual data, text, audio, or video data. You can perform data science modelling and use implementation operations by using tools like Microsoft R server, Anaconda Python, Jupyter Notebooks for Python /2.x , R , SQL Server 2017, Azure ML workbench, Julia, F# SDK and so on.

You can provision the Deep Learning VM in the Azure portal from the marketplace as an Azure Resource Manager (ARM) and by providing various details like the type of OS, user credentials, and the instance size of the GPU that's been accelerated on a deep learning machine:

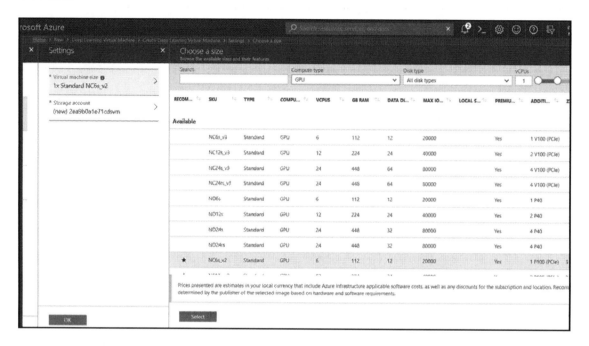

More details on the Azure DLVM from the marketplace can be found at the following link: `https://azuremarketplace.microsoft.com/en-us/marketplace/apps/microsoft-ads.dsvm-deep-learning`.

Open source deep learning frameworks

The details of various open source deep learning frameworks that are used in enterprise situations can be seen in the following table:

Software	Innovator	Platform	Software license	Open source?	CUDA (GPU) support	Platform interface
CNTK	Microsoft research	Windows and Linux	MIT	Yes	Yes	Python, C++ , C#, and CLI support
TensorFlow	Google Brain	Linux, macOS, and Windows	Apache 2.0	Yes	Yes	Python(NumPy) and C/C++

Theano	University of Montreal	Cross-platform	Apache 2.0	BSD license	Yes	Python
Caffe	Berkeley AI	Linux, macOS, and Windows	BSD license	Yes	Yes	Python and Matlab
Apache MXNet	Distributed ML community	Ubuntu, macOS, Windows, AWS, Android, and iOS	Apache 2.0	Yes	Yes	C++ , Python, Matlab, JavaScript, R, and Scala

In-depth analysis of Microsoft deep learning tools

Microsoft has brought out extensive new deep learning toolkits which can be utilized to speed up advances in areas like text analysis, speech/voice recognition, and image classification by applying the cognitive toolkit known as CNTK, which can be run on-premise or in Azure GPU instances. The Azure Cognitive toolkit has support for binding to BrainScript and Python (versions 2.7, 3.5, and 3.6 at the time of writing), C++, and the .NET managed C# platform.

The following are the features of CNTK 2.0 in deep learning:

- An extension facility for the CNTK function for the extraction, feature engineering, and scoring of optimizer ML algorithms in a variety of languages like Python, C#, and C++.
- The integration of TensorFlow models for visualization in CNTK.
- Several pre-trained models are available as samples.
- Support for image recognition via the use of the FAST R-CNN algorithm on GPU instances (for example, Nvidia Tesla CUDA, and cuDNN).
- The availability of a performance profiler for Python and BrainScript.
- Autoscaling feasibility of deep learning projects on Azure by running on kubernetes clusters. The autoscaling facility on Kubernetes provides both pod-level scaling (out of the box) as well as node-level scaling. **Horizontal pod scaling (HPA)** is a major feature of running CNTK models on AKS, as this automatically scales the number of pods in the clusters based on your requirements and also takes care to specify several node metrics like the percentage of CPU utilization and % of memory availability based on being scaled out or in.
- Support of VS tools for AIs, which provides easy local installation for most, if not all, deep learning libraries (for example, Tensorflow, MXNet, Keras, Caffe2, Theano, Torch, Pytorch, Chainer (with GPU cuda support as cuPy), XG-Boost, Scikit-learn, LIBSVM, **Open Neural Network Exchange (ONNX)**, Core ML Community Tools (coremltools), Microsoft ML tools, tf2onnx, Netron, and so on).

More details on AI tools for Visual Studio and its supported ML/DL libraries can be found at the following GitHub link: `https://github.com/Microsoft/vs-tools-for-ai/blob/master/docs/`.

Overview of Microsoft CNTK

Microsoft CNTK is a commercial-grade open source toolkit that's used for deep learning and specifies the neural network structure as a series of computational directed graphs. It was introduced by Microsoft speech researchers (Dong Yu et al.) in 2012, open sourced in 2015, and published on Codeplex. On GitHub, the source code base of CNTK has been available under a permissions license from 2016. CNTK provides the flexibility of ease of use, is fast, and composes simple building blocks into complex networks. This deep learning toolkit is 100% production ready and gives state-of-the-art accuracy, making it efficient and scalable to any CPU/GPU processing platform. It incorporates the popular training models of feed-forward DNNs, CNN, and recurrent neural networks (RNNs/LSTM). Stochastic gradient descent (SGD) and error back-propagation are developed with CNTK for automated model differentiation and parallel execution of training models across CPU/GPU instances.

The GitHub public repository for CNTK is available at, `https://github.com/Microsoft/CNTK` and contains multiple examples, pre-trained models, documents, and relevant toolsets.

The architecture building blocks of CNTK

The **open neural network exchange (ONNX)** format that's supported by CNTK as the first deep learning toolkit has a shared open source model representation for framework interoperability and optimization. ONNX also extends support for moving trained models between frameworks such as CNTK, Caffe2, Apache MXNet, and PyTorch.

The top-level command blocks of CNTK, which are CNTK configuration files, define what actions are to be carried out with related information. The configuration parameter classifies what command blocks are to be implemented, and in what order context, if more than one command block is defined.

Architecture-wise, CNTK configuration parameter command blocks consists of the following:

- **Input reader block**: Specifies the building concepts of the network from the corpus and by loading an existing model
- **Network layer**: Defines the specified training algorithm to use

- **Learner layer**: Specifies the *where* and *how* to load the training modules and labels:

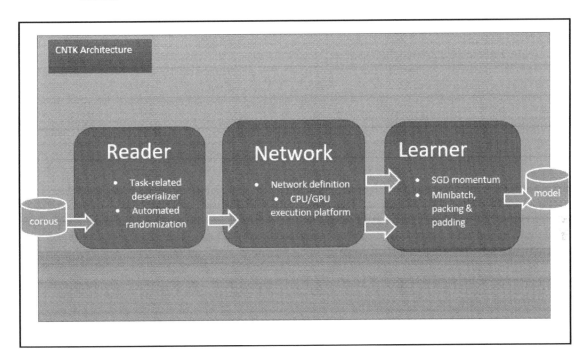

The most widely used configuration blocks of CNTK are as follows:

- Network layer building block:
    - **SimpleNetwork Builder**: Executes one of the network models with constrained customization
    - **BrainScriptNetwork Builder**: Implements a network based on the CNTK network description language (BrainScript), which provides benefits in network designs and neural network configurations
- Learners:
    - **SGD model**: It mainly applies the stochastic gradient descent algorithm for the training of the model.
- Input readers:
    - **CNTK Text format Reader**: Reads input text files which merge multiple input text files in the same format.
    - **LM Sequence Reader**: Reads input text files containing word sequences for predicting word sequences.

- **LU Sequence Reader**: Accepts input text-based files as word sequences, as well as its associated labels. This is mainly used for language understanding API building.
- **HTKMLF Reader**: Reads the input files in the format of HTK/MLF for speech recognition and voice synthesis applications.

Concepts on CNTK

The input, output, and parameters of CNTK are organized as *tensors*, where rank classifies each tensor. A tensor of rank 0 is associated as Scalar, a tensor of *rank 1* is specified as a Vector, and a tensor of *rank 2* is defined as a Matrix. There are some static and dynamic axes available for every CNTK. Static axes have the same length throughout the lifetime of the network. The dynamic network's static axes are defined as a meaningful grouping of tensors where a) their axes' lengths can differentiate from instance to instance, b) their axes lengths are typically unknown before each minibatch is represented, and c) the dynamic axes are ordered. The minibatch is called a tensor, and is called a dynamic axis or batch axis if its axis length varies from one minibatch to the next.

Developing and deploying CNTK layers in the Azure Deep Learning VM to implement a neural network

Microsoft CNTK is flexible and easy to use, and mainly applies simple building blocks to build complex layers quickly. One of the major utilities of CNTK is that it can be used as a backend for the Keras framework as well. From a few benchmark results, we can see that CNTK is generally faster than Google's TensorFlow and up to 5-10 times faster than recurrent/LSTM networks.

To get started and build the CNTK building blocks of Azure Deep Learning GPU instances, we need to provision the DLVM from an Azure portal that supports GPU instances. You can provision the DLVM from the Azure Marketplace by selecting **Create a Resource | New**, and then typing `Deep Learning Virtual Machine` in the search bar, as demonstrated in the following screenshot:

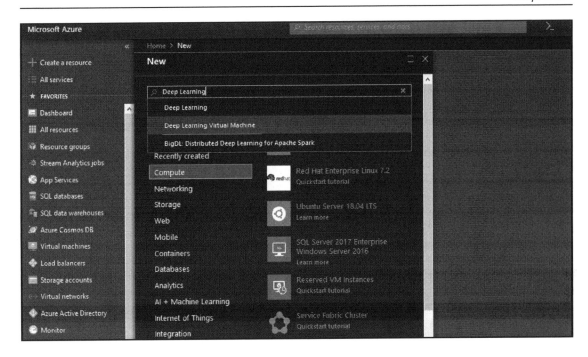

Next, by providing the appropriate VM details, such as OS type (Windows/Linux), user credentials, and resource group, you may choose the required GPU instance size, for example, NV6 or NV12, or, if a sufficient quota is available in your Azure subscription, then you can try out the instance sizes such as NC6sv3 (for example, 6 core GPU, 112 GB RAM, and 12 data disks) and NC12sv3 (for example, 12 core GPU, 224 GB of RAM, 24 data disks, and 40k disk IOPS availability).

Azure deep learning is accessible either through the remote desktop (RDP) mode (port 3389), or SSH mode (port 22).

CNTK inputs and variables declaration

The foremost exceptional thing about the deep learning framework is its ability to handle input datasets, declared variables, and performance management on computational graphs. In this CNTK demo on the Azure Deep Learning VM, three layers will be associated so that they can recognize a MNIST dataset of handwritten digits.

CNTK variables section

In the MNIST dataset classification problem, a flattened 28 x 28 pixel value scale input and its associated ten labels are present for classification. In CNTK, the variables could be declared to capture data, as follows:

```
import cntk as Cognitive
  from cntk.train import Trainer
  from cntk.io import MinibatchSource, CTFDeserializer, StreamDef,
StreamDefs
  from cntk.learners import adadelta, learning_rate_schedule, UnitType
  from cntk.ops import RELU, element_times, constant
  from cntk.layers import Dense, Sequential, For, default_options
  from cntk.losses import cross_entropy_with_softmax
  from cntk.metrics import classification_error
  from cntk.train.training_session import *
  from cntk.logging import ProgressPrinter


  input_dimension = 784
  number_output_classes = 10
  number_hidden_layers = 2
  hidden_layers_dimension=200
  feature_val = Cognitive.input_variable(input_dimension)
  label_val = Cognitive.input_variable(number_output_classes)
```

These types of `input_variable` functions are declared, just like the placeholder variables in TensorFlow. However, Microsoft CNTK eliminates the necessity to identify the number of sample/batch sizes and users can also supply the dimensions for each evaluation sample. In the case of a convolution neural network task, users can assign `input_dimension = (1,28,28)` for a flattened 28 x 28 = 784 pixel input and 10 output labels or classes.

Data readers for CNTK

Microsoft CNTK provides a few helper modules to assist in getting training data into an acceptable format and having it read into the model in a minibatch context. `CTFDeserializer()` is a type of function in CNTK that can read input text files in a special CNTK format (where data comes in a sample per line with a pipe/delimiter). Another one is the `StreamDef()` function, which acts like a dictionary object.

Using the `CTFDeserializer()` function, the CNTK file format is read in the following way:

```
from cntk.io import MinibatchSource, CTFDeserializer, StreamDef, StreamDefs

path =
"C:\\Users\\CNTK\\Examples\\Image\\DataSets\\MNIST\Train-28x28_cntk_text.tx
t"

reader_train_val = MinibatchSource(CTFDeserializer(path, StreamDefs(
  features=StreamDef(field='features', shape=input_dimension),
  labels=StreamDef(field='labels', shape=number_output_classes))))
```

In this function, the `CTFDeserializer()` function defines the path from where the data is to be read. Here, I've used the MNIST dataset, which I've downloaded from the following link: `https://github.com/Microsoft/CNTK/tree/v2.0/Examples/Image/DataSets/MNIST`.

After downloading the dataset, the `install_mnist.py` file should be executed using the following Python command:

```
python install_mnist.py
```

Upon executing this command, the following output files will be available in the training folder for the MNIST dataset:

- `Train-28x28_cntk_text.txt`
- `Test-28x28_cntk_text.txt`

Another argument that's used in this reader operation is the `StreamDefs()` argument, which is a dictionary collection object that assigns a set of keys to different types of `StreamDefs()` objects.

For training purposes, the CNTK object needs to be set up, which can draw some random minibatch samples from the `CTFDeserializer()`. The `MinibatchSource()` is the object and, for utilizing it, `CTFDeseralizer()` can be used as a serializer that can retrieve random minibatch samples from serialized input data models of a particular size that can later be specified in the `training_session()` object. The `MinibatchSource()` object can be defined as follows:

```
reader_train_val = MinibatchSource(CTFDeserializer(path, StreamDefs(
  features=StreamDef(field='features', shape=input_dimension),
  labels=StreamDef(field='labels', shape=number_output_classes))))
```

Operations in CNTK

Similar to TensorFlow, Microsoft CNTK allows operations that are nodes in a computational graph. These nodes and operations provide support for flows. CNTK specifies operations from graph multiplication and division to softmax and convolutional operations. There is a need for the explicit evaluation of the operation code via the `eval()` method on the operation runtime. Though most of these operations are not explicitly evaluated, it's evaluated implicitly during the final layer's network execution.

For example, in the MNIST dataset, a simple CNTK operation is performed to scale input features. This scaling is achieved by using 1/256 ~ 0.00390625:

```
# Instantiate the feed forward classification model
scaled_input = element_times(constant(0.00390625), feature_val)
```

Here, a constant of 0.00390 is declared, as well as the usage of `element_times()` operations for multiplying it by the input variable features. The input dataset is scaled between 0 and 1.

Layers of the Microsoft CNTK

The Microsoft Cognitive Toolkit provides us with the capability to provision neural network layers, which provides many layer features such as Dense, Convolution, MaxPooling, Recurrentm, and LSTM. For example, in an MNIST dataset, the standard neural network classifier consists of some densely connected layers such as the input layer, the first hidden layer, the second hidden layer, and the final output layer:

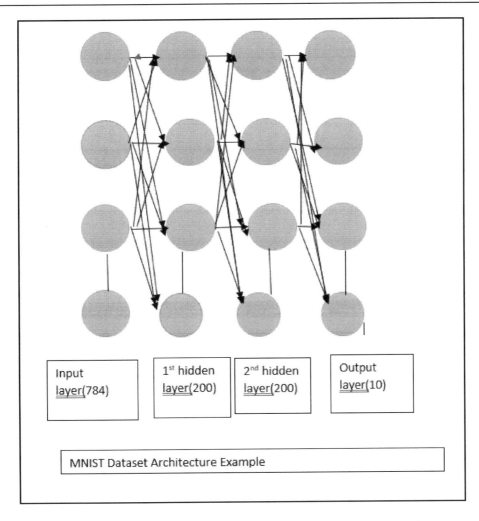

| Input layer(784) | 1ˢᵗ hidden layer(200) | 2ⁿᵈ hidden layer(200) | Output layer(10) |

MNIST Dataset Architecture Example

Fundamentally, the input layer consists of 784 flattened pixel input layers that are proceeded by two hidden layers of size 200 and a final output layer on which a softmax has been activated. The layers are designed as follows:

```
from cntk.layers import Dense, Sequential, For, default_options

with default_options(activation=relu, init=Cognitive.glorot_uniform()):
 z = Sequential([For(range(number_hidden_layers),
 lambda i: Dense(hidden_layers_dimension)),
 Dense(number_output_classes, activation=None)])(scaled_input)
```

For building a densely connected neural network, the Dense() function needs to be declared. The node's activation also has to be defined via rectified linear units or RELU. CNTK manages all relevant neural connections and takes care of input tensor dimensions. It defines the inclusion of weight and bias variables internally, and, unlike TensorFlow, we don't need to declare explicitly.

CNTK layer provision helpers

To make network definitions more streamlined, CNTK provides some helper functions/object classes, such as the Sequential() module, which is similar to the Sequential( ) paradigm in Keras. It also allows you to sequentially stack layer after layer on top without specifying output, which is then passed to the next layer as the input of the next:

```
from cntk.layers import Dense, Sequential, For, default_options

with default_options(activation=relu, init=Cognitive.glorot_uniform()):
 z = Sequential([For(range(number_hidden_layers),

lambda i: Dense(hidden_layers_dimension)),
 Dense(number_output_classes, activation=None)])(scaled_input)
```

There is the presence of the layers.default_options() module in CNTK, which can assist in streamlining, and which is used in more complicated networks. Activation functions are no longer required here, but default_option is used for the output layer since it allows us to apply softmax in the loss function. The same initialization of the glorot_uniform() function is specified in each layer:

```
def simple_mnist():
 input_dimension = 784
 number_output_classes = 10
 number_hidden_layers = 2
 hidden_layers_dimension = 200

# Instantiate the feedforward classification model
 scaled_input = element_times(constant(0.00390625), feature_val)

with default_options(activation=relu, init=Cognitive.glorot_uniform()):
 z = Sequential([For(range(number_hidden_layers),
 lambda i: Dense(hidden_layers_dimension)),
 Dense(number_output_classes, activation=None)])(scaled_input)
```

CNTK modules for losses and error handling

The CNTK library has a full set of loss functions and error handling modules to train the model. This range classifies from standard cross entropy and squared error to cosine distances such as lambda ranks. For classification purposes, the `cross_entropy_with_softmax` option can be applied:

```
ce = cross_entropy_with_softmax(z, label_val)
```

Here, the output layer, `z`, is supplied with a labelled output variable value and the cross entropy loss is calculated with softmax precision on `z`.

Next, for accessing errors on the test set, the training model has to be used. For the classification task, the `classification_error()` function has to be used:

```
pe = classification_error(z, label_val)
```

Input training models in CNTK

CNTK has various options for performing training, such as simply calling a dictionary containing input and output training sets:

```
input_map = {
  feature_val: reader_train_val.streams.features,
  label_val: reader_train_val.streams.labels
  }
```

The `MinibatchSource()` object that's been used here calls `reader_train`, and is where you can access the streams/data by using the dot notation.

A `ProgressPrinter` also needs to be defined, and this is where an object allows you to design output metrices such as loss and classification errors. The progress writers can be instantiated as well:

```
# Instantiate progress writers.
 progress_writers_val = [ProgressPrinter(
 tag='Training',
 num_epochs=number_sweeps_to_train_with)]
```

The `tag` argument specifies the demonstration of a value in the log that's been attached in each update. The total number of epochs during model training is counted by a counter, and is declared by `num_epochs`.

Instantiating the Trainer object

In order to set up the `Trainer` object, we need a module that trains the model and feeds it into a number of information layers, such as the output layer and the prior layer, which is used to train a computational graph structure. Then, we need to utilize the loss function that's going to be used for computing gradients where optimizers such as stochastic descent, and Ada Grad can be used:

```
#Instantiate the trainer object to drive the model training
lr = learning_rate_schedule(1, UnitType.sample)
trainer = Trainer(z, (ce, pe), [adadelta(z.parameters, lr)],
progress_writers_val)
```

Defining the training session object

The CNTK library has a marvellous way of expressing the `training_session()` object and its minibatch initialization. It associates defining the input data, logging, `num_sweeps_to_train`, samples per sweep, and so on:

```
# Training config
minibatch_size_val = 64
number_samples_per_sweep = 60000
number_sweeps_to_train_with = 10

training_session(
trainer=trainer,
mb_source=reader_train_val,
mb_size=minibatch_size_val,
model_inputs_to_streams=input_map,
max_samples=number_samples_per_sweep * number_sweeps_to_train_with,
progress_frequency=number_samples_per_sweep
).train()
```

In this `training_session()` object, all of the optimization and parameter learning is going to occur in the source, and is where we can extract minibatch data that's used as the `reader_main MinibatchSource` object.

Once you execute the training, the output is shown on the progress writer, as shown in the following screenshot:

The CNTK testing model

For testing the CNTK training model, we need to load `Test-28x28_cntk__text.txt` in the path retrieved from the MNIST dataset. We need to set up `MinibatchSource` to read our test data, and we also need to assign input maps to the test data:

```
# Load test data
 path =
"C:\\Users\\CNTK\\Examples\\Image\\DataSets\\MNIST\\Test-28x28_cntk_text.tx
t"

#Reading of data using MinibatchSource
reader_test_val = MinibatchSource(CTFDeserializer(path, StreamDefs(
  features=StreamDef(field='features', shape=input_dimension),
  labels=StreamDef(field='labels', shape=number_output_classes))))

#mapping of input dataset using feature & label
input_map = {
  feature_val: reader_test_val.streams.features,
  label_val: reader_test_val.streams.labels
  }
```

The `MinibatchSource` object used here extracts the minibatch from the reader object by using `next_minibatch()`. This assists in executing a bunch of minibatches from the test dataset to estimate the average classification error. These values can also be fed into minibatch data as batch processes to the trainer object so that you can find the classification error for a particular batch:

```
#Test data for trained model
test_minibatch_size_val = 1024
num_samples = 10000
num_minibatches_to_test = num_samples / test_minibatch_size_val
test_result_cntk_final = 0.0
for i in range(0, int(num_minibatches_to_test)):
 mb = reader_test_val.next_minibatch(test_minibatch_size_val,
input_map=input_map)
 eval_error = trainer.test_minibatch(mb)
 test_result_cntk_final = test_result_cntk_final + eval_error
```

The CNTK operation Python code can be executed in VS Tools for AI on VS code by using the Microsoft DSVM or DLVM, which comes with pre-configured environments, including deep learning environments such as CNTK, Keras, MXNet, TensorFlow, and Caffee2.

The following is a screenshot of running a CNTK simple convolution neural network implementation demo that's been executed on the VS AI platform of Microsoft DLVM:

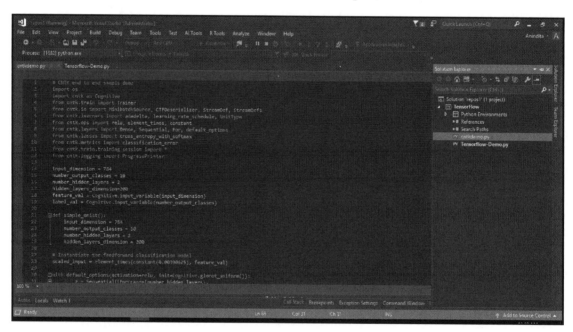

The Microsoft CNTK library can be installed via Python, or via a manual process, in both Windows and Linux environments. The library comes pre-installed with Microsoft Data Science VM and DSVM images. Algorithms with CNTK can be executed in CPU or GPU mode on the cloud by using the NVIDIA Tesla CUDA VM.

 More details regarding setting up CNTK on your machine can be found at the following link: `https://docs.microsoft.com/en-us/cognitive-toolkit/Setup-CNTK-on-your-machine`.

Deploying CNTK tools by using Azure Containers (Docker)

For running CNTK Jupyter Notebooks on Docker containers and pulling CNTK images from Docker, make sure that you use a Linux-based VM or Azure Linux Data Science/DLVM.

The latest build of CNTK can be pulled using a Docker container that's using Azure DSVM via the following command:

```
docker pull microsoft/cntk
```

`docker pull microsoft/cntk:2.6-gpu-python3.6` can be used for a GPU-specific version of Python. The Nvidia-docker driver is required for the execution of GPU versions of CNTK Jupyter Notebooks:

```
anbasa@dsvm-ubuntu: ~
root@dsvm-ubuntu:/home/anbasa# docker pull microsoft/cntk
Using default tag: latest
latest: Pulling from microsoft/cntk
3b37166ec614: Pull complete
504facff238f: Pull complete
ebbcacd28e10: Pull complete
c7fb335lecad: Pull complete
2e3debadcbf7: Pull complete
05448701b97f: Pull complete
5ae481ed00fd: Pull complete
6a7d72f99d0e: Pull complete
ec49014d6ac0: Extracting   325.9MB/473.9MB
20287b0857db: Downloading  8.583MB/62.83MB
ee2b81267240: Downloading  8.583MB/3.85GB
```

To run CNTK Jupyter Notebooks in the Docker container of the Azure Deep Learning VM, the CNTK container needs to be created and started with the IP port exposed in detached mode in the default port `8888:8888`:

```
docker run -d -p 8888:8888 --name cntk-jupyter-notebooks -t microsoft/cntk
```

Then, the following command starts and activates the CNTK for Jupyter Notebooks. You need to expose port `8888` in the **network security group (NSG)** configuration settings for inbound network rules:

```
docker exec -it cntk-jupyter-notebooks bash -c "source /cntk/activate-cntk
andand jupyter-notebook --no-browser --port=8888 --ip=0.0.0.0 --notebook-
dir=/cntk/Tutorials --allow-root"
```

The output screenshot looks like it does in the following image:

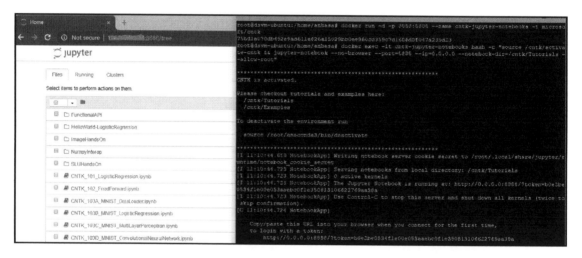

More details on executing CNTK in GPU mode on Docker containers in a Linux environment can be found at the following link: https://docs.microsoft.com/en-us/cognitive-toolkit/CNTK-Docker-Containers.

Keras as a backend for Microsoft CNTK

Keras is a high-level neural network API that's written in Python that abstracts complex configurations and builds production grade training models using matrix algebra. Keras is capable of executing on top of Microsoft CNTK, Google TensorFlow, or Theano, and has been developed with aim of enabling fast experimentation in a sequence or a graph of standalone, fully configurable modules:

- Keras supports both convolutional and recurrent networks and executes on CPU/GPU.
- After CNTK activation, Keras can be simply installed by using `pip`. The `keras.json` file can be used as the backend of CNTK.
- Update `keras.json` at `%USERPROFILE%/.keras` on Windows, or `$HOME/.keras` on Linux:

```
{

    "epsilon": 1e-07,

    "image_data_format": "channels_last",

    "backend": "cntk",

    "floatx": "float32"

}
```

- The environment variables for Windows and Linux are as follows:
    - **Windows**: `set KERAS_BACKEND=cntk`
    - **Linux**: `export KERAS_BACKEND=cntk`

An overview of the Microsoft Machine Learning Library for Apache Spark (MMLSpark)

The Microsoft **Machine Learning Library for Apache Spark** (**MMLSpark**) assists in provisioning scalable machine learning models for large datasets, especially for building deep learning problems. MMLSpark works with SparkML pipelines, including Microsoft CNTK and the OpenCV library, which provide end-to-end support for the ingress and processing of image input data, categorization of images, and text analytics using pre-trained deep learning algorithms. They also train and retrieve scores from classification and regression models by applying featurization.

Environment setup for MMLSpark

The following prerequisites are mandatory for setting up MMLSpark library for deep learning projects on Azure:

- The MMLSpark library can be used with the Azure ML workbench
- MMLSpark can also be integrated with the Azure HDInsight Spark cluster
- Use of a Databricks Cloud
- Use of an Azure GPU VM
- Use of the Spark/pyspark/Scala(SBT) package
- Use of a Docker container

Execution of MMLSpark notebooks using a Docker container

In order to execute MMLSpark Jupyter Notebooks by using a Docker container, you can run the following command in a PowerShell prompt:

```
docker run -d --name my-mmlsparkbook -p 8888:8888 -e ACCEPT_EULA=yes
microsoft/MMLSpark
```

The execution output of the MMLSpark Jupyter Notebook running on a Docker container appear as in the following screenshot:

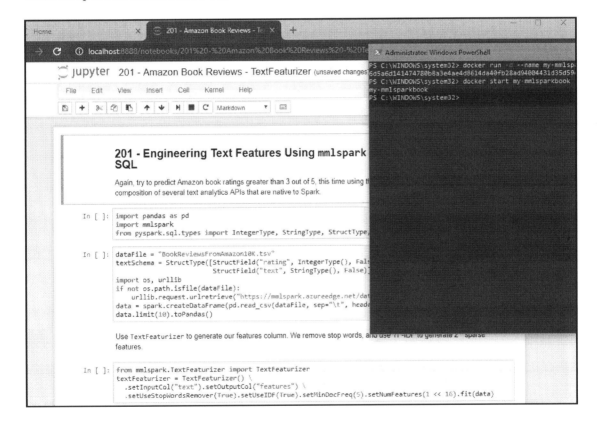

Here, the notebook is tagged with the name `mmlsparkbook` and is accepting the EULA agreement by default. Next, the Docker container needs to be started and activated for `mmlsparkbook`, which opens the MMLSpark notebooks at the following URL: `http://localhost:8888`:

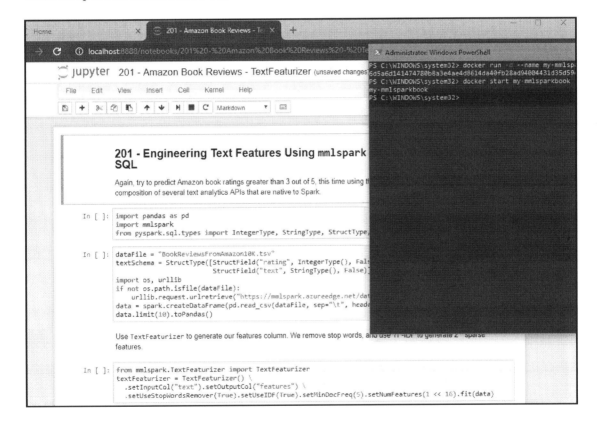

Azure HDInsight Spark cluster setup for MMLSpark

The MMLSpark library can be installed by using an existing Spark cluster and applying the `--packages` options, as follows:

- `spark-shell --packages Azure:MMLSpark:0.13`
- `pyspark --packages Azure:MMLSpark:0.13`
- `spark-submit --packages Azure:MMLSpark:0.13 MyMMLSparkApp.jar`

Similarly, it can be applied for Spark contexts as well, which can be done by using MMLSpark in AZTK in the `.aztk/spark-default.conf` file.

More details on the MMLSpark library can be found at the following GitHub link: `https://github.com/Azure/MMLSpark`.

Overview of TensorFlow on Azure

TensorFlow is an open source, deep learning library that was introduced by Google and is used for solving a range of tasks. TensorFlow was introduced to fulfill the requirement of building and training complex neural networks in order to detect and decipher patterns, recognitions, and correlations, similar to that of the learning process of the human brain. Google introduced the TPU (Tensor Processing Unit) cloud platform for running the TensorFlow Python API and utilizing TensorFlow graph units.

In order to get started on TensorFlow with Azure, the two easiest options are as follows:

- **Using Deep Learning toolkit for Data Science VM (Deep Learning VM)**: Provides a Windows GPU version of mxnet, CNTK, TensorFlow, and Keras that's able to run on a GPU-NC, N-series, or FPGA infrastructure.
- **Using Data Science VM for Azure**: Support for CNTK, TensorFlow, MXNet, Caffe, Caffe2, DIGITS, H2O, Keras, Theano, and PyTorch is installed by default, and has been configured so that it's ready to use along with the support of NVidia CUDA, and cuDNN. Jupyter Notebooks and VS tools with AI are preconfigured as well.

Simple computation graph on TensorFlow

The TensorFlow library is based on computational graphs, such as $a = d * e$, $d = b + c$, and $e = c + 2$, and so this formula can be written as $a = (b+c) * (c+2)$, as shown in the following diagram:

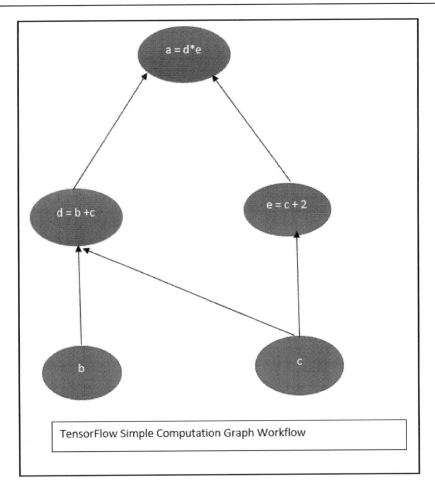

TensorFlow Simple Computation Graph Workflow

The preceding graph computation can be parallelized by executing ($d = b + c$ and $e = c + 2$) and by splitting the calculations on both CPUs and GPUs. For complex deep learning problems, especially in Convolutional Neural Network (CNNs) and **Recurrent Neural Network (RNNs)** architectures, this is essential. The concept behind TensorFlow is to have the capability to provision these computational graphs in code and allow significant performance improvements via parallel operations in order to gain sufficient efficiency.

A simple TensorFlow calculation such as $a = (b+c) * (c+2)$ can be computed using simple declarations of variables and constants:

```
import TensorFlow as tensorf
 import numpy as np
  from TensorFlow.examples.tutorials.mnist import input_data
```

Constants and variables are declared as follows. TensorFlow constants are declared by the `tensorf.constant` function, and variables are declared by the `tensorf.Variable` function:

```
def run_simple_tensorGraph():
 # first lets declare a TensorFlow constant
 constant = tensorf.constant(2.0, name="constant")

 # Next Create TensorFlow variables
 b = tensorf.Variable(2.0, name='b')
 c = tensorf.Variable(2.0, name ='c')
```

TensorFlow allows you to refer to the type of constant/variable from the initialized value, but it can also be set explicitly by using the optional `dtype` argument. TensorFlow also supports `tf.float32`, `tf.int32`, and so on.

TensorFlow operations

TensorFlow supports a bunch of operations so that it can initialize the graph's structure:

```
#Declare few TensorFlow operations
d = tensorf.add(b, c, name='d')
e = tensorf.add(c, 2, nname='e')
a = tensorf.multiply(d, e, nname='a')

#setup the initialization of variables
init_operation = ttensorf.global_variable_initializer()
```

In order to run the operations between the variables, we need to start a TensorFlow session, such as `tensorf.Session`. The TensorFlow session is an object where all such operations can run. In the TensorFlow session `run` function, the operation initializes variables that need to be initialized. Next is an operation. This needs to be run and can be executed with the `tfsess.run(a)` command. We can assign the output to `a_graphout` so that it can be printed:

```
#Start the Tensorflow Session
 with tensorf.Session() as tfsess:
 #initialize the variables
 tfsess.run(init_operation)
 #computation of the output from the graph
 a_graphOut = tfsess.run(a)
 print("Variable a is the value of {}".format(a_graphOut))
```

Declaration of the TensorFlow placeholder

TensorFlow assigns the basic structure of data by using a placeholder variable declaration such as the following:

```
def run_simple_tensorGraph_multiple():
 #first lets create a constant for TensorFlow
 constant = tensorf.constant(2.0, name="constant")

#Next create those TensorFlow variables
 b = tensorf.placeholder(tensorf.float32,[None, 1], NameError='b')
 c = tensorf.Variable(1.0, name='c')
```

Neural Network Formation using TensorFlow

TensorFlow specifies the Neural Network Formation for solving complex real-life problems, especially on CNNs or RNNS. For example, we can use the MNIST dataset TensorFlow package, where the dataset contains a 28 x 28 pixel grayscale image with approximately 55k rows, 10k testing rows, and 5k validation handwritten digit rows:

```
def nn_example():
 mnist = input_data.read_data_sets("MNIST_data/", one_hot=True)

# Python optimisation variables
 learning_rate = 0.5
 epochs = 10
 batch_size = 100
```

For training data and parameters, the placeholder variables can be provisioned:

```
# declare the training data placeholders
# input x - for 28 x 28 pixels = 784
x = tensorf.placeholder(tensorf.float32, [None, 784])
# now declare the output data placeholder - 10 digits
y = tensorf.placeholder(tensorf.float32, [None, 10])
```

Here, the x input data layer consists of 28 x 28 = 784 pixels and y nodes like 10 digits. Also, for a neural network, the weight and bias also need to be initialized. In TensorFlow, there is the possibility of an L-1 number of weights/bias tensors or graphs:

```
# now declare the weights connecting the input to the hidden layer
 W1 = tensorf.Variable(tensorf.random_normal([784, 300], stddev=0.03),
name='W1')
 b1 = tensorf.Variable(tensorf.random_normal([300]), name='b1')
 # and the weights connecting the hidden layer to the output layer
 W2 = tensorf.Variable(tensorf.random_normal([300, 10], stddev=0.03),
```

```
name='W2')
 b2 = tensorf.Variable(tensorf.random_normal([10]), name='b2')
```

First, we need to declare some variables for `W1` and `b1` for the weights and bias for the connections between the input and hidden layer, where the neural network will have 300 nodes in the hidden layer. The size of the weight tensor, `W1`, is `[784, 300]`. Similarly, TensorFlow supports the NumPy random normal function, which assigns to provision a matrix of a given size that's populated with random samples. In a similar manner, the weight variable, `W2`, and the bias variable, `b2`, connect the hidden layer to the output of the neural network.

The output of the hidden layer is calculated by using the `relu` function (by applying the rectified linear unit):

```
# calculate the output of the hidden layer
hidden_out = tensorf.add(tensorf.matmul(x, W1), b1)
hidden_out = tensorf.nn.relu(hidden_out)
```

The weight multiplication with the output from the hidden layer, and the addition of a `b2` bias value, is applied by using the softmax activation for the output layer. This can be found via the TensorFlow softmax function `tf.nn.softmax`:

```
# now calculate the hidden layer output – in this case, let's use a
softmax activated
# output layer
y_ = tensorf.nn.softmax(tensorf.add(tensorf.matmul(hidden_out, W2), b2))
```

For the optimizer, we need to include a cost or loss function. The cross entropy cost function is used for this purpose. Here is how we set up the optimizer in TensorFlow:

```
# add an optimiser
 optimiser =
tensorf.train.GradientDescentOptimizer(learning_rate=learning_rate).minimiz
e(cross_entropy)
```

The gradient descent optimizer is supplied by TensorFlow alongside a learning rate that's used to specify the minimized cross entropy cost operation that has been provisioned. The function is going to perform gradient descent and back propagation as follows:

```
# finally setup the initialisation operator
 init_operation = tensorf.global_variables_initializer()

# define an accuracy assessment operation
 correct_prediction = tensorf.equal(tensorf.argmax(y, 1),
tensorf.argmax(y_, 1))
 accuracy = tensorf.reduce_mean(tensorf.cast(correct_prediction,
```

```
tensorf.float32))

# add a summary to store the accuracy
  tensorf.summary.scalar('accuracy', accuracy)

merged = tensorf.summary.merge_all()
  writer = tensorf.summary.FileWriter('c:\\users\\anbasa\\source\\repos')
```

The correct prediction operation provides `correct_prediction`, which utilizes TensorFlow. `tensorf.equal` provides a true/false reading depending on the arguments of the Boolean value. `tensorf.argmax` works in the same way as the NumPy `argmax` function, since it returns the index of the maximum value in a particular tensor or vector.

Henceforth, the `correct_prediction` operation assigns a tensor of size (mx1) true or false, designating whether the neural network is correctly predicting the digit value.

TensorFlow training

For provisioning the TensorFlow training, first, the TensorFlow session needs to be set up and initialize the variables.

It also provides the details from a minibatch training scheme that can be executed for the neural network. It also calculates the number of batches to run through in each epoch by calculating each training epoch and initializing an `avg_cost` variable. TensorFlow supplies an MNIST dataset that has a utility function, such as `next_batch`, which makes it easier to extract batches of training data:

```
# start the session
  with tensorf.Session() as tfsess:
  # initialise the variables
  tfsess.run(init_operation)
  total_batch = int(len(mnist.train.labels) / batch_size)
  for epoch in range(epochs):
  avg_cost = 0
  for i in range(total_batch):
  batch_x, batch_y = mnist.train.next_batch(batch_size=batch_size)
  _, c = tfsess.run([optimiser, cross_entropy], feed_dict={x: batch_x, y:
batch_y})
  avg_cost += c / total_batch
  print("Epoch:", (epoch + 1), "cost =", "{:.3f}".format(avg_cost))
  summary = tfsess.run(merged, feed_dict={x: mnist.test.images, y:
mnist.test.labels})
  writer.add_summary(summary, epoch)

print("\nTraining complete!")
```

```
writer.add_graph(tfsess.graph)
print(tfsess.run(accuracy, feed_dict={x: mnist.test.images, y:
mnist.test.labels}))
```

The output of the TensorFlow Neural Network code is executed via VS tools for AI on a Microsoft data science VM using GPU. It shows the progress in terms of the average cost, and while the training is being completed, the accuracy operation to retrieve the accuracy of the trained network in each epoch is used:

```
C:\Anaconda\python.exe                                                    —    □    ×
Please use tf.one_hot on tensors.
Extracting MNIST_data/t10k-images-idx3-ubyte.gz
Extracting MNIST_data/t10k-labels-idx1-ubyte.gz
WARNING:tensorflow:From C:\Anaconda\lib\site-packages\tensorflow\contrib\learn\python\learn\datasets\mnist.py:290: DataS
et.__init__ (from tensorflow.contrib.learn.python.learn.datasets.mnist) is deprecated and will be removed in a future ve
rsion.
Instructions for updating:
Please use alternatives such as official/mnist/dataset.py from tensorflow/models.
2018-09-23 11:14:56.945713: I T:\src\github\tensorflow\tensorflow\core\platform\cpu_feature_guard.cc:140] Your CPU suppo
rts instructions that this TensorFlow binary was not compiled to use: AVX2
2018-09-23 11:14:57.329082: E T:\src\github\tensorflow\tensorflow\stream_executor\cuda\cuda_driver.cc:406] failed call t
o cuInit: CUDA_ERROR_UNKNOWN
2018-09-23 11:14:57.339371: I T:\src\github\tensorflow\tensorflow\stream_executor\cuda\cuda_diagnostics.cc:158] retrievi
ng CUDA diagnostic information for host: dsvm-packt
2018-09-23 11:14:57.346002: I T:\src\github\tensorflow\tensorflow\stream_executor\cuda\cuda_diagnostics.cc:165] hostname
: dsvm-packt
Epoch: 1 cost = 0.605
Epoch: 2 cost = 0.237
Epoch: 3 cost = 0.173
Epoch: 4 cost = 0.140
Epoch: 5 cost = 0.115
Epoch: 6 cost = 0.096
Epoch: 7 cost = 0.086
Epoch: 8 cost = 0.069
Epoch: 9 cost = 0.065
Epoch: 10 cost = 0.051

Training complete!
0.9788
Press any key to continue . . .
```

By way of an approximation, ~98% accuracy comes out of TensorFlow, which can be further improved by using regularization and over fitting, selecting the correct parameters (via a brute-force search example), and speeding up the training process.

The Accuracy function is used to calculate how often predictions match with the labels based on two local variables such as `total` and `count`, while the `whereas` accuracy operation is used to update the metrics.

Execution of TensorFlow on Azure using Docker container services

TensorFlow can be executed using Docker container services on top of Azure Linux virtual machines. The endpoint needs to be exposed in the NSG port 8888, and the following command, which initializes a Docker container running TensorFlow inside a Jupyter Notebook, needs to be executed:

```
docker run –d –p 8888:8888 –v /notebook:/notebook xblaster/TensorFlow-
jupyter
```

Running TensorFlow containers on an Azure Kubernetes Cluster (AKS)

A sample Kubernetes cluster on the **Azure container service (AKS)** is provisioned by using the open source toolkit DLWorkspace (https://microsoft.github.io/DLWorkspace/). The repository provides standard Azure VMs on CPU/GPU. The sample k8 cluster and Alluxio-FUSE-enabled k8 pods can be created.

The sample pod configuration is available at the following GitHub link: https://github.com/jichang1/TensorFlowonAzure/tree/master/ Alluxio.

TensorFlow jobs can be executed on the parameter server pods and worker pods by using the following commands:

```
python tf_cnn_benchmarks.py --local_parameter_device=gpu --num_gpus=2  --
batch_size=128  --model=googlenet  --variable_update=parameter_server --
num_batches=50  --cross_replica_sync=False  --data_name=imagenet --
data_dir=file:///alluxio-fuse/  --job_name=ps --ps_hosts=10.255.2.2:2222  -
-worker_hosts=10.255.0.2:2222 --task_index=0
```

Other deep learning libraries

Microsoft provides samples of deep learning tools across Theano, Caffe, MXNet, Chainer, PyTorch, and Keras on datasets such as MNIST and CIFAR10. The following are the prerequisites to run these samples:

- You need Visual Studio 2017 with VS tools for AI and the MNIST dataset. The VS tools for AI are available to download from **Extensions and Updates** under **Tools**:

- An NVIDIA GPU driver/CUDA 9.0/cuDNN 7.0, as applicable, and Python 3.5/3.6. Python 2.x is still not supported (as of the time of writing).
- The deep learning libraries that need to be installed include NumPy, SciPy, Matplotlib, ONNX, CNTK, TensorFlow, Caffe2 , MXNet, Keras, theano, and PyTorch:

- The GitHub link for the AI samples repository is available at `https://github.com/Microsoft/samples-for-ai`.
- **Apache MXNet**: Apache MXNet is a scalable deep learning library that's used to train and deploy deep neural networks that are available to scale across GPU or CPU. MXNet offers support for Azure. More details on MXNet are available at `https://mxnet.incubator.apache.org/`.
- **Caffe**: This deep learning framework provides expressions, speed, scalability, modularity, openness, and huge community support for building and training complex neural networks. Caffe 2.0 is pre-installed in Azure Deep Learning toolkits and DSVM.
- **Theano**: This is a Python-based deep learning library that's used for the evaluation of complex mathematical, statistical expressions by using the NumPy-esque syntax and is compiled by using CPU/GPU architectures.
- **Pytorch**: Pytorch is again a Python-based scientific computing framework that's used for Numpy executions on GPU and Deep Learning interactive research. Pytorch allows for interactive debugging with clean dynamic graphs with a mixture of high-level and low-level API support. This works for **Artificial Neural Networks (ANNs)**, Regression, and **Convolution Neural Networks (CNNs)**.
- **Chainer**: An open source deep learning library based on Python that's used for NumPy and CuPy `libraries.supports` CUDA implementations and intuitive, flexible DL frameworks that allow the use of feed-forward nets, convnets, recurrent nets, and recursive nets. More details can be found at `https://chainer.org/`.

Summary

In this chapter, we have learned about deep learning methodology and the tools that are supported on the Microsoft Azure AI platform. We have demonstrated various AI tools, such as CNTK, MMLSpark, and TensorFlow, as well as its execution process on Azure deep learning toolkits/data science VMs, along with other open source deep learning libraries and utilities.

In the next chapter, we will be looking at a step-by-step overview of integrating other Azure services with the Microsoft AI platform.

11
Integration with Other Azure Services

In addition to using Azure AI services directly, Azure also provides options for using these services from other non-AI services. Many Azure AI services provide REST API interfaces that can be consumed from other services. AI services can thus be used as subcomponents of other apps to provide insights and predictions. Many non-AI services in Azure have built-in integration with AI services, so that AI components can often be added to apps with a few clicks.

Some AI services do not include any automation features. Recurring tasks, such as retraining ML models or running batch workloads, require integration with other services that offer these features. In the following sections, we will present various options for launching AI jobs automatically. In addition to traditional time-scheduled workloads, Azure services also provide objects called triggers to launch tasks after a certain event has occurred. Triggers allow services to react to events in a specific way, for example, processing the contents of a blob file after it has been created or modified.

In this chapter, we will learn how to integrate Azure AI services with four non-AI services:

- Logic Apps
- Azure Functions
- Data Lake Analytics
- Data Factory

With these services, it is possible to build complex application pipelines where the ML model is just a part of the solution. In Azure, integration between different services is made as easy as possible, without compromising security. Getting results is therefore quick and efficient, and developing Azure applications can be a lot of fun!

Logic Apps

Azure Logic Apps is a graphical tool for automating various types of tasks, such as getting data from a Web API and saving it in cloud storage. Logic Apps can be developed without writing a single line of code, so no programming skills are required. However, Logic Apps provides some basic functionality for programming languages, such as conditional execution and iterative loops.

Logic Apps is meant for light-weight tasks that do not require complex logic or lightning-fast performance. Such tasks could include sending an email when a SharePoint list is modified, or copying files between Dropbox and OneDrive if the files have been modified.

For AI development, Logic Apps provides a number of basic functionalities. There are built-in modules for Cognitive Services APIs and Azure Machine Learning Studio Web Services APIs. In combination with storage triggers, it is possible to develop simple data pipelines with data movement and ML scoring steps. Logic Apps are developed with the Logic Apps Designer, a web-based graphical editor. The designer can be accessed from the Logic Apps resource in the Azure portal by clicking **Edit**, as follows:

Logic Apps contains a wide range of templates for various tasks. These templates are a good starting point for developing your own apps.

Triggers and actions

Logic Apps is based on two main concepts: triggers and actions. Triggers are listeners that are constantly waiting for a specific kind of event. These events could be created when a new file is created in a `Blob` folder, or they could occur every day at the same time to automate daily tasks. Actions are routines that are executed every time the trigger fires. Actions usually take some input data, process it, and finally, save or send the result somewhere.

Logic Apps supports all Azure Data Storage services: Data Lake Storage, Blob Storage, Cosmos DB, and so on. For example, the **Blob Storage** trigger executes Logic Apps every time a new file is added to a directory or a file in the directory is modified. We can then take the file as input to Logic Apps, process the contents of the file, and save the results back to the Blob.

The Logic Apps Designer contains many Cognitive Services actions: the **Computer Vision API**, **Custom Vision**, **Text Analytics**, and so on. To see the full list, search for the cognitive actions when creating an action, as follows:

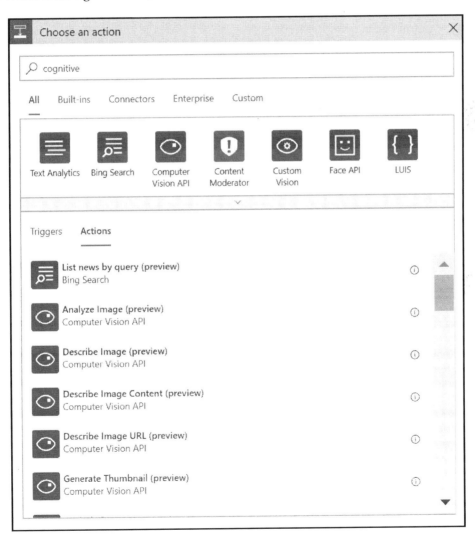

There are also a few Azure Machine Learning Studio actions. These can be used to score examples or retrain ML models, as follows:

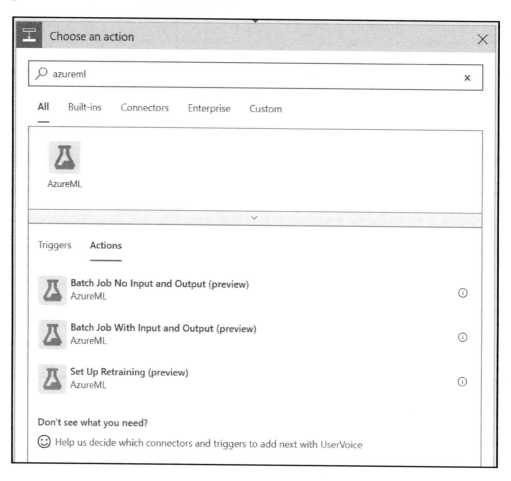

The connectors might have been updated since the time of writing, so check the latest information in the official documentation from Microsoft.

Twitter sentiment analysis

Social media has become an everyday tool for many organizations. In addition to advertising themselves on these platforms, monitoring discussions about a company brand provides important information about how customers see its products and the image of the company.

In this section, we'll show how to create an app that reads tweets containing the keyword *Azure* and saves those tweets in cloud storage. This is a real-world data acquisition scenario: once the tweets get stored in the cloud permanently, we have started to collect history data about the company's brand. As a next step, we could start creating analytics and machine learning models based on this data. These models could include topic analysis or looking for users who have a big influence on opinions, for example.

To complete this example, you will need a Twitter account, the Azure Cognitive Services Text Analytics API, and an Azure Storage account. The Twitter account is needed for reading tweets from the Twitter API. The Text Analytics API performs the actual sentiment analysis, and the Storage account is used to store the tweets in the cloud permanently.

Once you have created a Logic App in the Azure portal, open the Logic Apps Designer and choose the **When a new tweet appears** trigger to start developing your app. Provide your Twitter account details to connect to Twitter. You also need to specify how often Logic Apps will call the Twitter API to get new tweets. The default is 3 minutes.

After the Twitter trigger has been configured, we can add actions to the pipeline by clicking the **New step** button. The Twitter trigger produces a stream of tweets that can be processed further or saved to permanent storage. In this example, we perform sentiment analysis on the tweets. In other words, we try to understand whether the tweet has a negative or positive tone. For example, if someone has been unsatisfied with our company's service, they might tweet angry feedback that would be counted as a negative tweet.

Similarly, another user could tweet a recommendation for our company because they received good customer service, which would be considered a positive tweet.

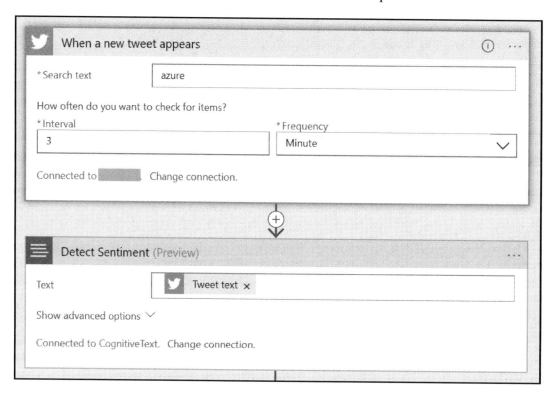

Before proceeding, make sure that you have the Cognitive Services Text Analytics API set up and running in Azure. Then, follow these steps to create the Logic App pipeline:

1. Add a new **Text Analytics Sentiment Detection** action module after the trigger.
2. Clicking on the **Text** field in the new module, you should see a list of parameters. Note that the Twitter API response contains a lot of other information besides the tweet text and the tweeter's user name.
3. For the **Text** field, we choose the **Tweet text** parameter to be analyzed by the text analytics API.
4. We want to store the results of the sentiment analysis in the cloud. In this example, we use Blob Storage as the permanent storage facility.
5. To save the results in the Blob, add the **Create Blob** action after the **Text Analytics** action.
6. Configure the blob module according to your environment, and choose the parameters that you wish to store in the blob file.

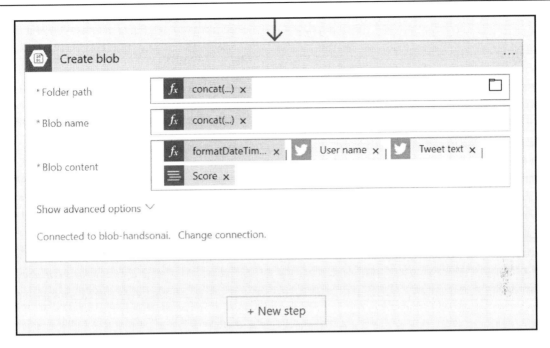

With these steps, we have achieved the end result. We have set up an app that reads tweets periodically, performs sentiment analysis on the tweets, and saves the results to cloud storage.

Note that in the last module (**Create blob**), we have set dynamic expressions for the fields. It is usually good to distribute the blob files in separate directories, according to time, for example, in our example, we store all the tweets for a single day in the same directory. This can be achieved with the following expression:

```
concat('handsonai/twitter/', formatDateTime(utcNow(), 'yyyy-MM-dd'))
```

The preceding expression creates a blob directory for each day under the base directory handsonai/Twitter, using a flat hierarchy (all months and years in the same folder). For the date, we used the UTC timestamp, which is produced when the Logic App processes the file.

The blob filename is also parameterized according to time. We also add a unique identifier for the tweet, which is returned by the Twitter API:

```
concat(formatDateTime(utcNow(), 'yyyy-MM-dd_HH-mm'), '-',
body('Detect_Sentiment')?['id'], '.csv')
```

For the blob content, we have chosen the `timestamp,` `tweeter username,` `tweet text,` and `tweet sentiment score` (a number between 0 and 1) fields. Note that, here, the pipe | character has been used to separate the fields in the CSV file, instead of a comma. This is handy since the tweets contain a lot of commas.

Once you save the app, it will be started and the trigger will start listening to events. After a while, you should start to see new files in the destination folder. Each file should contain a single tweet in the following format:

```
2018-09-21 11:10:58|azure_rivers|RT @toonzone: Watch: Space Dandy: Episode
7 -- Dandy Does Combat (Clip) ... https://t.co/FxkiSwTglo
https://t.co/hUcbmYSzR9|0.5
```

We can see that the file contains the timestamp, the user name, the tweet text, and the sentiment score separated by the pipe character, as we specified earlier. The sentiment score is a number between 0 and 1, where 0 indicates a completely negative tweet, and 1 a completely positive tweet. In the preceding case, the sentiment detection model seems to think that the tweet text is completely neutral, since the score given is exactly halfway between positive and negative.

This concludes our example: we have set up a periodic data fetch that reads tweets, uses cognitive services to get a sentiment score for each tweet, and finally, saves the tweet and the score in cloud storage.

Note that your app will consume the Azure resource bill every time a tweet is processed. You might want to disable your app from the portal after you are finished experimenting with it. This way, the app will not be deleted and you can continue development later. Disabling the app will stop the pipeline, but it can be restarted anytime by clicking the **Enable** button.

Adding language detection

In the previous example, we created a workflow that reads tweets with a specific keyword, performs sentiment analysis on them, and saves the results in Blob Storage. If you completed the example and looked at the results more carefully, you might have noticed that the tweets can contain many different languages, because our keyword (Azure) is not specific to any language. In this example, we show how to add language detection to the pipeline and filter out all tweets that are not in a particular language.

1. To begin the example, create a new Logic App in the Azure portal, open the Logic Apps Designer, and choose the same trigger as a starting point as we did in the previous example (when a new tweet appears).

2. Add the Detect Language module from the Text Analytics API. For the **Text** field, choose the **Tweet text** parameter to be analyzed by the Text Analytics API. The output of this module will contain the list of languages detected from the tweet. Note that the default number of detected languages is 1. This can be changed in the advanced options for the module, if the text is expected to contain more than one language:

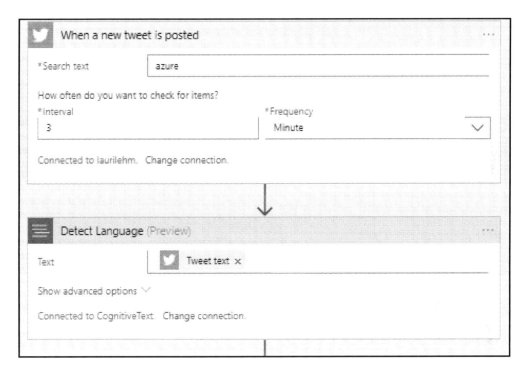

3. Once the tweet language has been detected, we need to add a module that chooses only tweets that are in a certain language. For this purpose, create a new step in the pipeline, search for `Control` actions and choose the `Condition` action.

4. When the `Condition` module has been added to the pipeline, we must specify the filter condition using the three fields in the module. The first field indicates which value we would like to compare, the second field specifies the condition type, and the last field contains the value against which to compare. For the first field, choose the `detectedLanguages` item. Note that the detect language module returns the languages as a list, even if we are only detecting one language. The `detectedLanguages` item refers to each item in this list. Therefore, the Logic Apps Designer will add a new `For each` control module to the pipeline and the previously created `Condition` module will be placed inside the `For each` module. The `For each` module iterates through all the values in the `detectedLanguages` list, if there is more than one language detected.

5. Now that our `Condition` module is placed inside the `For each` module, we can change the first field of the `Condition` module to `Language code`. The second field should be set to `is equal to` and the last field should contain the two-letter language code. To keep English language tweets only, we set the parameter to `en`. Note that the language detection module might not be able to detect all languages, so check the list of available languages in the latest Microsoft documentation.

6. After the condition module, the pipeline now branches into two directions, depending on whether the condition is `true` or not. In the `true` branch, we can add any processing steps for the English language tweets. In the `false` branch, we can specify what to do with the rest of the tweets. In this example, we use the sentiment detection pipeline that was developed in the previous example to process the English language tweets. We are not interested in the non-English tweets, so we can just ignore them by leaving the false branch empty. After completing all these steps, the pipeline appears as follows:

Once you save the app, the trigger will start to run and the tweets will be saved to the Blob. Since we used the same modules for sentiment detection as we did in the previous example, the format of the files should be identical, with the exception that only English tweets are saved to the Blob.

Azure Functions

While Logic Apps provides a fast way to automate tasks, its collection of actions is limited to pre-selected options that cannot be customized. Moreover, the programmability of Logic Apps is quite limited, and the development of more complex programs is not necessarily any easier than writing code. If more flexibility is needed, it might be more productive to develop applications with Azure Functions. Functions can be developed with multiple programming languages familiar to web developers.

Azure Functions is a serverless coding platform in the cloud, where the underlying operating system has been virtualized. This means that many maintenance tasks, such as updating the operating system or language versions, is managed by the platform and the user does not need to worry about those tasks. On the other hand, the user cannot change the language version used by the system, so breaking changes in the language specification can also break the application unless the code is accommodated to the new version.

This platform provides a complete programming environment for web applications. It can be used to automate many backend tasks, and even to create simple backend APIs for web apps. Using native and external libraries, the Functions app can connect to a wide variety of services both in Azure and in external networks. Load balancing is also managed by the platform, so that resources are scaled up automatically if the application receives unexpectedly high traffic.

Azure Functions can be developed with three different development environments: the Azure portal, VS Code and Visual Studio. The Azure portal experience is convenient for small scripts and tests, but it lacks many features of proper code editors. To develop Azure Functions in VS Code, you must install the Azure Functions extension from the **Extensions** tab in the left-hand menu:

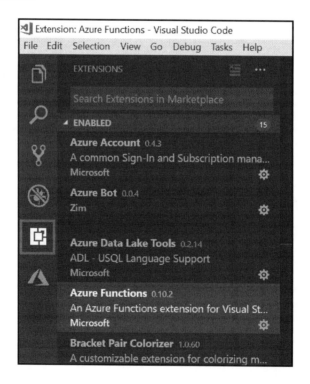

This will allow you to develop and deploy Azure Functions inside VS Code, without visiting the Azure portal. For Visual Studio, install the Azure Functions tools to get the same functionality.

The languages currently available in Azure Functions v2 are C#, F#, and JavaScript. Java is in preview phase in Azure Functions v2, but is not available in v1. Perhaps the biggest drawback of using Azure Functions for AI development is the lack of Python support. Python support was an experimental feature in Azure Functions v1, but there is no availability in v2 at the time of writing. Check the latest updates in the official Microsoft documentation. If you need to use AI features inside a C# function, consider the Cognitive Services libraries or the ML.NET package provided by Microsoft.

There are two ways to develop Azure Functions with C#: C# scripts (`.csx` files) and C# class libraries (`.cs` files). If you create a new function in the Azure portal, it will be created as a C# script that can be edited directly in the portal. C# class files can be created with IDE tools (VS Code or Visual Studio). There are some subtle differences between these ways of working, but they will not be discussed here.

With its versatile integration features, Azure Functions can be easily incorporated into various Azure services. For example, Logic Apps can call Azure Functions to perform some calculations that are too complex for Logic Apps to handle. Azure Functions provides a lightweight platform for performing small and modular tasks, without having to worry about the underlying server infrastructure.

Triggers

Azure Functions triggers work with the same principle as the Logic Apps triggers introduced in the previous section: they listen to a certain event and initiate the function every time the event occurs. For example, an HTTP trigger executes the function every time the web URL of the function is called. A schedule trigger can execute the function periodically, for example, once a day. One of the biggest strengths of Azure Functions is the trigger collection. The trigger collection allows you to respond to many different types of events, and the code-based approach makes it possible to react to those events with the full flexibility of programming languages.

For data-related tasks, the most useful triggers are the storage triggers. Similar to how Logic Apps can be triggered on blob events, Azure Functions can be triggered when files are added or updated in storage services such as Blob Storage or Cosmos DB. Consider a scheme where raw data is stored in the cloud, for example, JSON files that are produced by a web app, and we wish to convert those files into a columnar format to add them to a relational database, for example. Using Azure Functions with Blob Storage triggers, this task can be fully automated without any external services. Thus, Azure Functions provides another way to perform such format conversions, among other things.

One of the most interesting applications for Azure Functions is processing data from **Internet of Things (IoT)** devices. With event hub and IoT hub triggers, Azure Functions can be used as a downstream processing engine for data sent by IoT devices. The event hub and IoT Hub resources in Azure are data ingestion services that are capable of handling a large number of requests in a short time interval. They are designed for continuous data streams where the size of each message is small, but the number of messages can be large. Therefore, they are ideal services for receiving data from an array of IoT sensors that send their measurements in short intervals. The event hub and IoT hub triggers are set to fire every time a new event is received from the IoT devices, so we can use Azure Functions to define a processing routine for each event. This routine could include a scoring call to a machine learning service and saving the results in a database, for example.

For most trigger types, the trigger also passes some information about the event that fired the trigger. For example, a Blob Storage trigger passes the contents of the file that was created or changed, or a HTTP trigger passes the contents of a POST request. Handling different types of input data is made very simple in Azure Functions: depending on the source, a handle to the input data is passed as a parameter to the main function. In the following section, we will show an example how to read the contents of a blob file after the blob trigger has been fired.

Blob-triggered function

In this example, we'll demonstrate how to create a simple function that reads the contents of a blob file. We will not do any processing on the file; instead, we'll just print its contents in a log file.

When you create an Azure Functions service in the portal, it will create a number of resources in addition to the functions app itself. A storage account is needed to store logs produced by the functions app. The app service plan is a container resource that determines the pricing and the resource scaling of the app. Optionally, you can also create an app insights resource for monitoring your app usage. This is particularly useful for error analysis and tracking how often your app is triggered.

To begin development, first create a function app in the Azure portal. To create a new function, go to the newly created **Functions Apps** blade, choose **Functions** from the left-hand menu and press **New function**, as follows:

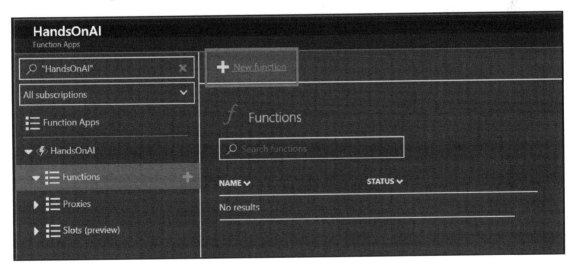

A list of triggers should appear on the screen. Choose the **Blob trigger** template to begin with. Configure the function according to your preferences, as follows:

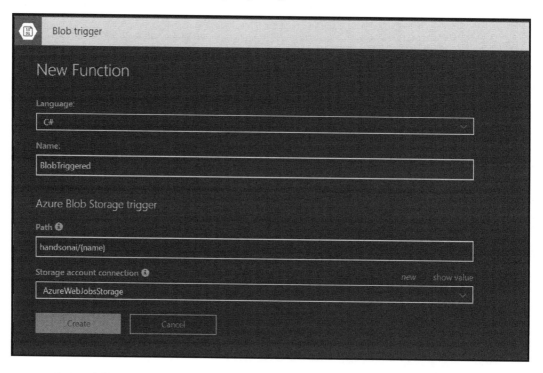

The **Path** parameter indicates the `blob` directory that we would like to monitor. In the preceding example, we are monitoring the `handsonai` subdirectory. Leave the `name` parameter as it is; it is a placeholder for the filename inside the directory. The filename parameter will be passed on to the function and it will be replaced by the name of the file that has been created or modified.

The storage account connection determines the Blob Storage account where the blob container resides. If you are using the same storage account that was created with the function app, you can just pick the default value from the drop-down menu. Otherwise, you have to specify a new connection for your storage account. Note that the storage account must be in the same geographical region as the Azure Functions service in order to use the blob trigger.

Clicking on **Create** initiates the function and opens the portal code editor. By default, the code should include a Run function with the following signature:

```
public static void Run(Stream myBlob, string name, TraceWriter log)
```

The Run function is the main entry point to the script. It is executed every time the trigger is fired; in this case, every time a file is created or modified in the directory monitored by the trigger. The script could also include other functions, but they are not executed unless called from inside the Run function.

The myBlob parameter contains the blob file contents as a stream object, which can be read in segments. This is especially handy for large files that do not fit in the processor memory. The name parameter contains the filename of the blob and log is an object that allows you to write diagnostic information to the application log. The log is stored in the Storage account associated with the Function app. If you run the function from the Azure portal, the log can be viewed from the context menus.

Note that the myBlob and name parameters are specific to the blob trigger. For different triggers, the input parameters would be different as well. The void keyword means that the function has no return value. In principle, the function could have a return value as well, for example, a status code returned with an HTTP response.

Next, replace the default function contents with the following script:

```
public static void Run(Stream myBlob, string name, TraceWriter log)
{
    log.Info($"Started processing blob {name} ({myBlob.Length} bytes)");
    var bufferLength = 1000;
    var buffer = new byte[bufferLength];
    myBlob.Read(buffer, 0, bufferLength);
    var fileContent = System.Text.Encoding.Default.GetString(buffer);
    log.Info($"File contents:\n{fileContent}");
}
```

The preceding function prints the blob name, the blob size in bytes, and the first 1,000 bytes of the blob. To print to the log, we use the log.Info() method. Note that there is no console output when we run the function in the cloud, so we must use the log to get any output from the program.

The `Stream.Read()` method is where we actually read the contents of the blob. Here, we do not use the return value of the method, which is just the number of bytes read from the file. The method does not return the contents of the blob as a return value; rather, it fills the `buffer` variable with the contents of the blob. In the preceding example, only the first 1000 bytes of the blob are read to the memory. This is to ensure that we do not end up filling up the memory if the file is very large. To process the whole contents of the file, a loop should be added to the function that reads the file contents in batches. The size of each batch would be determined by the `bufferLength` variable. This way, the memory footprint of the app would be constant, not dependent on the size of the input file.

When the script is saved, the log should show that the function has been compiled successfully. Now, creating a new file in the directory that is tracked by the blob trigger will trigger the function. For example, using a sample of the well-known Iris dataset, the log should show something similar to the following output:

```
2018-09-17T21:05:12.763 [Info] Started processing blob iris.csv (85 bytes)
2018-09-17T21:05:12.810 [Info] File contents:
5.1,3.5,1.4,0.2,Iris-setosa
4.9,3.0,1.4,0.2,Iris-setosa
4.7,3.2,1.3,0.2,Iris-setosa
```

In this case, the `iris.csv` input file contains only three lines (85 bytes), which fits in the buffer (1,000 bytes). If the file size was larger than the buffer size, only the contents that fit in the buffer would be printed.

Once you are finished playing with the function, you can disable it from the **Functions** tab, as follows:

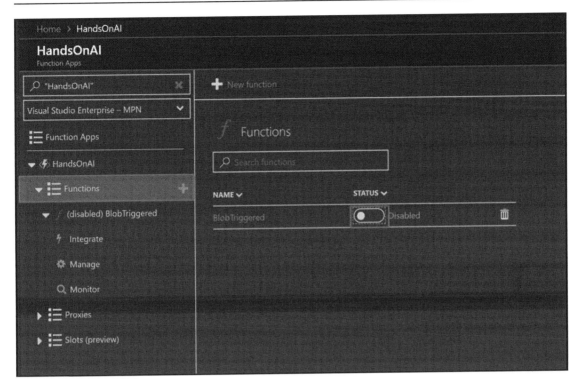

This way, the function will not consume any resources, but the code will be stored for later use.

In summary, we have created a function that tracks a certain blob directory and fires every time that files in the directory are created or modified. Note that the Function is billed by usage, so costs may become high if files are created in the directory with high rate by external applications. This might happen for example in IoT scenarios, where sensors send small events in short intervals, and a new file is created for each event.

Azure Data Lake Analytics

Azure Data Lake (ADL) is Microsoft's storage and analytics service for big data. It is capable of storing data on a petabyte scale and making efficient queries on the stored data. The storage and the analytics services are separate in Azure and the ADL service actually consists of two different products: **Azure Data Lake Storage** (ADLS) and **Azure Data Lake Analytics** (ADLA). In this section, we will focus on ADLA, but we will also touch on ADLS where appropriate.

Data Lake Storage is a file-based storage, with files organized into directories. This type of storage is called schemaless, since there are no constraints on what type of data can be stored in the Data Lake. Directories can contain text files and images, and the data type is specified only when the data is read out from the Data Lake. This is particularly useful in big data scenarios where the amount of data written to the Data Lake is large and running the data validation steps on the fly would be too resource-consuming. The data validation steps can be incorporated in the queries later when the data is read out, or they can be run periodically in batches.

ADLA is the query engine that enables you to make efficient queries against the ADLS. An ADLA account always requires an ADLS account behind it. This primary account is the default source for queries. ADLA queries are written with U-SQL, an SQL-like language with some programming features borrowed from C#. Some examples of U-SQL scripts that query data from ADLS and Storage Blobs follow.

In addition to the primary ADLS source, the ADLA instance can have secondary sources as well. You can add other ADLS accounts or Azure Storage Blobs from the **Data sources** tab in the portal, as follows:

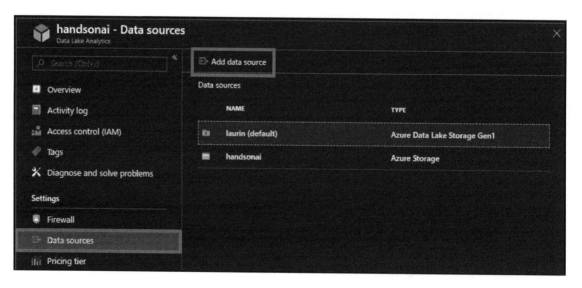

Once an account has been registered as a data source, it can be used in queries similar to the primary ADLS account. By using multiple data sources, you can avoid moving the data to a single Data Lake if your data resides in multiple Storage accounts.

As a side note, it is always possible to create an ADL Storage account without associating an ADLA account with it. But the ADLS would only act as a file storage in that case, without the ability to make queries against the file contents. Also, nothing would prevent you from creating multiple ADLA accounts that all use the same ADLS account as their primary source. This flexibility is possible because ADLS and ADLA are separate products in the Azure portal.

One of the biggest strengths of ADL is its user permission controls. Permissions can be set separately for each file and directory. If some data in the Data Lake is confidential and should not be visible to all users, it can be placed in a separate directory and the directory can be made visible only to a select group of users. Data Lake is also integrated with Azure AD, and permissions can be assigned to Azure AD groups instead of specific users. Role-based access control will not be discussed further here, as the focus is on analytics. To add users to the ADLA account, they should be granted a Data Lake Analytics Developer role using the Add User Wizard in the ADLA instance in the Azure portal.

The material in this section concerns Data Lake Storage Gen1 (Data Lake Store). ADLS Gen2 is in private preview at the time of writing. There might be changes in how ADLA works with Gen2, so check the latest information in the Microsoft documentation.

Developing with U-SQL

As mentioned previously, ADLA queries are written in U-SQL, a query language developed by Microsoft specifically for big data. Similar to many other Azure services, queries can be written and executed in the Azure portal, which is useful for small and quick tasks. For advanced development, there are extensions for VS Code and Visual Studio IDEs that offer more functionality.

Although writing U-SQL queries is in many ways similar to writing SQL queries, there are some differences as well. ADLA does not produce interactive output to the query editor as it does in SQL Server Management Studio, for example. The results are always directed to a certain output, which is usually a file in ADLS. To check the results of the query, it is necessary to open the output file from the cloud storage using the Azure portal or the Storage Explorer app. Moreover, the query syntax is sometimes closer to C# than SQL. For example, the equality operator in a WHERE clause is == as in C#, not = as in SQL. U-SQL commands are also always written in capital letters. An error will be thrown if the commands are written in lowercase, in contrast to SQL.

One of the greatest features of U-SQL is its extensibility. If the built-in commands and modules are not sufficient for a certain task, developers can make their own modules and import them to be used in U-SQL scripts. After modules have been registered once using the CREATE ASSEMBLY command, they can be used in U-SQL scripts, similar to the built-in modules. There are also open source custom modules available, which can be imported to add JSON support, for example.

In addition to importing C# modules, it is also possible to define custom C# code for a U-SQL script. By using so-called code-behind modules, we can write custom C# functions that can be called from the U-SQL script. Code-behind files have the same file name as the U-SQL script, except that the file ends with .cs instead of .usql. This is a more lightweight method of using custom C# code in a U-SQL script, but the code-behind files are not visible to other U-SQL scripts. If you need to use the same function in multiple U-SQL scripts, then it might be more efficient to register it as an assembly, as explained previously.

ADLA can also be used to execute Python and R code in a massively parallel fashion. This requires U-SQL extensions to be installed on the ADLA instance. For instructions and examples, see the official documentation.

U-SQL databases

Although ADLS is a file-based storage system, it also includes features that are familiar from relational databases, such as tables and views. An ADLA database is a collection of these objects. ADLA databases are useful for managing data in Data Lake Store, since they provide some useful features such as table indexes. On the other hand, ADLA database tables have strict schemas in place, so data must be validated before it can be entered into a table. Then, we have lost one of the biggest strengths of the Data Lake, namely the schemaless storage principle that was discussed at the beginning of the section.

When an ADLA resource is created, a master database is also created. This database is used as the default database for U-SQL queries. New databases can be created with the CREATE DATABASE command and a database can be changed with the USE DATABASE command. The contents of databases can be viewed in the catalog inside the ADLA Data Explorer.

There are two kinds of tables in U-SQL databases: managed and external tables. Managed tables are in many ways similar to SQL tables: a table consists of metadata (for example, table schema) and the data itself. In practice, the data is stored as structured files in a Data Lake Storage directory. Managed tables enforce a schema-on-write, meaning that it is not possible to enter data to the table unless it conforms to the table schema.

External tables are in some ways similar to SQL views: only the metadata is stored in the database, but the data itself can reside outside of Data Lake. External tables can refer to various Azure services: Azure SQL Database, Azure SQL Data Warehouse, or SQL Servers on virtual machines. In contrast to managed tables, external tables enforce a schema-on-read: the format of the underlying data can change after the schema is defined, because the schema is not enforced at the time of writing. If the schema of the data changes, the external table definition can be altered to match the new data.

Using a managed table instead of storing the data as files in directories has some advantages. For example, if your data is stored in a huge CSV file, it might be difficult to append new values to the file. This operation is possible with managed tables using the INSERT statement. (Note that the managed table is append only, without the possibility to update values.) Managed tables also have a clustered index defined, which can be used to make more effective queries.

Simple format conversion for blobs

In this section, we'll demonstrate the execution of U-SQL scripts in the Azure portal and integration with secondary data sources (Blob Storage). We will read a **CSV** (short for **comma-separated value**) file from a Blob Storage and write the whole contents of the file to another blob file in a **TSV** (short for **tab-separated values**) format. In other words, we'll perform a file format conversion from CSV to TSV. Such format conversions are common in data management, since different applications often require data in different formats.

The requirements for running this example are a Blob Storage account (with some data), and ADLS and ADLA accounts.

To read the input data, the U-SQL module Extractors must be used. ADLA supports a few different input formats, including CSV, TSV, and raw text. In addition to these built-in extractors, it is possible to import custom extractors for reading JSON data, for example. Users can also develop their own custom extractors to extend portability even further.

The output formats are specified by the Outputters module. The built-in outputters support the same formats as the input extractors. Similarly, users can develop their own outputters or import custom outputters.

To run scripts in the Azure portal, go to the ADLA instance and choose the **New job** tab. This will open the U-SQL script editor. Enter the following lines in the script editor:

```
DECLARE @blobAccount string = "handsonai";
DECLARE @blobContainer string = "handsonai";
DECLARE @blobInputFile string = "iris.csv";
DECLARE @blobOutputFile string = "output/iris.tsv";

// Construct paths for blobs
DECLARE @blobInput string = "wasb://" + @blobContainer + "@" + @blobAccount
+ "/" + @blobInputFile;
DECLARE @blobOutput string = "wasb://" + @blobContainer + "@" +
@blobAccount + "/" + @blobOutputFile;

// Define the query schema. This must correspond to the input data format.
@query =
    EXTRACT SepalLength float,
            SepalWidth float,
            PetalLength float,
            PetalWidth float,
            IrisType string
    FROM @blobInput
    USING Extractors.Csv();

// Define output location and data format
OUTPUT @query
    TO @blobOutput
    USING Outputters.Tsv();
```

Adjust this script according to your environment. The first lines of the script define the blob settings and the paths to the input and output files. The DECLARE statement means that we are defining U-SQL variables. The variables are referenced by the @ sign.

On the next lines, the paths to the blob files are formed. The WASB protocol indicates that we are referencing a blob account. Note that a blob account must be added as a secondary source for the ADLA account before it can be used for queries, as discussed in previous sections. If the default ADLS account is used instead, the blob prefix should be omitted and the plain ADLS path should be used.

The query expression is defined in a different way to variables: there is no DECLARE statement before @query. The query expression defines the format and the schema of the input data. This is the core principle of Data Lakes: the data can be stored in various formats and there is no schema enforced when adding new data. The schema is only enforced at read time, when the query is executed.

Lastly, the OUTPUT command is used to direct the query results to a permanent store. In this case, the results are saved back to the blob in TSV format. The amount of outputs is not constrained to one, as in this example. Nothing prevents the user from adding more output locations and doing some processing between them.

To test the script, add some data to the Blob Storage in comma-separated format. The script can be executed by clicking on the **Submit** button in the **New job** window. After the job has finished, there should be a new file ending in .tsv in the blob. Verify that it contains the same data as the original file, except that it is now tab-separated instead of comma-separated.

Integration with Cognitive Services

In previous sections, we saw how to integrate Logic Apps with Cognitive Services. We used the Text Analytics API to score the sentiment of each tweet and stored the results in Blob Storage. In this example, we'll show how to implement the same steps with ADLA. In addition to getting the sentiment score, we'll also extract key phrases for each tweet to get more insights.

Completing this example requires a Cognitive Services Text Analytics API account.

Before Cognitive Services can be used in U-SQL scripts, the ADLA instance must be registered with Cognitive extensions. This can be done in the Azure portal by opening the ADLA instance and choosing the **Sample scripts** tab, as follows:

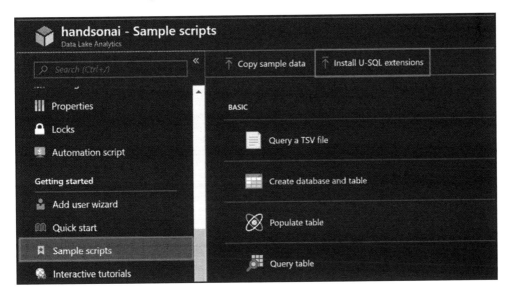

Once installation is successful, Cognitive extensions are ready to be used in U-SQL scripts. This means that the REFERENCE ASSEMBLY statement can now be used to import the Cognitive Services modules.

In this example, the input comes from a directory that contains multiple files. The query can be limited to match only some of the files in the directory, according to the filename. In this case, all CSV files in the input directory are chosen. The input files have the same format as the files that were produced by the Logic App in a previous example:

```
2018-09-22 11:55:20|Nadeem_ahamed_r|RT @msdev: .@JimBobBennett would like
to help you build #Azure #CognitiveServices speech API into your Android
app in this three part serie...|1
```

Create a new job and enter the following script:

```
DECLARE @inputFiles string = "HandsOnAI/twitter/2018-09-21/{*}.csv";
DECLARE @sentimentOutput string = "HandsOnAI/twitter/sentiment.csv";

REFERENCE ASSEMBLY [TextSentiment];

@query =
    EXTRACT Timestamp DateTime,
            Username string,
            Text string,
            SentimentScore float
    FROM @inputFiles
    USING Extractors.Text(delimiter:'|', quoting:false, silent:true);

// Extract the sentiment for each tweet
@sentiment =
    PROCESS @query
    PRODUCE Username,
            Text,
            Sentiment string,
            Conf double
    READONLY Username, Text
    USING new Cognition.Text.SentimentAnalyzer();

OUTPUT @sentiment
    TO @sentimentOutput
    USING Outputters.Csv();
```

The preceding script reads the input data using the `Extractors.Text()` module. The module options state that the values are separated by the pipe | character, the text values are not quoted, and that the `Extractor` should ignore all erroneous data instead of throwing an error and exiting (silent mode). This last property is useful if we don't need to worry about the errors.

The Cognitive Services modules are accessed through the `PROCESS` command. Since we referenced the assembly `TextSentiment` in the beginning of the script, the `Cognition.Text.SentimentAnalyzer` module is now available to be used for processing.

Finally, the username, tweet text, tweet sentiment, and the sentiment score are saved to the output (Data Lake directory). The output file should look like the following:

```
"treyjohnson","Delta got me this far.  Waiting on the MARTA train and then
a quick UBER to #SQLSatATLBI.  Feels like an episode of the Amazing Race!
#Evangelism #Azure #BusinessIntelligence
@ZAP_Data","Positive",0.74410326366140189
"LouSimonetti","RT @fincooper: Getting ready for #MSIgnite? Check out my
sessions BRK3267 and THR2104 in the schedule builder:
https://t.co/NYiEWCAfr5 . I'...","Neutral",0
```

Note that, in the preceding script, the output schema is defined after the `PRODUCE` statement. In this case, some fields in the input schema are ignored (`Timestamp`, `SentimentScore`). The output is enriched with the new sentiment and confidence values returned by Cognitive Services. The new confidence score can take values between −1 and 1.

In addition to sentiment detection, the Text Analytics API includes a number of other features. We can extract the most relevant key phrases from a text sample, in this case the tweet text. The `Cognition.Text.KeyPhraseProcessor` module can be used to extract the key phrases from the `Text` column, as in the following script:

```
// Add this to the beginning of the script
DECLARE @keyphrasesOutput string = "HandsOnAI/split_keyphrases.csv";
REFERENCE ASSEMBLY [TextKeyPhrase];

// Extract key phrases for each tweet
@keyphrase =
    PROCESS @query
    PRODUCE Username,
            Text,
            KeyPhrase SQL.ARRAY<string>
    READONLY Username, Text
    USING new Cognition.Text.KeyPhraseProcessor();
```

```
// Tokenize the key phrases
@split_keyphrases =
    SELECT Username,
           Text,
           T.KeyPhrase
    FROM @keyphrase
       CROSS APPLY EXPLODE (KeyPhrase) AS T(KeyPhrase);

OUTPUT @split_keyphrases
    TO @keyphrasesOutput
    USING Outputters.Csv();
```

The preceding script uses the CROSS APPLY statement to produce a new row for every item in the key phrase list.

By merging the preceding script with the previous script, we have created a simple data pipeline that reads tweets from CSV files, calls the Cognitive Services Text Analytics API to find the tweet sentiment and key phrases, and finally, saves the results in ADLS.

Azure Data Factory

Azure Data Factory (ADF) is a cloud data integration platform that allows you to automate various data-related tasks, such as copying data between data stores, running analytical workloads, and retraining machine learning models. It supports a wide range of different data stores, including products from other vendors. Via its integration runtime model, ADF can also connect to on-premises locations such as self-hosted SQL databases.

ADF can make use of many different types of computing resources in the Azure catalogue. These include Machine Learning Studio, ADLA, Databricks, and HDInsight. ADF can also make requests to any service that exposes a REST API, such as Cognitive Services.

Data Factory is developed with ADF Visual Tools, a web portal dedicated to development and management. After creating the Data Factory resource in the portal, you can open the Visual Tools by opening the **Author and Monitor** link on the **Overview** tab of the Data Factory instance.

Datasets, pipelines, and linked services

The three main concepts in ADF are datasets, pipelines, and linked services. Datasets represent data that is stored in a specific location, such as a file in Blob Storage or a table in an SQL database. Pipelines are procedures that copy or modify data between datasets. Pipelines consist of a sequence of activities that make transformations to the input dataset and produce the output dataset as a result. The most simple pipeline consists of two datasets, the input and output datasets, and a copy activity between them. This simple pipeline could be used to move data between data stores, for example, from an on-premises SQL database to an Azure SQL database.

The dataset definition itself contains information only about the format and the schema of data, not about the location of data. All the connection information is separated to modules called **linked services**. Linked ssrvices contain all the information needed for integration, such as connection strings, server addresses, and passwords. Every dataset must be associated to a linked service, otherwise, ADF would not know where the data resides. The linked services collection defines all the data sources that ADF can connect to. This collection includes many Azure, on-premises, and third-party products and services. The full list can be found in the ADF documentation and you can also request more connectors through the Azure feedback system, if your favorite service is missing.

Activities are tasks that move and transform data within the pipeline. These include control statements, such as loops and conditional execution, and computational tasks using various Azure services. The computational services include the Azure Batch service and many Machine Learning services, such as AML Studio, Azure Databricks, and Azure HDInsight. Therefore, Data Factory provides a great way to automate many AI-related tasks, including retraining ML models and running periodic analytical workloads. Similar to datasets, computational activities require a linked service definition that points to an existing computational resource in Azure.

It is also good to note that the use of storage and computational resources is not included in the Data Factory billing model. Data Factory billing includes data management only, and data transfer costs and computational costs are billed per service on top of the Data Factory bill. As general advice, it is always good to test pipelines with very small datasets and keep an eye on the costs as the amount of data grows.

File format conversion

Here, we'll show yet another way to perform a file format conversion in the cloud. To begin developing Data Factory pipelines, open the Data Factory Visual Tools portal and choose the *Author* tab from the left-hand menu. Create and configure the linked services for your Storage account(s), where the input and output data resides. After the linked services have been created successfully, create the datasets for the input files and output files and attach these datasets to the linked services.

When creating the dataset, pay attention that the configuration matches the format of your data. Also, make sure that you specify the data schema correctly.

When the datasets are configured, add a new pipeline to the Data Factory. To implement the file format conversion, only one activity is needed: the **Copy Data** activity (**Move & Transform** menu). Configure the Copy activity to use the previously created datasets as the source and the sink. Configure the **Mapping** blade to define the input and output columns, according to the dataset schemas. As a result, we have created a simple pipeline, as follows:

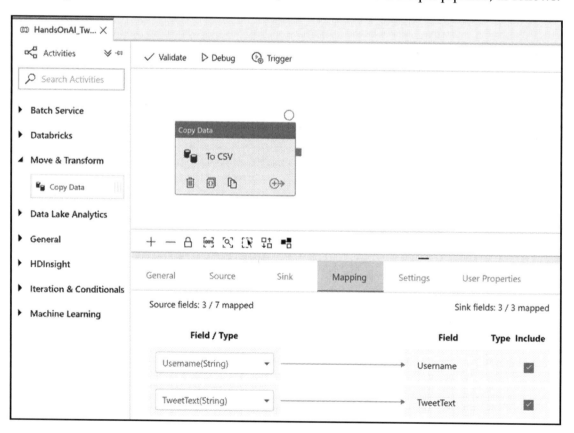

To run the pipeline, click on **Debug** or, alternatively, **Trigger**, **Trigger Now**.

Automate U-SQL scripts

In the previous sections, we developed U-SQL scripts to transfer and transform data in the cloud. The ADL Analytics engine does not include any automation functionality in itself, so we must use external services to automate such data workflows. ADF has the ability to trigger Data Lake Analytics jobs at regular intervals, so it is a good choice for automating U-SQL scripts.

Completing this example requires ADLS and ADLA account, and a U-SQL script to run. The first step is to create an ADLS linked service. The ADLS linked service is used to store the U-SQL script to run. The U-SQL script should be uploaded to ADLS so that it can be read by Data Factory during runtime.

There are two ways to authenticate with the ADLS instance: **Managed Service Identity (MSI)** and **Service Principal**. In this example, we will use the MSI authentication. The instructions for using the service principal authentication can be found in the documentation. When creating the linked service, take note of the service identity application ID, which is displayed on the screen as follows:

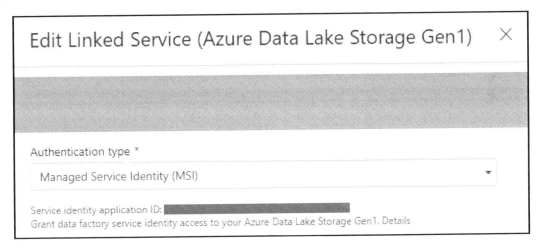

In order to modify the Data Lake contents, the Data Factory instance must have the correct access rights to the Data Lake. To grant these access rights, copy the application ID onto the clipboard and navigate to the Data Lake Storage in the Azure portal. From the **Data Explorer** view, open the directory where you want to store your data. Click on **Access** and add new permissions using the **+Add** button, as follows:

Use the service identity application ID to find the Data Factory account and grant all access rights (rwx) to this account. This gives Data Factory the rights to read and write files to the specified directory.

In addition to the destination directory, Data Factory also needs permissions for the parent directories. In this case, the x permission is sufficient. The easiest way to grant these permissions is to go to the root directory and grant the x access rights to the root and all its children directories. This means that the service account can navigate to all the subdirectories in the Data Lake, but it cannot read or write any files in these directories unless the rw rights are granted to these directories specifically. If you want Data Factory to be able to modify all files in the Data Lake, you can just grant rwx rights to the root directory and all its children directories at once. This way, you do not need to worry about the permissions anymore, since Data Factory has all the necessary permissions by default.

Next, create an ADLA linked service. For details about configuring the service principal authentication for ADLA, refer to the documentation.

The last step is to create a new pipeline and add a U-SQL activity to the pipeline. Configure the activity to use the previously created linked services for ADLS and ADLA, and specify the path where the U-SQL script can be found. Here is an example configuration:

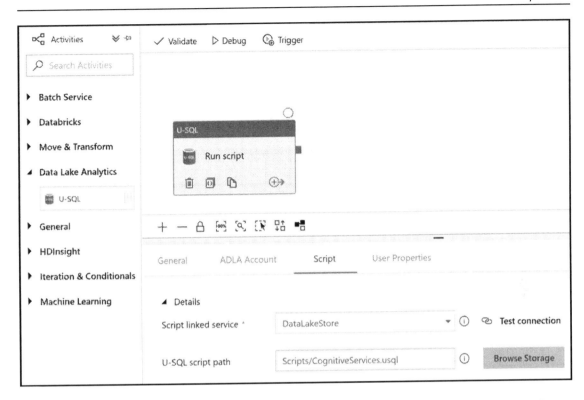

Note that the U-SQL module does not have any datasets associated with it. The input data and output data is specified in the U-SQL script, as explained in the section *Azure Data Lake Analytics*. It is possible to pass parameters to the U-SQL script, however. These can be specified under the advanced properties in the **Script** tab, and they will be available as variables in the U-SQL script. This is useful for passing filenames or table names for input and output data, for example.

Running Databricks jobs

Azure Databricks is a cloud-based machine learning service that is able to process heavy workloads with very high efficiency. Based on Apache Spark, it is designed for handling big data and high-throughput streams in real time. With ADF, it is possible to schedule Databricks jobs to run batch workloads periodically.

To complete this example, you need access to a Databricks Workspace. If you don't have an existing Databricks account, create one first in the Azure portal.

Once you have access to a Databricks Workspace, open Data Factory Visual Tools and create a Linked Service for Databricks. The Databricks linked service is of compute type. Choose the Databricks account to connect to and configure the linked services properties according to your environment. For the **Select cluster** option, choose **New job cluster**. This cluster will only be used to run a single Databricks script, after which the cluster will be terminated and it cannot be reused. If you run the pipeline multiple times, a new temporary cluster will be created every time the pipeline is run.

Note that you also need a secret access token, which is used by ADF to connect to Databricks. The access token should be stored by the Databricks administrator or it should be stored in Azure Key Vault. You can also create a new token by clicking on the information icon next to the **Access token** field:

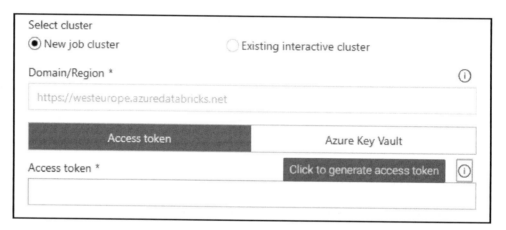

Once the Databricks linked service has been created successfully, we are ready to create the pipeline for a Databricks job. In the following, we demonstrate how to pass parameters from a Data Factory Pipeline to the Databricks job. We assume that you have an existing Databricks Notebook in the workspace. If this is not the case, go to the Databricks Workspace, create a new notebook, and enter the following script in the notebook:

```
file_name = getArgument("FileName")
print('File name: ' + file_name)
```

The preceding Python code reads the Data Factory parameter `FileName`, stores the value in variable `file_name`, and prints the contents of the variable to the output. If you already have a script that uses parameters, you must modify your script and use the `getArgument` function to get the Data Factory parameters as input.

Next, create the Data Factory Pipeline and add a Databricks Notebook module to your pipeline. Configure the module to use the previously created Databricks linked service and browse the Databricks Workspace to locate the Databricks Notebook to run. Since our script also uses Data Factory parameters, the parameter values must be specified in the configuration. Click to open the **Base Parameters** option and enter a value for the FileName parameter. The Data Factory Pipeline will now pass the value of the parameter to the Databricks script. The value of the parameter can also be set dynamically during runtime, using a pipeline parameter or a timestamp, for example:

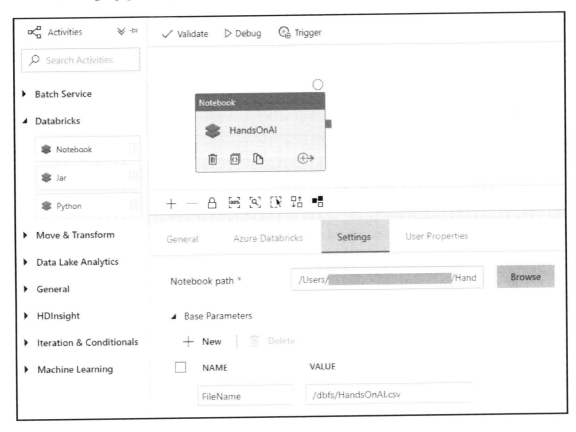

Similar to the U-SQL module, the Databricks module does not have any input or output Datasets. Data input and output must be handled in the Databricks script. The data can reside in the **Databricks File system (DBFS)**, for example. Azure Databricks also integrates with many Azure services, such as Data Lake Storage and event hub. See the official documentation for details about data sources and instructions on how to connect to them.

To finish the pipeline, click on **Publish** to save the changes. To run the pipeline, click on **Trigger Now** from the **Trigger** menu. After the pipeline has been executed successfully, check that the parameter value is printed correctly to the output. To view the job output, go to the Databricks Workspace and open the **Clusters** tab. Click on the job cluster that executed the script and review the output of the script.

Summary

As we have seen in this chapter, integrating Azure AI services with other non-AI services is easy and configuring these integrations can be done in a few simple steps. For codeless approach, Logic Apps and Data Factory provide tools to automate many data-related tasks. By leveraging AI services such as Cognitive Services or ML Studio Web Services, the incoming data can be enriched with insights and predictions produced by the AI services.

The trigger-based event handling system allows you to react to different kinds of events, for example when a new file is created or modified in cloud storage. The triggers can be used to launch data processing pipelines in scenarios where data moves infrequently and schedule-based data processing might introduce lags, since the system must wait for the scheduled time to lapse. With storage-based triggers, the data pipeline can be initiated automatically every time the source data is updated.

Data Lake Analytics is a batch processing engine that can make efficient queries against huge quantities of data. The U-SQL language combines SQL-style queries and C# commands as a highly flexible query language for Big Data. While the Data Lake Analytics engine does not contain an automation service in itself, Data Lake Analytics jobs can be launched from Data Factory by using the U-SQL module. This way all the triggers available in Data Factory can be used to automate Data Lake Analytics jobs.

In the next chapter will learn about Azure Machine Learning service launched by Microsoft.

End-to-End Machine Learning

12

In this chapter, we will learn about the new capabilities that were launched with the Azure Machine Learning service that can help data scientists and AI developers with **end-to-end (E2E)** machine learning.

When developing AI applications, we can use cognitive services, as described in `Chapter 3`, *Cognitive Services*. Alternatively, we can create custom machine learning models with our own data, because cognitive services won't work in every possible scenario. In cases such as these, we have to train our own machine learning algorithms. The Azure Machine Learning service has an SDK, CLI, and APIs that can help you to create these custom models.

In this chapter, we are going to learn how to use the Azure Machine Learning SDK for Python in order to carry out E2E machine learning.

Using the Azure Machine Learning SDK for E2E machine learning

As shown in the following diagram, the first step in E2E machine learning is **data preparation**, which includes cleaning the data and featurization. Then, we have to create and train a machine learning model in the **model training** step. After that, we have **model deployment**, which means deploying the model as a web service to perform predictions. The final step is **monitoring,** which includes analyzing how the model is performing and then triggering the retraining of the model.

The Azure ML SDK enables professional data scientists and DevOps engineers to carry out E2E machine learning. It allows us to seamlessly use the power of the cloud to train and deploy our model. We can start using the Azure ML SDK easily by installing it using `pip` in any Python environment. We can scale the compute for training by using a cluster of CPUs or GPUs. We can also easily track the run history of all experiments with the SDK. This run history is stored in a shareable workspace, which allows teams to share the resources and experiment results. Another advantage of the SDK is that it allows us to find the best model from multiple runs of our experiment, based on a metric that we specify, such as, for example, the highest accuracy rate or the lowest rate of errors.

Once we have a machine learning model that meets our needs, we can put it into operation using the Azure ML service. We can create a web service from the model that can be deployed in the Azure-managed computer or IoT device. The SDK can be installed in any IDE, so you can even deploy the model using VS Code or PyCharm if you do not use Jupyter Notebooks or Databricks. For development testing scenarios, we can deploy the web service to the **Azure Container Instance (ACI)**. To deploy the model in production, we can use **Azure Kubernetes Service (AKS)**. After the web service is deployed to AKS, we can enable monitoring and see how the web service is performing.

The following sample code shows how to use the SDK for E2E machine learning. Start by creating a workspace for your machine learning project. This will be created in your Azure subscription and can be shared with different users in your organization. This workspace logically groups the computes, experiments, datastores, models, images, and deployments that we will need for E2E machine learning:

```
from azureml.core import Workspace

ws = Workspace.create(name = workspace_name,
                       subscription_id = subscription_id,
                       resource_group = resource_group,
                       location = workspace_region,
                       exist_ok=True)
```

This workspace can be accessed either via code or in the Azure portal within our subscription. We can manage all logical components of the workspace and we can also manage user permissions. The following screenshot shows the components of a workspace as seen in the portal:

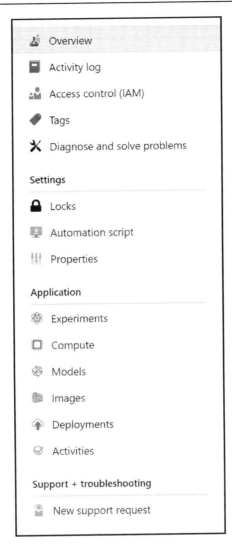

Once we have created a workspace, we can create a training compute that can scale automatically based on our training requirements. This compute can use either CPU or GPU, and we can use whichever framework we like. We can perform classical machine learning with scikit-learn, for example, or deep learning with TensorFlow. Any framework or library can be installed using `pip` and used with the SDK. We can submit experiment runs to this compute and we will see the results both in our environment and in the Azure portal. We can also log metrics as part of our training script. Here are some sample screenshots of how experiments run, and how corresponding metrics may appear in the Azure portal. We can also access these metrics using code with the SDK.

The following screenshot shows the number of experiments and the duration it took to run each experiment:

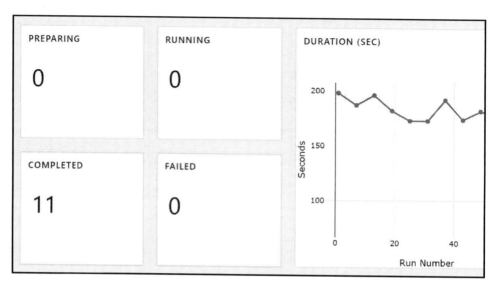

This screenshot shows the metrics that are being monitored within a particular run:

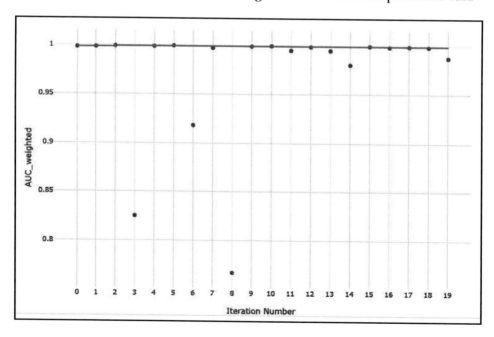

As mentioned, we can find the best run based on a particular metric of interest. An example of a code snippet used to find the best run is as follows:

```
best_run_id = max(child_run_metrics, key = lambda k: child_run_metrics[k]['au_roc'])
best_run = child_runs[best_run_id]
print('Best run is:', best_run_id)
print('Metrics:', child_run_metrics[best_run_id])
```

Once we have found the best run, we can deploy the model as a web service, either to ACI or AKS. To do this, we need to provide a scoring script and an environment configuration, in addition to the model that we want to deploy. Here is an example of code that can be used to deploy models:

```
# image creation
from azureml.core.image import ContainerImage
myimage_config = ContainerImage.image_configuration(execution_script = driver_file,
                                    runtime = runtime,
                                    conda_file = my_conda_file)

# Webservice creation
myservice = Webservice.deploy_from_model(
    workspace=ws,
    name=service_name,
    deployment_config = myaci_config,
    models = [mymodel],
    image_config = myimage_config
    )
```

When a model is deployed in production to AKS and monitoring is enabled, we can view insights on how our web service is performing. We can also add custom monitoring for our model. The following screenshot shows how the web service has performed over a few days:

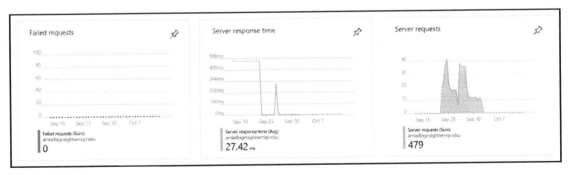

You can get more details about the Azure Machine Learning service at the following website: `https://docs.microsoft.com/en-us/azure/machine-learning/service/overview-what-is-azure-ml`.

You can also get sample notebooks to get started with the Azure Machine Learning SDK at the following website: `https://github.com/Azure/MachineLearningNotebooks`.

Summary

In this chapter, we have learned about the new capabilities of the Azure Machine Learning service, which makes it easy to perform E2E machine learning. We have also learned how professional data scientists and DevOps engineers can benefit from the experimentation and model management capabilities of the Azure Machine Learning SDK.

Other Books You May Enjoy

If you enjoyed this book, you may be interested in these other books by Packt:

Stream Analytics with Microsoft Azure
Anindita Basak

ISBN: 9781788395908

- Perform real-time event processing with Azure Stream Analysis
- Incorporate the features of Big Data Lambda architecture pattern in real-time data processing
- Design a streaming pipeline for storage and batch analysis
- Implement data transformation and computation activities over stream of events
- Automate your streaming pipeline using Powershell and the .NET SDK
- Integrate your streaming pipeline with popular Machine Learning and Predictive Analytics modelling algorithms
- Monitor and troubleshoot your Azure Streaming jobs effectively

Hands-On Data Warehousing with Azure Data Factory
Christian Cote

ISBN: 9781789137620

- Understand the key components of an ETL solution using Azure Data Factory and Integration Services
- Design the architecture of a modern ETL hybrid solution
- Implement ETL solutions for both on-premises and Azure data
- Improve the performance and scalability of your ETL solution
- Gain thorough knowledge of new capabilities and features added to Azure Data Factory and Integration Services

Leave a review - let other readers know what you think

Please share your thoughts on this book with others by leaving a review on the site that you bought it from. If you purchased the book from Amazon, please leave us an honest review on this book's Amazon page. This is vital so that other potential readers can see and use your unbiased opinion to make purchasing decisions, we can understand what our customers think about our products, and our authors can see your feedback on the title that they have worked with Packt to create. It will only take a few minutes of your time, but is valuable to other potential customers, our authors, and Packt. Thank you!

Index

Pytorch 271

Q

QnA Maker 70

R

R packages installation, on ML Services
   performing 191
R Server 15
R, with HDInsight 172
Recurrent Neural Network (RNN) 235
Resilient Distributed Dataset (RDD) 211
RevoScaleR 186
Root Mean Square Error (RMSE) value 225

S

scalable compute options
   in Azure 132
Search APIs 71
Search APIs, with Cognitive Services
   about 71
   Bing Autosuggest 71
   Bing Custom Search 71
   Bing Entity Search Bing News Search 71
   Bing Image Search 71
   Bing News Search 71
   Bing Video Search 71
   Bing Visual Search 71
   Bing Web Search 71
Service Principal 303
Spark ML 214
Spark MLib functions
   data exploration 219
   data ingestion 218
   running, in Jupyter 217
spark.mllib 214
Speech APIs 70
Speech APIs, with Cognitive Services
   Speaker Recognition 70
   Speech to Text 70
   Speech Translation 70
   Text to Speech 70
Speech to Text API 70
SQL Server Integration Services (SSIS) 184
SQL Server

connecting to 191
   data, reading from 190
SQL, in Azure Databricks
   data, displaying 209
   using 207, 208
Sum of Squared Error (SSE) 223

T

tab-separated values (TSV) 295
TDSP stages
   about 21
   business understanding 21
   customer acceptance 27
   data acquisition and understanding 23
   deployment 26
   modeling 25
Team Data Science Process (TDSP)
   about 20, 97
   tools 27
TensorFlow 262
TensorFlow, with Azure
   Data Science VM for Azure, using 262
   Deep Learning VM, using 262
   Neural Network Formation 265, 267
   overview 262
   simple computation graph 262, 264
   TensorFlow containers, running on Azure
      Kubernetes Cluster (AKS) 269
   TensorFlow execution on Azure, Docker
      container services used 269
   TensorFlow operations 264
   TensorFlow placeholder declaration 265
   TensorFlow training 267, 268
Text Analytics API 63, 65, 67, 69
Theano 271
tools, for TDSP
   AMAR tool 44
   IDEAR tool, for R 28
traditional machine learning
   verus, deep learning 234
two-class classification 151

U

U-SQL databases 294
U-SQL

developing 293

V

Vision APIs 52
Vision APIs, with Cognitive Services
    Computer Vision API 52
    Face API 60

W

web service
    deploying 126, 129

model, deploying 123
testing 126, 129

X

XDF format
    CSV files, converting to 189
    text, converting to 189
    using, in ML Services 190

Y

YARN 212

99035037R00190

Made in the USA
Middletown, DE
10 November 2018